Eldorado and the Quest
for Fortune and Glory
in South America

ALSO BY PETER O. KOCH
AND FROM MCFARLAND

*William Hickling Prescott: The Life and Letters
of America's First Scientific Historian* (2016)

*John Lloyd Stephens and Frederick Catherwood:
Pioneers of Mayan Archaeology* (2013)

*Imaginary Cities of Gold: The Spanish Quest
for Treasure in North America* (2009)

The Spanish Conquest of the Inca Empire (2008)

*The Aztecs, the Conquistadors, and
the Making of Mexican Culture* (2006)

*To the Ends of the Earth: The Age
of the European Explorers* (2003)

Eldorado and the Quest for Fortune and Glory in South America

PETER O. KOCH

McFarland & Company, Inc., Publishers
Jefferson, North Carolina

ISBN (print) 978-1-4766-8487-1
ISBN (ebook) 978-1-4766-4254-3

LIBRARY OF CONGRESS AND BRITISH LIBRARY
CATALOGUING DATA ARE AVAILABLE

Library of Congress Control Number 2021024762

© 2021 Peter O. Koch. All rights reserved

No part of this book may be reproduced or transmitted in any form or by any means, electronic or mechanical, including photocopying or recording, or by any information storage and retrieval system, without permission in writing from the publisher.

Front cover: Gold artifact on display in the Museo del Oro in Bogotá, Colombia (© 2021 Shutterstock / Milosz Maslanka); the Ciudad Perdida (Lost City) in Magdalena, Colombia (© 2021 Shutterstock / Alexandre Laprise).

Printed in the United States of America

McFarland & Company, Inc., Publishers
Box 611, Jefferson, North Carolina 28640
www.mcfarlandpub.com

To my beloved wife, Abelene Bilan Koch,
who has shared my adventures
in spirit and in person

No other race can be found which can penetrate through such rugged lands, such dense forests, such great mountains and deserts, and over such broad rivers as the Spaniards have done without help from others, solely by the valor of their persons and the forcefulness of their breed.
—Pedro de Cieza de León[1]

The difficulties of penetrating into these countries, where the path is to be broken for the first time, can only be conceived by one who has traveled over the roads already trodden. The broken and precipitous mountain track—the deep morass—the thick and tangled forest—the danger from the Indians, wild beasts, and reptiles—the scarcity of provisions—the exposure to the almost appalling rains—and the navigation of the impetuous and rock-obstructed river, threatening at every moment shipwreck to the frail canoe—form obstacles that might daunt any heart but that of the gold-hunter or the missionary.
—William Lewis Herndon[2]

"Shadow," said he,
"Where can it be—
This land of Eldorado"
"Over the Mountains
Of the Moon,
Down the Valley of the Shadow,
Ride, boldly ride,"
The shade replied,-
"If you seek for Eldorado!"
—Edgar Allan Poe[3]

Table of Contents

Introduction   1

1. The Germans of Venezuela   7
2. The Conquistadors of Quito   46
3. The Fortune Seekers of Santa Marta   55
4. Into the Golden Realm of the Chibcha   84
5. Unexpected Encounters   103
6. A Well Organized Expedition   122
7. Lost in a Lost World   131
8. An Altered Course   146
9. The Great River   156
10. An Interminable Wait   170
11. Into the Realm of Machiparo   182
12. The Amazons   189
13. Homeward Bound   208
14. The Final Voyage   218

Chapter Notes   233
Bibliography   239
Index   241

Introduction

In February of 1539, three separate European expeditions converged along a plateau in the Andes Mountains of central Colombia. These soldiers of fortune had set out from three different locations in search of a great treasure rumored to eclipse the extraordinary amount of gold and silver that fellow conquistadors had plundered during the recent conquests of the mighty empires forged by the Aztecs of Mexico and the Incas of Peru. To the many Spaniards who migrated to the New World during the early 16th century, the Americas appeared to be a vast realm of untold riches just waiting to be discovered, and there was certainly no shortage of ambitious and stouthearted men willing to risk everything, including their lives, for the chance to find fortune and glory.

From the distant Incan city of Quito there arrived an army of conquistadors led by Sebastián de Benalcázar, a veteran conquistador determined to find the legendary realm of El Dorado,[1] a Golden Man who lorded over Eldorado, a Golden City blessed with such an abundance of precious gold that its ruler would periodically cover himself entirely in gold dust prior to undertaking an elaborate ritual bath in a lake awash with a treasure trove of golden offerings accumulated over time.

The origin of the El Dorado tale can be traced to the coronation ceremonies of the Chibcha Indians, a tribe also known as the Muisca. The conquistadors of South America were told that a new chief of this distant region participated in an extravagant ritual in which his naked body was covered with a sticky resin and then coated from head to toe with finely ground gold dust. Afterwards, the golden chief was ceremoniously rowed out from a cave in a large reed raft to the very center of the sacred lake so that he could make an offering to the ancient deity that dwelled at the bottom of the lake. His loyal subjects encircled the rim of this hallowed lake, and each member of the tribe held a valuable item that was to be cast into the water as an offering to the fiery serpent-deity below. All solemnly looked on as the chief submerged himself until his body shed sparkling specks of gold that briefly fluttered atop the sacred water before sinking slowly down the great depths of the lake. Once the anointed chief had thoroughly washed off his splendid coating of precious gold and returned to shore, the reverent spectators hurled their golden trinkets and elegant emeralds into the water, an act which thereby confirmed him as their Grand Zipa.

Stories of the coronation of a new Chibcha chief quickly evolved into the oft-told tale of an omnipotent native ruler who lorded over a distant city made almost entirely of gold, and who bathed daily in a vast lake named Guatavita, a body of water laden with gold dust, precious stones, and numerous other valuable items. Located in Colombia, Lake Guatavita, which came to be known as the Lake of El Dorado, is believed to be a naturally formed sinkhole. Many conquistadors convinced themselves that another native empire awaited their discovery, one which surpassed the immense wealth of either the Aztec or Incan empires.

Tales of a mighty chief who lorded over a golden realm did not seem terribly far fetched to the conquistadors. Many who heard this intriguing tale of riches that awaited at Eldorado, including Sebastián de Benalcázar, were veterans of the conquest of Peru, and had seen with their own eyes the lavish amount of gold and silver summoned as ransom for the imprisoned Atahualpa, the Inca ruler who had been captured by Francisco Pizarro and his small army. Many had viewed the wealth of precious metals stored at the city of Cuzco, the Inca capital, and knew that many of the tribes who paid tribute to their Inca overlords had an abundance of gold and silver, much of which was worked into remarkable pieces of jewelry by highly skilled craftsmen. In addition, there were a few Spaniards who had served under Hernán Cortés during the epic conquest of the Aztec empire and had had an opportunity to marvel at the wealth of tribute collected and stored at Tenochtitlán. It therefore stood to reason that there were surely other rich native kingdoms that had not been conquered by the Incas. These rumors seemed credible enough for Sebastián de Benalcázar and his troops to abandon their post at Quito and seek out the distant realm of El Dorado.

Shortly after Benalcázar and his weary troops set up camp at the village of Neiva there arrived another expedition of conquistadors, which was under the command of a German officer named Nicolaus Federmann. This band of European fortune seekers hailed from Coro, a small Spanish settlement situated along the coast of Venezuela. German fortune seekers had recently earned a small foothold in the New World thanks to the political connections of the Welser family, wealthy entrepreneurs who provided the essential financing that helped secure the election of Charles I, the young king of Spain, as the newly anointed Charles V, the Holy Roman Emperor. While the Welser firm planned to settle and exploit the Venezuela region for all it was worth, they also had a far more ambitious plan in mind, which was to find a passage to the South Sea, a passageway that would lead to the untold riches of Asia. However, this objective would change once it was learned that Francisco Pizarro and his small army of conquistadors had conquered the wealthy civilization of the Incas. The new directive from the Welser group was to locate other golden empires that were surely hidden somewhere in the mountains or forests of South America. This quest led Federmann and his men to the village of Pasca, located just a few leagues from Bogotá.

Both Sebastián de Benalcázar and Nicolaus Federmann were shocked to discover that another European expedition had beaten them to the plains of Bogotá, the heart of the opulent Chibcha empire. Gonzalo Jiménez de Quesada and his soldiers of fortune had set out from Santa Marta, a small Spanish settlement situated along the coast of Colombia, to discover the Río Grande de Magdalena, where they expected to find native kingdoms every bit as rich with gold and silver as that of the Incas. It didn't take long for these Spaniards to unravel the native riddle, "Where the salt comes, comes the gold."[2] Quesada and his troops followed the native salt trail all the way to Bogotá, where they discovered that salt mined from Zipaquirá served as a form of currency for the Chibcha to purchase from neighboring tribes the various commodities they sorely lacked, a list which included gold.

Quesada and his men were deeply distressed to learn that they might have to share their magnificent find with two other expeditions. Oddly enough, even though these groups had set out from separate locations at different times and with armies of varying size, all three expeditions, according to some accounts, arrived at the contested realm with exactly 166 men. If these dubious reports were true then this chance encounter was truly one of the most amazing coincidences in the annals of exploration.

The officers and the rank and file of these three expeditionary forces spent the next several days resting and feasting while their respective commanders discussed their peculiar dilemma. As they contemplated what to do next, each officer surely reflected on the series of events that had led them to this remote place at that precise moment. The meetings between the three leaders were cordial; their spirit of cooperation was enhanced by the realization that after such a long and arduous search there was little, if any, incentive to return to their former posts. The three commanders agreed to return at the same time to Spain and place their trust in the decision of Emperor Charles V as to which expedition held a lawful claim to the land that rightfully belonged to the Chibcha.

While Quesada, Federmann, and Benalcázar were back in Europe embroiled in legal disputes over who had a bona fide claim to the region that many believed was the realm of El Dorado, Gonzalo Pizarro, the younger half-brother of Francisco Pizarro, led his own expedition to find this legendary region of untold wealth. Such a search seemed ever more enticing with the purported discovery of La Canela, a vast stretch of land the Indians claimed was home to plentiful groves of cinnamon trees, a spice that was worth its weight in gold to Europeans. He was accompanied on this expedition by Francisco de Orellana, a one-eyed soldier of fortune who hailed from Trujillo, Spain, the hometown of the Pizarro brothers.

With each passing day the men who enlisted in the Pizarro expedition encountered unforeseen events that tested their will and tried their souls. After several months of foraging across swamps and through dense vegetation the Spaniards found themselves hopelessly lost. In dire need of food and reliable native guides, Gonzalo Pizarro ordered Francisco de Orellana, his second-in-command, to head downriver in the boat used to transport supplies and soldiers too weak to continue on foot. Orellana was accompanied by some sixty men, a roster which included Gaspar de Carvajal, a friar who kept a journal of their adventures along a great river later renamed the Amazon. Unable to make their way back to Gonzalo Pizarro and the rest of the troops, Francisco and his men elected to proceed downriver in the faint hope of finding a passage to the ocean.

After enduring many travails throughout their eight-month long voyage down a vast, uncharted river, Orellana and the surviving members of his crew managed to reach a Spanish outpost. Francisco would return to Spain to provide an account of his wondrous adventure and speak of native reports regarding wealthy inland kingdoms. He also spoke of their encounter with a tribe of fierce female warriors, who surely had to be the legendary Amazons. Orellana sought the right to lead an expedition to conquer, colonize, and exploit the wealth of the region he had recently explored. After much consideration, his request was granted but the expedition ended in utter ruin, claiming the lives of many, including Francisco de Orellana.

Meanwhile, Gonzalo Pizarro and his remaining soldiers staggered back to Quito after an absence of two years. His army had been drastically reduced by hunger, exhaustion, and native assaults. All who managed to survive this horrendous ordeal were nearly naked, their long hair and beards were badly matted, and their shriveled flesh revealed skeletal frames. Some hobbled in with the support of another's shoulder, some used sticks or swords to support themselves, and a few crawled along the ground. All of the llamas, pigs, and natives that accompanied the expedition had perished during their futile search. Gonzalo Pizarro would blame the disastrous failure of his expedition on the treachery of Francisco Orellana, whom he believed had abandoned him and his men during their hour of need.

While these expeditions failed to find the legendary region they sought, the dream of discovering Eldorado and the realm of the Amazon warriors refused to die. In 1639, nearly one hundred years after the failed expedition of Gonzalo Pizarro and Francisco de Orellana, Father Cristobal de Acuna wrote, "Time will discover the truth, and if these are the Amazons made famous by historians, there are treasures shut up in their territory, which would enrich the whole world."[3] Blinded by greed, innumerable expeditions set out to find what others before them had failed to locate, each of which were doomed to give way to despair, disappointment, and death.

This story, which details the origin of the Eldorado tale and the various expeditions that set out to locate this mysterious land of untold wealth in South America, is divided into two parts. The first half of this book details the lesser known accounts of German interest in locating the wealth of a golden kingdom called Xerira and an elusive passage at Venezuela's Lake Maracaibo which allegedly led to the Pacific Ocean. The second section relates the Spanish efforts to discover the legendary realm of El Dorado. There was also the lure of a region that was home to many groves of cinnamon trees, a spice that was worth its weight in gold to Europeans. These quests for fortune and glory would lead to an encounter with fierce female warriors who were believed to be the Amazons of ancient Greek lore, and the discovery of the mighty river later named for the legendary Amazon tribe.

This book is meant to appeal to readers interested in the history of South America, the cultures of the various tribes that inhabited the regions explored by the conquistadors, the origins of the legendary tales of El Dorado and the Amazon warriors, and those intrigued by the ordeals of men who freely chose to participate in such an epic quest.

This work, like my previous books on the European explorations of the Americas, is part of an ongoing study of the chance encounters and interactions that took place between Old World explorers and the natives of the New World. Research for this study benefited greatly from a recent trip to South America, which included a voyage along the Amazon, the mighty river that lies at the very heart of this story.

1

The Germans of Venezuela

On June 28, 1519, Charles I, the 19-year-old king of Spain, was elected Holy Roman emperor. To secure this exalted title, seven European princes were each paid a handsome sum to assure his unanimous vote as the newly elected Emperor Charles V. In order to achieve the favorable outcome he so greatly desired, the young king of Spain borrowed heavily from several banking houses, a list that included prominent German mercantile and banking firms owned by the Fugger and Welser families of Augsburg. The Fugger family had served as royal bankers to Maximilian, Holy Roman emperor and grandfather of young Charles. They had enriched themselves through highly profitable banking and mining operations in Bohemia, Hungary and Tyrol while the Welser clan amassed a tidy fortune through sound investments in property and overseas commerce in goods, especially the highly-coveted spices of distant lands. To guarantee his election to the coveted post vacated by the death of his grandfather, Charles I borrowed 300,000 ducats from the house of Fugger and 141,000 ducats from Anton Welser in 1519, sums which were used to purchase the votes of the Electors of the Holy Roman Empire. Charles was compelled to pledge as collateral for these substantial loans nearly all the royal property of Castile he had inherited upon being crowned King of Spain.

Emperor Charles V decreed on November 15, 1526, that any of his European subjects were permitted to venture to the New World, provided they possessed a skill or service that would prove beneficial to the interests of the Crown. Suddenly, a once tightly closed door had swung wide open for German firms eager to gain a foothold in the Americas. This decision, however, was a source of bitterness for many Spanish colonists in the New World.

Finding himself deeply indebted to the house of Welser the emperor, on March 27, 1528, added fuel to his controversial decision by granting the German firm jurisdiction over a region in South America which extended from the coast of the Caribbean to the shores of El Mar del Sur (the South

Sea), a vast tract of land known as Venezuela. This region had been offered as collateral in 1526 for an additional loan the emperor desperately needed from the Welsers. Charles granted the right to the German firm "to discover, conquer, and populate" the region and import horses to aid in their quest. The emperor also decreed that he "wanted these discoveries made without men dead, or Indians robbed, or slaves taken. The Indians were not to be ordered to work in the mines against their will."[1]

While Spain still held title to Venezuela, the Welsers were allotted a generous four percent return of profits from the conquest and were exempted from paying new taxes. Instead of the customary royal fifth that was to be set aside for the Spanish Crown, a reduced figure of one-tenth of the gold mined for the next 10 years was expected to be shipped to the treasury of Spain. Additionally, the German firm was subject to all conditions set forth by the Casa de la Contratación, the institution that oversaw all aspects of trade within the Spanish colonies. In anticipation of this royal license, Bartholomew Welser founded a small trade depot at Santo Domingo on the island of Hispaniola in 1527 to prepare for the upcoming settlement and exploitation of the natural resources from Venezuela.

Bartholomew Welser first became aware of the untold fortunes that awaited in the New World after he had viewed an exhibit in Brussels of gold and other magnificent treasures Hernán Cortés had sent from Mexico to garner favor with Emperor Charles. In 1524 the Welser firm set up a branch office in Seville to handle trade in the Americas. Bartholomew expected to further enrich the family fortune by collecting a sizable sum mining gold and auctioning slaves in the New World.

It was widely believed that the greatest wealth of the New World was sure to be found in Colombia and Venezuela. The waters of the northern coasts of South America were known as the Sea of Pearls. Following Christopher Columbus's third voyage to the New World vast amounts of pearls were harvested from this region. A colony was founded near Venezuela in 1500 to procure pearls but was abandoned after the supply began to wane. However, the harvesting of pearls continued to prosper at Coche Island and the Island of Margarita.

In early 1528 Emperor Charles and the Council of the Indies signed an agreement authorizing the launching of a fleet to serve and protect a new settlement in Santa Marta, situated at the mouth of the Magdalena River in present day Colombia. The agreement called for the Welsers to dispatch an expedition numbering 300 men to Santa Marta within one year and to construct three fortifications with their own funds. They were to enlist 50 German miners who were to excavate the precious gold they expected to find in the native mines, and granted the right to import 4,000 black slaves over a four year span. Ironically, the region had once been the site of a failed experiment by Bartolomé de las Casas, the anointed *Apostle to the Indians*, to operate a state sanctioned encomienda where natives could live and work without fear of oppression. In 1529 the Welsers erected a factory in Seville to serve as their clearing center for trade dealings in the New World, which they were sure would prove to be a very lucrative business.

The Welsers appointed young Ambrosius Dalfinger as governor of their Venezuela territory. Of Swabian heritage, Dalfinger was born at the German city of Ulm in the year 1500. He hailed from a wealthy family that profited from the fabric trade, and was fortunate to have very close ties to the Welser firm. The newly appointed governor set sail from Santo Domingo in late January 1529 and arrived at Venezuela on the 24th of February. The Spaniards had a difficult time with Dalfinger's name and sometimes wrote it as Cinger, Alfinger, Micer Ambrosio or Jorge de Aspira. Even historians can't agree on his surname, as evidenced by the alternative usages of d'Aflinger, Thalfinger, and Ehinger.

Ambrosius Dalfinger, a giant of a man with fiery red hair, chose to settle at Coro, a small town founded by Spanish explorers in 1527 at the far northwestern coast of Venezuela, a site that overlooked the Caribbean Sea. The newly appointed governor was disappointed to discover that Coro was little more than a handful of thatched buildings, many incomplete, which were home to very few colonists. Juan de Ampiés founded Coro for the purpose of exporting brazilwood. Ampiés chose to abandon his settlement in favor of a stone house he had built at the island of Curacao. Alfinger arrested Ampiés when the founder made the mistake of returning to Coro. He was placed aboard a ship bound for Santo Domingo and ordered to never return to Coro.

The name of the town owes its origin to the Coro Indians who inhabited the area, but Dalfinger soon learned that most of the natives had been carried off or driven away by Spanish slave-raiders. This was a barren and dry region punctuated with sand dunes, cacti, and stunted trees. Thankfully, the nearby Rio Coro provided a plentiful supply of freshwater for the settlement that Dalfinger planned to turn into a major trading port for his employers, but instead Coro evolved into a base for launching expeditions in search of the elusive realm of El Dorado.

At the time, most European explorers thought that Venezuela was merely an island, albeit a very large one. The region received its name in 1499 when a Spanish expedition led by Captain Alonso de Ojeda sailed past the large inland lake of Maracaibo and saw native dwellings resting on stilts. Ojeda and his crew paid romantic homage to their discovery by christening it Venezuela, or Little Venice.

Many believed that Lake Maracaibo offered a passage from sea to shining sea, and the Welser firm therefore expected Dalfinger to thoroughly explore the lake to locate a strait that led to that vast body of water Vasco Núñez Balboa had christened El Mar del Sur, the Southern Sea, and which Ferdinand Magellan renamed El Mar Pacifico, or Pacific Ocean. Beyond lay the many splendid treasures of the Far East, the wealth of which the Welsers were eager to tap into.

Shortly after laying the foundation for his Coro settlement, Ambrosius Dalfinger rounded up 180 of the 300 men who had accompanied him to Venezuela and set out to reconnoiter the surrounding region. He brought along 100 Indians to serve as porters and guides. An important member of the Dalfinger expedition was a Spaniard named Esteban Martín, who served as interpreter and scrivener. The expedition departed Coro in late August 1529.

Shortly after losing sight of the coast, Ambrosius Dalfinger and his troops crossed a mountainous region that led to the eastern side of the lake they sought. They soon found themselves battling with the warlike Jirajara, a native people who had escaped the notice of Spanish slavers. The Jirajara, who did not take kindly to strangers trespassing on their land, were armed with clubs, which the Spaniards referred to as a macana, and long arrows, the heads of which were tipped with poison, which were shot from long bows as tall as a large man.

The expeditionary force lived off the food they brought with them, and when this was exhausted they had to rely on whatever items the natives told them were edible—mostly beans, squash, sweet potatoes, and the hearts of chonta plants. Occasionally, Dalfinger and his men were able to carry on trade with the Jirajara tribes who felt threatened by the presence of these strange looking and peculiarly attired intruders. They bartered little hawk bells, knives, scissors, and whatever else might interest the natives in exchange for food, particularly maize and manioc.

Dalfinger and his troops received a more welcome reception from the Bobure tribes living near or around the shores of Lake Maracaibo. This great lake is fed by numerous streams and rivers, the largest tributary being the Catatambo River. On September 5, 1529, the expedition reached the southern end of the Catatambo. The commander was able to procure from the Pemeno tribe a fleet of dugout canoes. The expeditionary force paddled 110 miles, at which point they reached the narrows. There the soldiers were forced into combat with the Ontos tribe. On September 8, after having successfully chased off the natives from their village, Dalfinger and his troops founded a settlement, which he christened Ulma, in honor of his hometown. Ulma was later changed to Maracaibo to pay tribute to the great lake.

Ambrosius Dalfinger and his men were inspired to continue their search after they sighted a number of natives wearing finely-crafted bracelets, earrings, and other jewelry items made of precious gold. They managed to accumulate—a portion by trade and the rest by force—the equivalent of 7,000 pesos of gold. After determining that these natives were not skilled enough to work gold in such a refined manner, Dalfinger sought to ascertain where they obtained such intricately fashioned articles. Esteban Martín learned from the natives that their gold came from tribes further inland who, besides gold, had tremendous stores of green stones, which the explorers correctly guessed were precious emeralds. The Indians stated that they traded their shells, pearls, coral, and cotton for the ornamental golden pieces possessed by the highland tribes. Esteban also learned that they had herds of fine-wool coated animals very similar to sheep. Esteban Martín told this story to Pedro Limpias, who became obsessed by these tales of a golden land. "I am convinced," said an historian who lived during this period, "that it was Pedro Limpias who brought the legend of El Dorado back to the colony of Coro."[2]

After ten months of probing every inlet and tributary of Lake Maracaibo without locating the expected passage to the Southern Sea, Ambrosius Dalfinger decided the time had come to return to Coro. The precious gold they obtained on this expedition came at a steep price—the loss of one hundred men.

In Search of the South Sea

The passage of so many months without news regarding the whereabouts of the Dalfinger expedition was disconcerting to the men stationed at Coro. Many feared that the governor and his soldiers had met an untimely end in this untamed land. The Welser office at Santo Domingo was eventually informed of this uncertain situation and the agents immediately sent word by ship to the Welser firm in Augsburg. In response to this disturbing report, Johannes Seissenhofer was named the new governor of the Venezuela region. Troubled by the pronunciation of the replacement governor's name, many Spaniards referred to him as simply John, the German.

Prior to the appointment of a new governor to their leased realm of Venezuela, the Welsers dispatched to Coro another expedition led by Nicolaus Federmann, a young German officer in their employ. Just like Ambrosius Dalfinger, Federmann was a Swabian from the city of Ulm, a region now part of the German state of Bavaria, and who also hailed from a family of considerable wealth. Nicolaus attended the prestigious Fondaco de Tedescshi in Venice, during which time he became fluent in Italian. Skilled in the arts and letters as well as the use of the sword, the worldly Federmann, following his graduation from the university, went to work for the

Welsers, who assigned him to their office in Seville. The young German stayed long enough in Spain to learn to speak and write Castilian. Only twenty-three when he arrived at Santo Domingo in December 1529, the blue-eyed Federmann was said to be slightly less than average height but of stout build. His thick red beard and matching fiery locks projected an aura of maturity well beyond his years. Nicolaus was well liked by the men who knew and served him.

Accompanied by twenty-four miners and a company of soldiers, Nicolaus Federmann reached Coro in March 1530, a time when Ambrosius Dalfinger was still exploring the region surrounding Lake Maracaibo. Seeing firsthand the desperate state of the settlement the young officer quickly returned to Santo Domingo to obtain supplies. Before returning to Coro, Federmann was able to enlist the aid of Sebastián Rentz, a fellow Welser employee who also hailed from Ulm. Shortly after his return three ships belonging to the Welsers docked at Coro carrying sorely needed supplies, additional men, and Johannes Seissenhofer. Federmann warmly greeted the new governor, who showed his heart-felt appreciation by appointing the fellow German as his right-hand man, a display of favoritism that did not sit well with the Spanish settlers.

On April 18, 1530, shortly after assuming their new posts at Coro, Johannes Seissenhofer and Nicolaus Federmann were surprised by the unexpected appearance of Ambrosius Dalfinger and his surviving band of soldiers, all of whom looked as if they were on the brink of death. Dalfinger had returned to Coro with little to show for the loss of 100 soldiers, a disappointment further compounded by the forfeiture of his post as governor. Johannes Seissenhofer, the new governor, died soon afterwards, which allowed Ambrosius Dalfinger to return to his rightful post.

Governor Dalfinger named Federmann as interim Lieutenant-Governor of the Realm, Captain-General of the military, and alcalde (mayor) of Coro. These appointments were made prior to when a delirious Dalfinger, who had failed to fully recover from the many travails of his expedition, boarded a ship bound for Santo Domingo, where he expected to either recover or prepare for his eternal rest. Before leaving Venezuela, the fever-stricken Dalfinger instructed Federmann to lead an expedition to Lake Maracaibo to build up and settle the town he had recently founded, and to seek out the elusive passage to the South Sea. Dalfinger imparted to Federmann his knowledge concerning encounters with natives as well as the terrain of the region. In contrast to other conquistadors, the young German commander would prove himself mature enough to treat the natives more humanely.

Nicolaus Federmann noted in his memoirs, "Here I was staying in Coro with too many idle soldiers on my hands. And I decided to travel myself towards the South Seas, hoping I could achieve something useful there. So I prepared all that was necessary for such expedition. I left on 16th September 1530 together with one hundred Spanish foot soldiery and sixteen cavalry."[3] The expedition was accompanied by two monks and one hundred native porters who had been pressed into service. Bartolomé de Santillana was left in charge of the Coro settlement while Federmann sought to locate the elusive route to the Pacific, the gateway to the wealth of the Spice Islands.

With only the vaguest notion of which path to follow, the Federmann expedition headed southwestward through a tropical forest by adhering to the route of the Coro river. They soon entered the region inhabited by the Caquetios tribe. This once populous Arawak speaking people had been decimated by the European introduction of the highly infectious strain of smallpox and the violent raids of Spanish slavers. The once coastal tribes had sought sanctuary in the foothills where they cultivated fields of maize, manioc, and sweet potatoes. They were adept at separating salt and collecting shells from the sea to barter with other tribes for sorely needed goods. The natives concocted a poison for their arrows, derived from the toxic barbasco root. This toxin was also used to stun freshwater fish for easy collection. Federmann and his men were shocked to see that the Caquetio practiced ritualistic cannibalism; prisoners of war were fattened, sacrificed, and then consumed.

Federmann and his troops departed the realm of the Caquetio and proceeded to ascend the steep slopes of the Sierra de San Luis in order to reach the domain of the Jirajara, the same tribe that Dalfinger had encountered without much trouble. Nicolaus knew of them from his talks with the governor, and he made sure to send an interpreter ahead to alert the Jirajara of their approach and sincere desire for peaceful relations. The German commander and his troops managed to pass among the riverine Caquetio and the inland tribe of the Jirajara without incident. He even received a small offering of gold objects from the latter tribe. Nicolaus was also able to enlist 150 natives to serve as porters, guides and interpreters. Seven days and thirty miles after leaving Coro the expedition came upon the border of a wilderness region that Federmann described as "a no-man's land and deserted." Ahead lay the mysterious lands of the Ayoman.

It was toward the end of September before the expedition entered the region inhabited by the Ayoman, an unfamiliar tribe. To prevent the natives from running away with all of their food, Federmann launched a lightning raid on the first Ayoman village he happened upon. Once their victory was complete, Nicolaus and his men quickly won the confidence of the natives with an offering of trinkets, which included handfuls of colorful glass beads. Day after day, the soldiers came upon one village after another. In some instances, the settlements were abandoned, but the natives were kind enough to leave an adequate supply of maize, yuca, sweet potatoes for the invaders to feast upon. Since the Ayoman were of relatively small stature Federmann surmised that they were intimidated by the superior height of the Europeans.

Federmann and his men reached the Tocuyo River on October 1, 1530, a waterway roughly seventy miles from Coro. While the horses were able to wade across this deep river the swift and powerful current necessitated the use of balsa rafts to deposit the army on the other side of the Tocuyo. The soldiers now found themselves at a region called Carahana, where they were fortunate to barter for both food and gold.

Several members of the expeditionary force suddenly fell ill and had to be carted in hammocks, most being victims of the intense heat and humidity. To maintain the pretense that the European explorers were immortal, Federmann conveyed to the tribes encountered along the way that his sickly soldiers were great and powerful lords who needed to be transported throughout the land.

The German commander decided to follow a path into the thick forests of the Matatere hills to investigate native tales of a tribe of dwarfs who inhabited this uncharted region. As they continued toward some neighboring hills, Federmann and his men were startled by the sight of some six hundred diminutive Ayoman warriors prepared for battle. The blare of conch-shells and the beating of drums were a prelude to a flight of arrows that streamed toward the soldiers. Federmann claimed that all of their enemy were no more than 30 inches high "but well proportioned in relation to their height."

Federmann ordered his men to hold their fire, and when the natives finished their volley of arrows the commander sent three of his conscripted natives with an offering of assorted trinkets to emphasize his desire for peace. They were accompanied by a monk who read aloud the *Requirement*, which declared Emperor Charles V had been granted rights to these lands of the Americas and therefore all inhabitants must submit to the will of the Pope, King, and Spain to ensure peace; otherwise a war without mercy would be waged upon them.

Refusing to yield, a number of natives were killed in the ensuing confrontation, and as many as 150 were taken prisoner before the Ayoman chief sued for peace. Since the captured natives were too small to serve as porters Nicolaus presented all with trinkets before he freed them. The ruler expressed his appreciation with an offering of golden items. According to Federmann, "The chief presented me with a girl dwarf, four spans high, beautiful and with fine proportions and figure. He said that she was his wife—for (such a gift) is normal among them as a confirmation of peace. I accepted her, although she was distressed and crying much, for she believed she had been given to devils."[4]

A five-day march southward led the expedition past the lands of the Ayomans and into the realm of the Gayon, who were sworn enemies of the Ayomans. In their first meeting with the Gayons there was an exchange of gifts, which Federmann believed was evidence that the natives recognized his friendly intentions. However, when the natives abandoned their village, the commander believed they were preparing for an attack. Federmann sent fifty soldiers on a predawn raid that succeeded in capturing eighty men and women.

A similar raid, however, on the village of the chief was not so easy. Seven soldiers were wounded, and one was killed, which marked the expedition's first loss of life since leaving Coro. The dead soldier was buried in secret to conceal from the natives that they were also mortal. Five days of continuous assaults ended when Federmann's soldiers captured the chief and forty-three of his subjects, all of whom were enslaved to serve as replacements for the native porters who had deserted them.

The expedition continued to the upper stretch of the Cojedes River, a region that was home to the Xaguas. Federmann wrote, "The Xaguas are water-people, live without clothing, more like fish than men. Since they live mostly in the water, one cannot see their pathways. When the water is high they have no fear of being attacked. For the Indios, the journey is only a day and a half by water to the village but for us it took four days with all those horses and equipment."[5]

Nicolaus Federmann employed the same night raid tactic that had proved so effective against the Gayon tribe. The frightened Xaguas fled when they saw the approach of these peculiar looking men and their even stranger looking beasts of burden. A few fleeing natives were captured, and Nicolaus handed them gifts of glass beads while trying to make it clear that he merely wished to pass through their lands. The commander's kindness soon paid off handsomely. On the 25th of October, Federmann and his men were invited to a place called Coari, where they were met by the chief and eight hundred of his subjects who proceeded to shower them with gifts of gold and bountiful offerings of deer meat, manioc, and maize. They also granted Nicolaus permission to cross over their lands.

The list of interpreters grew in direct proportion to the number of tribes they encountered who spoke a different dialect. Federmann summed up the language barrier by stating, "There is no doubt that before each could understand and transmit to the fifth what I had ordered, each would have added or omitted something. Of every ten words I spoke, scarcely one would arrive exactly as I desired. I considered this a great hindrance. It often impeded our discovery of many secrets of the land—the principal object of our journey."⁶

The dense tropical forest eventually gave way to the open plain of Barquisimeto. It was here that Federmann and his men encountered numerous villages inhabited by an offshoot tribe of the coastal Caquetio. The first village they came to was quite large, which Nicolaus estimated was home to some 4,000 people. The commander also learned there were 23 fortified villages along the river, each approximately one mile apart. He was warned that at a moment's notice the tribes could muster a combined force of thirty thousand warriors. The native men were described as rather tall and well proportioned and the women were so pleasing to the eyes of the soldiers that they dubbed the region *The Valley of the Ladies*. What pleased the troops even more was the discovery that these Indians possessed a significant amount of gold that they were willing to trade. Federmann and his men were able to collect 3,000 pesos of pure gold by swapping knives, axes, glass beads, and other inexpensive items they had brought for trade.

Finding himself once again among the more familiar tongue of the Caquetio tribe, Federmann wrote: "I heard news of another sea, called South or Midday Sea, which was exactly the one we hoped to find and which was the main reason for our journey. It is said that plenty of gold, pearls, and emerald jewels are to be found there. The inhabitants of the villages had told us a lot about this, but they insisted that they themselves had never been to the Midday Sea; they had only heard about it through their forefathers. But we considered this only an excuse, so that they would not have to guide us."⁷

Inspired by this latest piece of intelligence, Federmann immediately set out to find this route to the other sea. The South Sea, which the German commander believed he was close to sighting, was more than six hundred miles to the west. The course that the soldiers followed was actually a path toward the Caribbean Sea. During this stage of the expedition some sixty conquistadors became too ill to either walk or ride the horses and therefore had to be carried by the natives on stretchers made of hammocks. Nicolaus also felt poorly: "I tried not to show how miserable I felt, with sick and defenseless men, who were not really fit for traveling, and amidst people in whose friendship I could no longer trust, if they had seen us weak and sick."⁸

Soon after reaching the fertile savannah that was home to the Cuiba Indians, the two hundred conscripted Caquetio porters promptly dropped their burdensome bundles and returned to their homeland. Forced to carry their own weight, the weary and hungry soldiers used a field of tall corn stalks as cover for launching an attack on the unsuspecting inhabitants of a Cuiba village. The lightning charge of the cavalry and the swift advance of the accompanying foot soldiers quickly provided Federmann complete control of the village. Fifty natives died in defense of their village and an additional sixty were taken prisoner, while four soldiers were felled by arrows dipped in poison. Once he was able to reach a peaceful accord with the Cuibas, Nicolaus freed all the prisoners and presented each with gifts of hawk bells, knives and glass beads. The grateful Cuibas reciprocated with offerings of golden ornaments and food. They also promised to provide Federmann with porters and guides to assist him on his quest. The German commander and his troops remained at the village for nine days.

A dispute between Nicolaus Federmann and Antonio de Naveros, the royal treasurer responsible for ensuring the required *quinto reál*, or royal fifth, of acquired treasure was set aside for the Crown, erupted in anger. Naveros complained that Federmann was not keeping an accurate record of the gold acquired on this expedition. He also protested the burning of an Indian village without the obligatory reading of the *Requirement*. Federmann put an end to these protests by clapping the treasurer in irons and sending him back to Coro. During the two-month journey back to the settlement, the shackled treasurer was felled by a poison arrow that pierced his throat.

Resuming his search for the elusive route to the Southern Sea, Federmann wrote: "We travelled through the territory of the Cuiba, as the Gayon, the inhabitants, said that within three days we could reach a pueblo from where one could see the South Sea. So I sent five men on horseback and twenty-five on foot to go to the village, Itabana, if they could get there unhindered."[9]

After marching for three days Federmann's advance party reached a village situated near the banks of the Coaheri River. The settlement was inhabited by the Guaicari, a tribe of expert fishermen who traded their freshwater catch with the Caquetio. The soldiers heard stories from these Indians about other white men with beards who had sailed downriver in a ship—which the Indians believed was a large floating house—but added that they heard all had been killed by hostile tribes.

Encouraged by this scouting report which seemingly confirmed they were very near the South Sea, Federmann and his men hastened their pace along the path of the river. On January 23, 1531, the expedition came upon the Atacari (Atacan), a tribe that dyed their skin black. Since the surrounding region was mostly swampland, Federmann decided to continue on to Itabana with a small company of his fittest troops, which amounted to a mere thirty foot soldiers, eight horsemen, and two hundred Indian porters. The rest of the soldiers, who numbered mostly the sick and lame, remained behind to await the return of their comrades.

Federmann and his small expeditionary force passed through a

"Yuracares Indians Shooting Fish" (from *Exploration of the Valley of the Amazons*, published 1854 under the direction of the U.S. Navy for the U.S. House of Representatives).

number of villages where the residents were "all armed and unfriendly." A warm reception, however, awaited them at Itabana. While enjoying the native cuisine during discussions with the chief as to the precise whereabouts of the South Sea and the possible location of other Christians in this region, the commander and his men heard "a cock crowing and the clucking of chickens." The chief stated that the rooster and hens had been obtained in trade with a neighboring tribe. Since chickens were not indigenous to the Americas, Federmann speculated they were a sign that the expedition of Sebastian Cabot, which had sailed to South America three years earlier, had passed this way, but his guess was off course by several thousand miles.

It was in this region that Federmann and some of his soldiers climbed a hill and saw what appeared to be a lake and speculated that this seemingly vast body of water rested near the Pacific Ocean. What they visualized through the morning mist was merely the edge of the great plains that had been flooded by torrential rains. After hearing more stories from the natives that the South Sea was very close and noticing that the marshes and swamps ahead were impassable on foot, Federmann decided he was simply chasing a chimera and that the time had come to return to the village of Itabana.

As they made their way back to where the bulk of the troops anxiously awaited their return, Federmann and his company of soldiers suddenly found themselves being bombarded by long arrows dipped in poison. A host of bellicose Indian warriors ominously painted in red and black swiftly advanced upon them from the river. The commander ordered the crossbowmen to answer with a volley of their deadly bolts. One of the shots apparently felled their chief, because the natives ended their attack once they noticed he had been killed. All of the soldiers except for four were wounded in this brief, but very violent encounter. Nicolaus suffered a wound to the shoulder and one of the horses was felled by an arrow tipped with poison. Managing to gain control of the nearby village the weary and wounded troops sought shelter in the house of the dead chief. Federmann realized the time had come for their return to Coro.

While passing through the province of the Coquetios, Nicolaus noted that he was stricken with fever: "So we travelled from one village to another. My fever was so heavy that I could hardly sit on my horse. So we went on and on, until we came to the last village of the Coquetios. There were occasional fights along the way and I had to order my soldiers to stab a chieftain who would have run away and raised the alarm in the other villages against us."[10] Federmann's alternating chills and fever forced the expedition to camp at the village for 16 days, while the commander struggled to stay alive.

Federmann slowly recovered and once he felt strong enough the expeditionary force resumed its march back to Coro. They returned by the same path, which led them to the friendly Cuiba and Caquetio tribes. The commander then chose to switch course and follow the Yaracuy river. They were slowed by a native attack and a recurrence of Federmann's fever.

The men soon reached a Ciparicato village where a skirmish occurred that led to the death of the chief and others, as well as the capture of a great many inhabitants who could not flee in time to save themselves. After gaining control of the village the commander and his weary troops sought shelter in the house of the dead chief. A group of hidden warriors unleashed a volley of arrows at the intruders. Five soldiers were wounded, including Federmann, who was struck in the shoulder. In response, Nicolaus and his men attacked a group of warriors barricaded inside a high storage structure. Knocking out a support beam caused the building to collapse, and out rushed a number of armed warriors eager for revenge. Nicolaus was caught off guard and knocked to the ground by a blow from the blunt side of a warrior's macana. Luckily, one of the soldiers came to his rescue and killed the warrior just as he was preparing to finish off the wounded commander. Federmann remained unconscious for two hours.

The expedition's situation turned even more grim during its effort to cross the Sierra de Arroa. It was at this point that Federmann and his men were suddenly, and quite unexpectedly, deserted by their Indian guides. Finding themselves hopelessly lost, one of the soldiers climbed a tree in an effort to get a bearing. He spotted a savannah which all agreed they must make an effort to reach. The soldiers left the path of the Yaracuy and, trusting to the guidance of their chained Indians, headed northward into the dense jungle that was home to the fiercely independent Ciparicoto natives. After failing to find any villages to replenish their rapidly dwindling supply of food, many soldiers suspected they had been tricked by the natives. Nicolaus and his comrades were near the brink of starvation. The equally hungry dogs of the expedition sought to help by cornering a large jaguar. The beast killed two dogs before it was finally slain by the famished soldiers. "The meat had a strong smell," Federmann describes, "but we were so hungry we could have eaten anything. Although the jaguar was the size of a six-month-old calf, there were so many of us there, with the Indios, that each got as his share of the jaguar a piece no larger than two walnuts."[11]

The conquistadors came to a small stream which they followed to a deserted village where there was an ample amount of food to quell their ravenous hunger. After a rest of two days the soldiers resumed their trek to Coro. They soon reached another abandoned village where enough food and water had been left behind to fill their bellies for the final leg home. Federmann and his troops returned to Coro on March 17, 1531. They had lost ten men on the expedition but managed to return with enough samples of gold and tales of rich kingdoms to kindle the desire for another treasure hunt.

The Disastrous Second Expedition of Governor Dalfinger

Nicolaus Federmann was surprised to see Ambrosius Dalfinger among the crowd of Coro citizens waiting to receive him. The governor had returned to Venezuela on January 27, 1531, following a six-month convalescence at Santo Domingo. Upon his return to Coro, Dalfinger was angered by the news that Federmann had ignored his directive and instead chose to risk the lives of many of his men in a personal quest for fortune and glory. An official inquiry was established once the young commander returned. Nicolaus gave a written account that he hoped would justify his actions, but the governor decided the impudent officer needed to be punished.

After Governor Dalfinger banished him from the region for a period of four years Nicolaus Federmann returned to Seville in the company of his good friend Sebastián Rentz. Hoping to return to the good graces of the Welsers, Nicolaus made his way to Augsburg, and there he wrote *Historia Indiana*, an account of his adventures in South America. Federmann eventually succeeded in brokering a new deal that granted him a small salary and permission to spend seven years in Venezuela.

Ambrosius Dalfinger was bitten by the gold bug shortly after he banished Federmann. The governor heard stories of a region called Xerira (Jerira), where the natives were said to have such an abundance of gold that they freely traded this precious metal for items of seemingly lesser value. Ambrosius did not bother to relay this tale to the Welsers. A newly arrived dispatch from the Royal Audience was viewed by Dalfinger as justification for launching an expedition in search of this golden realm: "We entertain the hope that the governor of Venezuela, who more than one year and a half ago explored behind the jurisdiction of Santa Marta, will now continue to search for the other sea, and should he survive, discover much new land."[12]

Governor Dalfinger departed Coro on June 9, 1531, in another effort to find a route to the South Sea and a first attempt to locate the wealthy region of Xerira. This journey occurred during a period when the conquistador Francisco Pizarro was preparing for his third expedition along the Pacific coast of South America in search of golden kingdoms he had heard about while serving under Vasco Núñez de Balboa at Panama. The governor commanded 130 foot soldiers and 40 cavalry, many of whom were veterans of the previous expedition. Dalfinger was also joined by Pedro Limpias, a soldier who some cite as the instigator of the El Dorado legend, and Esteban Martín, a veteran officer who knew the native languages well enough to serve as an interpreter. Martín also kept a personal record of the expedition.

Esteban Martín noted that the governor "took with him lines of Indians carrying food and baggage, and they all went tied around the neck with the same cord; as the rope made a ring or loop around each head, it was not possible to release one of them without beginning with the first in line; for this reason, when an Indian grew tired, they cut off the head, if he did not cut it himself, without undoing the chain or calling a halt."[13]

The German commander and his band of Spanish conquistadors headed back to the settlement he had founded a year earlier at Lake Maracaibo. Since the path was already known to them, the governor and his troops had little difficulty finding their way back to the lake. The expedition encountered several tribes during this trek to Ulma, many rich in their own way, but not with precious gold.

In September, following a brief stay at Ulma, Dalfinger was fully prepared to resume his search for the golden realm of Xerira. The soldiers now had the additional support of many Indian porters supplied by the Pemenos, a tribe that submitted to the conquistadors after being read the obligatory *Requirement*. They marched up the banks of the Socuy River, where the mild vegetation soon gave way to a dense jungle.

The expeditionary force soon reached the serene Upar Valley, in what is now part of Colombia. It was in this region that they happened upon the cascading waters of the Rio César, which was named for Francisco César, a conquistador who led an expedition that discovered the river, and who died and was buried along this waterway. Dalfinger and his men followed the southwestern course of the river. They encountered along this fertile region a number of tribes who were kind enough to provide them with food and some offerings of gold. Some tribes, however, proved less hospitable and attacked the explorers.

Continuing along the banks of the Río César the conquistadors eventually reached a vast grassland where there were many villages, which were home to the Chiri Indians. The soldiers were attracted to the small crescent-shaped gold jewelry that dangled enticingly from the pierced noses of many natives. Several brief battles occurred in this region, each of which Dalfinger's men easily prevailed, thanks to a combination of superior weapons and combat tactics, and the menacing charge of the horse.

It was in this region that Dalfinger once again heard of the Xerira, the tribe said to possess prodigious amounts of gold. He learned through interpreters that the tribe could be found in the highlands to the south. The governor was told that in addition to a plentiful supply of precious gold, the Xerira possessed vast quantities of salt, cotton cloth, and green stones, the latter of which were presumed to be emeralds. As was often the case, the conquistadors heard what they wanted to hear or were told what they desired to learn. The natives occasionally spun tales shrewdly designed to lead the European invaders away from their land.

With only an inkling of which direction to follow, Dalfinger led his men in search of the rich and mysterious lands of the Xerira. The conquistadors again followed the course of the Río César, which soon deposited them at an enormous lagoon named Zapatosa. The soldiers slogged their way through this vast marshland that was a habitat for flocks of various birds, particularly egrets, flamingos, herons, spoonbills, and kingfishers. The lagoon was also home to a multitude of frogs and schools of manatees, the latter referred to as sea cows by the Europeans. The most frightening sight, by far, was the host of man-eating crocodiles that freely roamed the lagoon. A day's march from Zapatosa brought the expeditionary force to the banks of the Yuma, an extremely wide river that Dalfinger and his men decided to call the Magdalena. At this point, the governor and his men had been away from Coro for nine months.

Their situation changed for the better when Dalfinger and his troops encountered the friendly Pacabueyes, especially those residing at the Tomara settlement. The conquistadors first stayed at the village of Pauxoto and then marched thirty miles to Tomara, a large settlement estimated to have had more than a thousand thatched huts. The soldiers feasted on a variety of fruits and the flesh of deer, iguana, and partridge, but it was gold that truly gratified their appetite. Esteban Martín wrote, "In some eight days we obtained by gifts or by raiding, over 20,000 castellanos (91 kilos). ... All the Indians of this town of Tomara work gold. They have their forges and anvils, little hammers, and scales with which they weigh gold. The hammers are of a black stone or metal like emery, the size of eggs or smaller. The anvils are like average-sized cheeses, and the scales are made of a bone like ivory or of a black wood. They are notched like our balances, and they can weigh from half a castellano to fifty castellanos on them."[14]

Like so many other conquistadors, Dalfinger was overcome with a compulsive desire to get his hands on every last ounce of gold the natives possessed. The governor sought to satisfy his cupidity by taking a chief hostage and demanding a huge ransom of gold. Such was the case when Dalfinger and his men happened upon Tamalameque, an ancient native trade center, where he was welcomed with open arms by a kindly chief and his loyal subjects. Tribes from near and far came to Tamalameque to barter their goods, and the European soldiers used this opportunity to trade their trinkets for much needed food and greatly desired pieces of gold. Chief Cumujagua housed the visitors in a village encircled by lagoons, but the friendly atmosphere was poisoned when Ambrosius seized the chief and demanded the tribe hand over all its gold in exchange for his release. The natives responded to his demand with a full-scale assault. An armada of canoes transporting three thousand armed warriors painted with red and black dyes and adorned with brightly colored feathers attacked the soldiers. Dalfinger and his troops were able to drive off the warriors with a tactical charge of the horses. Emboldened by their success, the soldiers moved to conquer a nearby village ruled by a chief named Nicaho. Dalfinger and his men were surprised, but relieved, to see the warriors, who greatly outnumbered them, choose to surrender without a fight.

The conquistadors spent several months in the region inhabited by the Pacabuey natives. They eventually reached a site that Dalfinger called Pauxoto, whereupon he decided to send back to Coro the worst of his wounded and lame soldiers. This group was charged with transporting the large sum of gold already acquired on this expedition, and to carry a message requesting reinforcements and supplies. Antonio de Navarro, the

Spanish accountant, recorded that the treasure included "one thousand seven hundred and twenty-three ornaments, large and small; one thousand earrings in gold filigree; two thousand, five hundred and three neck ornaments; thirteen grams of gold arm bracelets; sixteen figures of eagles; four pieces called cemies; a golden head of an eagle; nine golden figures of women in fine gold; a great head-shaped cemi enveloping a great emerald diadem."[15] It was hoped that this collection of treasure would entice others to join the expedition.

Captain Iñigo de Vascuña and twenty-eight soldiers were selected to haul this treasure trove back to Coro. One of the soldiers was Francisco Martín, the brother of the historian of the expedition. Captain Vascuña, who was expected to return with new recruits, left for Coro with his small company of men on January 6, 1532, the celebratory day of Epiphany. With so few men, the captain was instructed to follow a different route back home, one that would, hopefully, bypass some of the more hostile tribes. Dalfinger wanted Vascuña to pass over the hills of Perijá to search for a lake the Indians had told him about, and to determine if this was a region worth exploring.

While awaiting Captain Vascuña's return, Governor Dalfinger and his men made camp at the native settlements of Pauxuto and Tomara. Seeking another cache of precious gold, the conquistadors launched a raid against an Araucana tribe residing in the shade of the tree-lined slopes along the Sierra Nevada de Santa Marta. Two costly discoveries were made on this foray: the Araucana did not own any gold; but they did possess an arsenal of poisoned arrows. One soldier suffered a lingering death from his festering wound. Esteban Martín was also wounded but managed to survive because he knew, as he stated, "how to mend myself."

In early April, the German commander marched his Spanish troops back to the lagoons of Tamalameque. When they reached the Magdalena, the natives told Dalfinger that on the other side of the wide river lived the Cindahuas, a tribe rich with gold extracted from the many creeks of their land. An envoy of Indians was dispatched across the river to announce the arrival of the Europeans. They returned the following morning with nine ambassadors of the Cindahua who presented Dalfinger with a gift of "nine pounds of gold, all of the finest quality."[16]

While waiting for reinforcements, Dalfinger and his men managed to collect another sizable pile of gold. When Captain Vascuña failed to return after an absence of three months, a gravely concerned commander sent Esteban Martín and a band of soldiers back to Coro to muster additional troops. Martín and twenty soldiers departed on June 24, 1532, a full year after they had left Coro. In addition to learning the reason for Vascuña's delayed return, Dalfinger wanted Esteban to make sure the new recruits included skilled carpenters who could bring their own tools and nails for the building of a brigantine to navigate upriver in search of golden kingdoms.

The new mantra for the conquistadors who remained behind was to follow the well-established salt trail, for this they were told was the path to finding the gold they so greatly desired. While at Tamalameque, Dalfinger sent out scouting expeditions to seek evidence that supported this account. White salt had been found in small baskets at the Tamalameque trading center and the conquistadors were eager to know exactly where it came from.

Meanwhile, Esteban Martín returned in July with 82 recruits, additional native porters, essential supplies, and numerous trinkets for trade. However, Martín was unable to discover what had become of Captain Vascuña, his brother Francisco, and the treasure, after learning from the colonists that they never reached Coro.

Governor Dalfinger decided to investigate reports of a wealthy native settlement called Comiti, which rested further inland, and set out at once along the salt trail with his reinforced army. Their march along the right bank of the Magdalena River was slowed by the sweltering heat and humidity and a host of mosquitoes and flies that drove the men nearly mad with their constant biting at their exposed skin.

The conquistadors were confronted by the Xiriguana, a tribe that fiercely defended its independence. Four soldiers and one horse died from wounds incurred during this conflict. Hoping to avoid further confrontations with the Xiriguana, Dalfinger led his men away from the river and towards the mountains to resume his blind quest for gold. Esteban Martín was sent ahead to scout the region for a path suitable for the horses, but the Spaniard and his accompanying soldiers were forced to turn back after coming under heavy attack from an unidentified highland tribe that did not take kindly to trespassers. The expedition continued on to a region where there was no food to replace the supply they had already exhausted. Esteban wrote that the men satisfied their ravenous hunger by feasting on horses that had died from hunger and exhaustion "and ate them right down to their hides, roasted and boiled: anyone with a piece of tripe or hide made something good to eat from it."[17] Shortly thereafter, the conquistadors came to a small village and seized the food and forced many of the inhabitants to serve as their porters.

Esteban Martín was sent on another reconnaissance mission, this time accompanied by 70 armed soldiers. They soon came upon the settlement of Elmene, which comprised fifty huts, and from there the soldiers ventured high up into the mountains where they made camp along the pass. "We all thought we would die of cold there. When dawn came the next morning we found most of the sierra covered in snow, and we were almost frozen and frostbitten."[18]

Martín and his men returned to the main camp after an absence of ten days to report on their findings, particularly the village of Elmene, which could provide the famished troops with food and water. Dalfinger marched his men to Elmene but the natives saw their approach and decided to deprive the soldiers of room and board by setting fire to their village. Fortunately, the famished soldiers managed to find still intact the fields where the tribe cultivated maize, yams, and potatoes, the latter being an unfamiliar food item which they called *earth truffles*. A group of men who had gone off to collect additional food were surprised by a band of natives who waited in ambush, and with their sharp cane knives they lopped off the heads of three conquistadors.

The soldiers suspected that the natives of this region were cannibals, especially after having made a disturbing discovery: "These Indians have a custom of keeping ornaments in their houses, the heads, arms and legs of dead Indians, with the bones removed, stuffed with grass and with the fingers and nails (still attached). We did not know whether these were Indians whom they had eaten or dead members of their own people."[19] At one of the villages Dalfinger and his men were shocked by the sight of a home built with human remains.

Hostile natives were not always the worst enemy confronting the conquistadors; nature had its own brutal arsenal. Mosquitoes, sweat flies, ants, and even vampire bats plagued the explorers at nearly every turn. The men also suffered from a pesky sand flea known as the nigua, which likes to burrow under the nails of human and animal toes to lay their nits. Many of Dalfinger's men were weakened by the mysterious onset of alternating chills and fever, which are symptomatic of malaria. A few were stricken with yellow fever, a fatal illness that caused them to vomit uncontrollably. And some were infected with a mysterious and often fatal fever known as *verrugas*, a disease carried by the sting of a regional fly that infected the skin with unsightly pustulating sores.

The ascent of the steep mountain chain was accompanied by a bone-chilling cold, intensified by biting winds. Such travails proved too unbearable for many members of the expedition, especially the near naked Indians—many of whom died or deserted during this difficult trek. The horses also suffered greatly during this climb, and those that died were quickly consumed by the famished soldiers. Dalfinger and his men did not know they were only a few days march from the outer realm of the Chibcha, the source of the El Dorado tale that was not yet familiar to them.

The final ascent of the mountain range deposited the expedition on a vast tundra blanketed with snow and chilled by icy winds, a bleak region

1. The Germans of Venezuela

Cannibals of South America (Library of Congress).

that soon served as a burial ground for eight soldiers, 120 Indians, and one negro servant, all of whom perished from either cold, fatigue, or hunger. Heavy rains added to the misery of those mired in a treeless region where they were unable to start a fire to warm themselves. Because there was no one left to carry their provisions, the soldiers had to leave behind many supplies and items deemed expendable. The troops finally reached a region where there were many villages from which they could confiscate food. Some of these settlements were quite large, containing as many as 600 huts.

The Indians of the highlands saw that these intruding soldiers were growing weak from exhaustion and lack of food. They had been victimizing stragglers for some time but soon decided they were strong enough to face the frail foreigners head-on. The greatest danger to the soldiers was the fact that these warriors were armed with spears and arrows, the tips of which were dipped in poison. The commander and his men were able to muster enough strength to fend off their attackers. Shortly thereafter, Dalfinger realized that his feeble and starving soldiers could not continue this difficult trek and shifted from a southward to an eastward course.

For three days the conquistadors made their way down this mountainous region, a descent of some 13,000 feet, which led them into a dense forest. They soon found and followed the course of the Río Zulia, a path that eventually delivered the expedition to a region where the natives cultivated corn. The famished soldiers spent several days feasting in these fields while fighting off the inhabitants who did not wish to share their corn with these interlopers.

As Esteban Martín was preparing for an early morning reconnaissance of this hostile region, he was surprised to learn that Governor Dalfinger wished to accompany him on this dangerous mission. The two set out with a small company of men and after passing both sight and sound of the main camp the scouting party suddenly came under heavy attack. A slew of arrows flew at them from every direction. The soldiers found themselves engaged in a desperate fight for their lives as they hurriedly made their way back to camp. Esteban was wounded in the hand by an arrow, and his horse was struck with five arrows and died once their encampment was reached. All of the scouts were wounded, and the soldiers soon realized, to their great horror, that these arrows were dipped in a poisonous concoction. Dalfinger was wounded in the neck—the arrowhead having pierced his throat. Immediate steps were undertaken to save the commander. The arrow was removed, and knowing that the tip was poisoned, the wound was sucked in a desperate effort to remove the deadly venom. The lesion was then cauterized with a heated blade and an unguent made from the fat of a dead Indian was applied.

Despite their best medical attention, the poison had already entered Ambrosius Dalfinger's bloodstream. The lethal venom quickly spread through his body, which swelled in a most painful and grotesque manner. Delirious and writhing in agony, the commander held on for four days before finally succumbing to the deadly toxin. The soldiers had to bury their dead governor beneath the roots of a ceiba tree at a village near the Zulia River. The valley where he died was later remembered as the Valley of Ambrosius.

Meanwhile, Esteban Martín was near death from his wounds, and the soldiers waited for more than a week to see if their comrade, who was now their commander, would live or die. Once Esteban had recovered and felt strong enough to travel, the survivors undertook the long journey back to Coro.

The expedition continued to the southern end of Lake Maracaibo, following a course that led the conquistadors into several more skirmishes. They came upon a region inhabited by the Pemones, a tribe that spoke the

Carib language—a dialect that Martín could somewhat understand. The natives told Esteban that there was another man like them living amongst a tribe just a few miles away. He decided to investigate this claim and sent an officer named Francisco de Santa Cruz and a few soldiers downriver to the village where this mysterious man supposedly resided. They were surprised to find Francisco Martín, the soldier who had accompanied Iñigo de Vascuña on the mission to bring the gold back to Coro and to recruit more men. Francisco was at first mistaken for an Indian because he was "...stark naked as he was born, with his genitals exposed, and dyed, with his beard plucked like an Indian and his bow and arrows and lance in his hand."[20] The two Franciscos were good friends and once they each realized who the other was they warmly embraced one another.

After successfully bargaining for his freedom, Francisco Martín, the lone survivor of the twenty-five who had accompanied Captain Vascuña on the journey to Coro, was brought back to camp. Following a joyous reunion with his comrades and his brother Esteban, Francisco proceeded to tell them a chilling tale. The route they had chosen to follow was one barren of villages. They had counted on finding native settlements to provide them with food and able-bodied men they could compel to serve as porters. With no natives to shoulder the weight, the additional ten to twelve pounds of gold that each soldier had to carry became too much of a burden to bear. Every step of the way the company of men grew weaker from exhaustion and lack of food. They came to a broad river, which they attempted to descend in crudely constructed rafts. One of the rafts capsized in the rapids and a portion of their precious gold was swept away. Some soldiers resumed the journey by land while the others continued to travel by raft. The next day those who struggled along the riverbank happened upon the bodies of several comrades who had been struck down by arrows. The others aboard the raft were missing, the only remaining evidence was the bloodstained clothes that had been left behind. The survivors pressed on. Several men wanted to leave the burdensome gold but Viscuña would not hear of leaving behind so much treasure. The captain and his few remaining soldiers continued on for another week, at which point even Viscuña conceded they could no longer carry this added weight of gold. He decided to bury the gold in a basket beneath a large ceiba tree that they marked with cuts from their swords. The plan was to come back later to dig up the treasure, but the opportunity to return never came to pass.

By this time the soldiers were so deprived of food that they saw no choice but to resort to cannibalism in order to keep from starving to death. A captured Indian woman was killed, butchered, and eaten by several soldiers. Soon thereafter, Captain Viscuña, who could no longer walk because of a festering wound to his foot, was abandoned. Two other dying soldiers remained behind as did the officer's servant. The captain and his ailing comrades temporarily kept death at bay by murdering and eating a native lad who had served the expedition.

The few remaining members of the expedition trudged back to the river where they were greeted by a flotilla of canoes carrying a great many armed warriors. The natives took pity on the emaciated Europeans and provided them with a healthy offering of their food. Seven Indians remained with them while the others said they would return with more food before guiding them to the lake. Shortly after the departure of the natives aboard the canoes, the soldiers deluded themselves into believing there was treachery afoot and assaulted the Indians as they slept. All but one native managed to escape. The soldiers took the bound Indian with them and hiked to a gully where they made camp and gathered wood for a fire. The Indian was killed and then chopped into pieces and roasted over the fire. After feasting on human flesh, the contented conquistadors slept the night away.

Crippled by an infestation of worms that had burrowed deep into a wound on his foot, Francisco Martín could no longer keep up with his comrades and therefore was left behind. Francisco managed to crawl to the riverbank where he latched onto a log and floated downstream to a village where he was rescued and tended to by kindly natives. After three months Martín was almost fully healed, and he managed to slip away with a group of Caprigueri Indians from Lake Maracaibo who had come by canoe to this village to trade their salt for maize. He spent a month with the Ciprigueri at their village along the lake, but before he had a chance to escape Francisco was traded to the Pemeos tribe for the price of a gold figurine. Martín spent a year living with the Pemeos; he took an Indian wife and earned his keep as a shaman. However, Francisco was never fully accepted as a member of the tribe. On three separate occasions he was tied to a stake to await his execution, but in each instance he was saved by the passionate pleas of his wife.

Soon after being reunited with Francisco, Esteban Martín marched the men back to Lake Maracaibo, and after a brief respite they resumed their march to Coro, which they reached on November 2, 1533. Of the hundreds of soldiers and natives who had set out on this expedition two years earlier only thirty-five returned to Coro. While the mission, which also resulted in the loss of the governor, failed to find the passage to the South Sea, the conquistadors did return with 40,436 pesos de oro (184 kilos of gold). An expedition was sent the following year to locate the gold buried beneath the tree marked by Captain Vascuña, but it was unsuccessful. To this day the whereabouts of this gold has eluded numerous treasure seekers.

The Failed Quest of Georg Hohermuth

On January 9, 1534, the galleon *Santa Maria de Campo* docked at Seville. On board this treasure ship was the obligatory royal fifth sent by Francisco Pizarro, which was part of the royal ransom intended to spare the life of Inca Atahualpa. The magnificent gold and silver works of art were shown to Emperor Charles V, who was far more impressed with the monetary value and therefore ordered them to be melted and made into coin. The ruler, however, yielded to demands to put them on public display in Seville before being destroyed. This astounding treasure trove of gold and silver bullion, and exquisite artifacts eclipsed the vast sum of riches obtained during the conquest of Mexico and rejuvenated interest in the search for other golden kingdoms of the New World. The Welser firm, which had serious doubts about finding rich native empires after learning of the death of Micer Ambrosius Dalfinger, decided that such a search was now worthy of their best effort.

The 27-year-old Georg Hohermuth von Speyer was chosen by the Welser group to replace the deceased Ambrosius Dalfinger as governor of Venezuela. Born on May 18, 1508, this young soldier of fortune hailed from a prominent German family of the city of Speyer, a river port town situated on the left bank of the Rheinpfalz. Georg Hohermuth traveled to Seville to recruit men for his colony. The newly appointed governor reached Coro in January 1535. Finding it difficult to pronounce the name of their new governor, the Spaniards referred to him as Jorge de Espira.

Several weeks later Nicolaus Federmann arrived from Santo Domingo aboard a Welser ship carrying 200 horses for Governor Hohermuth's benefit. The German officer had just completed his four-year banishment imposed by Ambrosius Dalfinger and was bitterly disappointed over not receiving the appointment as governor. Federmann had remained under contract to the Welsers and the firm believed Hohermuth could use an officer of his experience. There were mixed feelings among the colonists at Coro about the return of the red-haired officer.

Federmann's second departure for the New World from Sanlúcar had been accorded much fanfare: There was a procession of musicians, priests carrying lit candles, Dominican and Franciscan friars, cavaliers, and officers. The parade included infantry units, skilled carpenters, tailors, and shoemakers. Nicolaus's troops included Castilians, Germans, Flemings, Albanians, Englishmen, and Scots. All marched to a Franciscan convent to swear their allegiance to the emperor, as well as Federmann. The fleet sailed to Santo Domingo before heading to Coro. Once there, Nicolaus was eager to resume his exploration of the surrounding northern jungle region of Venezuela.

Per Georg Hohermuth's instructions, Nicolaus Federmann set out in August 1535 with a company of soldiers, and several hundred Caquetió Indians compelled to serve as porters, on an expedition to ascertain and establish the territorial line that separated the Welser grant from that of the Spanish settlement at Santa Marta. Federmann proceeded to Lake Maracaibo where he enlisted the aid of Spanish settlers who were still there. Legal entanglements with the Spanish courts and military threats from the Spanish governor of Santa Marta forced Federmann to abandon his post and return to Coro, but not before Governor Hohermuth had returned from his expedition.

While Federmann was preparing to fulfill his duties, Georg Hohermuth mounted his own expedition to find the elusive golden kingdom of Xerira. The governor's second-in-command was Andreas Gundelfinger of Augsburg. Since he lacked experience in this kind of military affair, Hohermuth made sure to bring along a number of veterans who could advise him. Included in this group was Esteban Martín, one of five Spanish captains who served on this mission. Governor Hohermuth departed Coro on May 12, 1535, in the company of 409 soldiers, 80 horses, and a great many native attendants and guides to probe the regions previously explored by Ambrosius Dalfinger and Nicolaus Federmann.

Rodrigo de Bastidas the Younger, the Archbishop of Santo Domingo, was appointed by the Welser firm to govern the affairs of the settlement while the two German officials were busy exploring. Rodrigo was the son of Rodrigo de Bastidas, a conquistador and New World merchant who had close business ties with Hernán Cortés. Bishop Bastidas sailed from Santo Domingo, and after his arrival at Coro he reported on the dismal state of the settlement: "It was part of my infirmity to have to see the place's great poverty. And we went to our church and there found poverty and ruin. Everything smelled and appeared of sovereign impoverishment.... The *pueblo* has fifty cottages, or a few more, and there are not four *bohios* [huts] which could be described as reasonable. The church is covered with the poorest kind of straw ... and at present people do not have shirts with which to dress themselves."[21]

Another important member of the Hohermuth expedition was a young German nobleman named Philipp von Hutten. Born in 1511 to an influential family in Frankfurt with close ties to the Welsers, Philipp reached the New World in 1535 to make a name for himself: "After having passed a great part of my life among friends, I want to come back with my name and my family honored, so that no one laughs at me."[22]

A cousin of the renowned scholar and poet Ulrich von Hutten, Philipp kept a record of his experiences on this adventure, which survived in the letters he wrote to family members, particularly Bernard von Hutten, his father, who was a prominent official at Konigshofen. In a letter to his older brother Maurice von Hutten, bishop of Eichstatt, Philipp expressed why he felt compelled to venture to the New World: "God is my witness that, in this journey, I have not been for a second moved by a desire for wealth, rather I have been affected by a strange dream. It seemed to me I could not die in peace without having seen the Indies."[23] In the case of Philipp von Hutten, the spirit of inquiry overshadowed any desire for fortune and glory.

The first month of the Hohermuth expedition was spent hunting for natives whom the Europeans could force into servitude as porters. The conquistadors followed the coastal desert before turning inland to the more verdant Tocuyo valley, the same region that Federmann and his men christened the Valley of the Ladies, in honor of the lovely females of the Coquetio tribes. A number of women were captured during a conflict at a Guarjibo village and Governor Hohermuth bartered their release for an end to hostilities. The natives left the conquistadors alone long enough for them to leave their land. Hohermuth and his troops periodically raided villages in order to procure food, natives, and anything else they deemed worth taking.

Unable to locate a passage that would lead them over the mountain chain, the Hohermuth expedition made its way to the llano, a vast sea of grass that stretches some one thousand miles southward to the upper stretch of the Amazon River. This flat and nearly treeless plain has but two seasons, both of which are extreme. The dry season brings torrid temperatures that bakes the earth and dries up the rivers and streams. This is followed by the rainy season, which restores the grass and refills the muddy banks that are home to many crocodiles, frogs, lizards, and snakes.

On June 20, 1535, Governor Hohermuth and his troops reached the river Acarigua and the village of the same name. It was in this region that a Spaniard by the name of Orejón made the grave error of going by himself to hunt deer along the vast plain. Caught up in the excitement of the chase, he inadvertently ventured far from the sight of his comrades and soon realized he didn't know the way back. Concerned soldiers fired arquebus shots to help guide Orejón back to camp, but without success. The lost soldier managed to find a native hut in which to pass the night. As he slept, returning natives snuck in and lopped off his head with his own sword.

Meanwhile, search parties were dispatched to find the missing Spaniard. Esteban Martín located Orejón's horse but not its owner. Juan de Cárdenas returned to camp with Orejón's sword and 30 natives "among whom were some who had witnessed the death of the Christian. (Hohermuth) had these eaten by the dogs in the presence of the rest; and the others were divided among the Christians."[24]

The expedition continued across the vast plains, a desolate region never before explored by Europeans. Greatly outnumbered, they were attacked along this route by a menacing force of between 500 and 600 Coyón warriors. A charge of the cavalry was enough to disperse the natives, putting an end to this threat.

By August 1535, the rigors of the search for rumored native kingdoms of gold had sapped the strength and will of nearly half the army. Exhaustion, starvation, malaria, and pneumonia, the latter of which was brought on by the dampness of the rainy season, claimed a heavy toll. In early November a mysterious illness raged through the camp that afflicted the soldiers, natives, and even the horses. Many natives died, as did eight soldiers and nine horses. All faced the insufferable pangs of hunger. Andreas Gundelfinger, Esteban Martín, and some of the healthier soldiers foraged for edible food such as maize and yucca. Philipp von Hutten, who kept a diary during the expedition, wrote that yucca "was a food dangerous alike to the ill and the well since they were not accustomed to it."

It was decided that the expedition could make better progress by leaving the weakest of the lot behind under the command of Andreas Gundelfinger, while Esteban Martín took 130 relatively healthy men to locate a passable route through the mountains. Unsuccessful in this effort, Martín and his men rejoined Gundelfinger's force. The weary conquistadors then marched toward the Masparro River where they happened upon the villages of the Masparro tribe. Four soldiers died during this march. By mid-January, the governor realized many of his men were too ill to continue on and decided to send the weakest back to Coro, seated upon the feeblest of the surviving horses.

Governor Georg Hohermuth and the remaining 199 soldiers pressed on with their search for native empires flush with gold. His expedition crossed the Apure River toward the end of February, and the Arauca at the beginning of March 1536. The tribes of this latter region proved friendly and were kind enough to bring maize and fish to feed these strangers who had tread upon their land. The conquistadors were unaware of the fact that they were very close to the lands of the Chibcha, a nation of tribes in possession of vast quantities of gold. On March 12, 1536, having trekked five hundred miles in the nine months since they departed Coro, the explorers entered a region that was home to many jaguars. Two horses and one native were killed and devoured by jaguars during this dangerous and terrifying crossing.

The expedition reached Sarobai on March 19, 1536, a village where the famished soldiers were able to trade their trinkets for sorely needed food, mainly maize and yucca. The natives proudly showed the governor and his men the ornaments they possessed, which were made of pure gold. Esteban questioned the chief as to the source of this precious metal. The ruler told him that they obtained this gold through trade with a tribe that lived among the mountains. This chief was named *Wakiri* but Martín heard it as *quay-quiri*, which to him sounded very much like Xerira, the golden realm they had been searching for. The chieftain claimed to have seen the gold himself and offered to guide them to this land of untold riches, a pledge that lifted the sinking spirits of the weary soldiers.

With the native ruler as his guide Esteban Martín felt confident that, this time, he would finally find the mysterious route up the Andes mountains. They searched for several days but once again Martín failed to find a safe passage over this seemingly impenetrable wall of rock. Little did they knoy they were but 40 miles from Sogamoso, a village rich with gold and emeralds that stood at the far eastern fringe of the Chibcha realm, the source of the El Dorado legend.

The Hohermuth expedition proceeded to follow the southerly course of the mountain range, a path fraught with extreme peril. They encountered a tribe at the edge of the llanos who did not take kindly to strangers. Very likely the Guahibo, they attacked while the governor and his troops pitched camp at their village. They set fire to the hut where the chained native porters were placed. The stench of the dead forced the soldiers to depart at once. They would have to cross several large rivers during this stage of the expedition.

It was April of 1536 when the expedition reached the Upia River, where they expected to find numerous villages of Arauak speaking tribes residing along this waterway. Unable to cross this raging river, swollen by the steady downpour of the rainy season, the conquistadors were forced to make camp for eight long months.

On Christmas Eve 1536, a band of soldiers captured some natives who were in possession of some finely crafted gold and silver jewelry. Esteban Martín questioned them about where these metals could be found, and, just like before, the Indians told him it came from tribes who inhabited the highlands. They were very near the trade routes of the Chibcha, but again a difficult terrain stood between them and the fortune they sought. Martín once again volunteered to lead a company of fifty men in search of a pass through a range of mountains soaring to the dizzying heights of around 11,000 feet. Esteban was convinced they were on the right track after he encountered other Indians who wore gold and silver ornaments. The scouting expedition suddenly came under attack from warriors who hurled spears and darts at them. The natives defended themselves with shields made from the thick hides of the tapir. Martín ordered a retreat back to camp after losing several men and horses to these hostile natives.

Once again, Georg Hohermuth heard from a native chief that salt and other precious items were obtained from a tribe that dwelled in the mountains. Juan de Villegas was dispatched with forty soldiers, but he soon returned to report that the mountains were far too steep for the horses to climb.

In January of 1537 the expedition resumed its march along the llanos, which they christened San Juan, by following a southerly course toward the equator, the tropical region many believed was the birthplace of gold—an equatorial theory first promoted by Aristotle. The soldiers passed through a fertile region situated between two rivers where they were greatly relieved to find large fields of maize and yucca being cultivated by the natives inhabiting this region.

The route followed by the conquistadors led them to one of the larger trade regions of the Chibcha. They soon happened upon an isolated structure, some two hundred yards long, which served as a trading post for bartering items between the tribes of the mountains and the tribes of the plains. Hohermuth and his men also learned that this trading post doubled as a temple where human sacrifices were performed to honor the gods. The Chibcha swapped the gold they acquired in trade with other tribes for small children of the Guahibos, whom they used for ritual sacrifices. It was here that Georg Hohermuth had his men erect a large cross to proclaim the new settlement of Neustra Señora (Our Lady), a colonial outpost later called San Juan de los Llanos.

The conquistadors continued on a path that would lead them to the Río Guaviare, a tributary of the Orinoco. They soon crossed the Río Ariari, which deposited them on an elevated plain that was home to a great many native villages. The governor was elated to hear from Chief Guaygueri of the Cauicuri tribe, "March two moons more, and you will reach a town where the Indians eat from vessels of gold and silver, where the land is flat and smooth and the wind urges flocks of fat sheep [llamas] across peaceful cultivated fields."[25] Hohermuth went in search of this promising land, which sounded much like the realm of the Incas, but found nothing remotely resembling this fanciful claim.

The Hohermuth expedition continued southward, a difficult trek that eventually brought them to the Rio Guaybero, a river that Philipp von Hutten called the Bermejo. All the rivers that the conquistadors had previously encountered were tributaries of the Orinoco, but now they had entered a region where the rivers flowed directly into one immense waterway referred to as the Great River, which was later named the Amazon.

It was during this phase of the expedition that many of Hohermuth's men fell ill from eating manioc, and soon thereafter several suffered a painful death from food poisoning. They had learned the hard way that the sweet manioc, or cassava, of the previous region gave way to a bitter and poisonous breed of cassava. The prussic acid of the manioc had to be washed and grated away prior to cooking in order to be fit for human consumption.

Hohermuth and his men cautiously entered the lands of the Huitotos, a tribe determined to drive off the soldiers from Coro. The conquistadors had to endure the brunt force attacks of warriors who had no fear of the horses, which marked the first time they had encountered natives who were not afraid of their mounts. The horses, however, were terrified of the sling shots flung by the natives. A captured Indian told them that if they headed west and faithfully followed that route for three or four weeks; or roughly eighty miles, they would reach a region rich with earthly delights. The governor followed the native's advice and headed west. After a march of two days the soldiers reached the Papamena River (also spelled Papamene, which was probably the Güejar) where they discovered a large village. The natives told Hohermuth a similar account of trade with a tribe just beyond their land that was rich with gold, silver, and llamas, a tale that convinced the governor he was finally on the right track.

Governor Hohermuth also heard the story of a kingdom of woman warriors living much further upriver, which sounded suspiciously like the legendary Amazons of ancient Greek lore. "Wherever they got this nonsense," wrote a skeptical Philipp von Hutten, "it is impossible to say."[26]

At the edge of the Caqueta River, a tributary of the Great River, the expedition became bogged down by torrential rains. They had traveled 1,200 miles and were now very near the equator. Unable to cross the 400-foot-wide river, Hohermuth had Martín take 40 soldiers and two native guides to search for a pass that would lead them to the rich tribes they kept hearing about. Martín and his men would spend four days blazing a trail in a forest tangled with vegetation. On the second day the trusted native guides deserted them. Esteban and his men stumbled upon an old Indian trail, which they followed for two days. On the second night they sighted a fortified Choque village, which Esteban Martín ordered his men to attack under cover of darkness. The natives fought back with such fierce determination that Esteban realized they would rather die than surrender. The fatigued soldiers attempted to withdraw but were attacked along the path by warriors from a neighboring Choque village. All of the conquistadors were wounded in this confrontation and two were killed.

Esteban Martín, whose body was riddled with arrows, and three other soldiers were so badly injured that they had to be carried on litters during their frantic escape. Two of the severely wounded men had to be abandoned, and the third died on the way back. Despite their best efforts to save him, Esteban soon died. The loss of Martín was viewed as a devastating blow to the expedition, for besides being their trusted interpreter and intrepid pathfinder, this well-liked and respected Spanish officer was the one everyone, including Governor Hohermuth, turned to for advice.

Following the death of Esteban Martín, nearly everyone expressed a desire to turn back, but Hohermuth encouraged them to continue their quest. The expedition had to slog through the swamps of the Choque region, where many of the men took ill. Each day saw more men and horses sicken and die, the latter viewed as the greater loss to the expedition. While the bulk of the army rested, Hohermuth took twelve horses and forty of the healthiest men and went ahead to search for the rich tribes they had heard about. Their quest abruptly ended when they reached a river that was far too wide and swift to cross. The governor returned to camp where he found that his men were on the verge of mutiny.

Even though he was sure they were very close to finding the fortune they had long sought, Governor Hohermuth listened to the complaints of his men and, after taking into account the shortage of food and supplies; the hostile nature of the natives; the steady rains that dampened their clothes and spirits; and the rapidly deteriorating physical and psychological state of his men, he decided the time had come to return to Coro. The army started back on August 13, 1537.

The return march along the same path was slowed by a constant need to forage for food. The swollen waters of the Wangari River forced the weary soldiers to make camp for two months. Thankfully, the natives along the river were kind enough to provide them with food. Philipp von Hutten wrote, "Many of us were without our swords, we had no more crossbows to defend ourselves. When we had started out we had more than sixty crossbows and twenty blunderbusses, now they were lost or unserviceable."[27]

Several soldiers died during this long and arduous march back to Coro, and the dead were left where they fell because the survivors were simply too weak to give them a proper burial. Most of the horses died from exhaustion and lack of salt. By retracing their steps, the conquistadors expected to find food at the native settlements encountered previously but were disappointed to discover that many of these villages were either abandoned or burned to the ground. Hohermuth and his men reached the Ariari River in January 1538; it had taken them 5 months to make this rugged journey of 165 miles. Here they were able to obtain from the local tribes enough fish and corn to satisfy their ravenous appetite.

Where Is Federmann?

When Georg Hohermuth reached the Apure River he learned from the natives that several months earlier another group of white men had passed this way. At first the commander and his weary troops thought the natives were simply telling tales, but their detailed description of a white man with a fiery red beard and equally vibrant hair atop his head convinced them that Nicolaus Federmann was nearby with sorely needed reinforcements and provisions. After spotting tracks of horses passing in the opposite direction, the governor dispatched Philip von Hutten and twenty soldiers to find Federmann. Unfortunately, Hutten and his men were stopped in their tracks by the flooding of the Apure, and therefore compelled to return to camp with news that further dampened the spirits of the troops.

"Only God and ourselves," wrote Hutten, "know the privations, the misery, the hunger, the thirst which we have suffered in these three years. I am full of admiration for the human spirit that it could withstand for so great a length of time these fearful exertions. We are forced to eat insects, snakes, frogs, lizards, worms, herbs, roots, as well as devour human flesh, which is contrary to natural law.... We were so reduced at one time that we boiled and ate the deer-hides which the Indios used for their shields."[28]

On May 27, 1538, Governor Georg Hohermuth's three-year search for the elusive kingdoms of gold came to a close when the disappointed survivors of the expedition hobbled into Coro. Captain Gundelfinger led an advance group of forty-nine emaciated soldiers. Governor Hohermuth followed close behind with eighty-five near naked soldiers; three hundred men who originally set out on this expedition failed to return. There was little to show for their ordeal except for a small amount of gold and numerous tidings of woe and want. Hohermuth was displeased to learn that Federmann was not there to greet him, and angered by the fact that his second-in-command had set off on his own expedition.

Georg Hohermuth wrote to Emperor Charles V, "I marched more than five hundred leagues, as far as the Choques, and, being no more than twenty-five leagues from what I sought, I found myself so weakened in men, horses, and arms that I had to go back to recuperate in order to renew the march."[29] Unfortunately for the governor, his rapidly deteriorating health prevented him from leading another expedition. Shortly thereafter, a delirious Georg Hohermuth had to be transported to Santo Domingo for treatment, but his health continued to falter, and on June 11, 1540, the governor of Venezuela was laid to rest. Despite all the horrors and deprivations endured, many of those who survived were willing to sign on for yet another expedition.

It was, indeed, Nicolaus Federmann and his troops who passed by the Apure River during the governor's desperate hour of need. However, Federmann was not coming to rescue Hohermuth and his men, but instead was leading his own expedition in search of golden kingdoms. Prior to setting out on his own excursion in May of 1535, Hohermuth had instructed Federmann to reconnoiter the rich Maracaibo region previously explored by Ambrosius Dalfinger. From the very beginning the expedition was tormented by a virulent illness that claimed the lives of many soldiers-of-fortune. The march inland was also plagued by fierce attacks from natives of the lands they passed through. Hunger and thirst imposed a heavy toll that further diminished the expedition's numbers.

After much difficulty, the Federmann expedition reached the far fringe of the Upar Valley, which was home to the friendly Pacabuey Indians. The conquistadors were greatly disappointed to discover that most of the gold of the region had already been looted by Ambrosious Dalfinger, as well as Spanish soldiers from Santa Marta. Like a good soldier, Federmann followed the governor's instructions to the letter: He founded an outpost at Rio Itacha, very near the border of the Spanish region of Santa Marta. Unfortunately for Federmann and his troops, Pedro Fernández de Lugo, the Governor of Santa Marta made it clear he would forcibly expel any and all trespassers, especially men who hailed from the Welser province of Venezuela. Besides the might of his army, Governor Lugo had the backing of the *Audiencia* in Santo Domingo, which had recently ruled that the valley of Pacabuey was the boundary line of the Santa Marta settlement. Realizing that he was outmanned, outgunned, and legally outmaneuvered, Nicolaus Federmann headed back to Coro in September of 1536. The German commander left behind a contingent of soldiers camped at the Carora hills to protect the Welser claim.

Once back at Coro, Federmann and others heard rumors that a large expedition, under the command of Gonzalo Jiménez de Quesada, was preparing to set out from Santa Marta in search of native kingdoms of extraordinary wealth. After a wait of nearly a year without hearing any word from Georg Hohermuth, many at Coro, including Nicolaus Federmann, believed that the governor and his followers had perished in the wild. Nicolaus decided that the time had come to lead his own expedition to find the golden kingdom supposedly located in the Xerira Valley.

Nicolaus Federmann set off on his expedition in December of 1536 without bothering to obtain permission from the Welser firm or waiting any longer for the return of Governor Hohermuth. He was accompanied by approximately 200 soldiers-of-fortune and 500 native laborers. This outing was ostensibly organized to locate, reinforce, and provision the expedition of his missing commander. Many suspected that Federmann, after having left Coro, purposely veered his men off the established route to avoid a possible meeting with the returning soldiers under the command of Georg Hohermuth. Nicolaus was eager to explore the rumored riches that awaited at a region along the Meta River.

One of the German commander's officers was Pedro Limpias, a

conquistador of questionable character. This proud Spaniard did not care for the Welser firm and their German soldiers of fortune. Federmann had characterized Limpias "as a man of sordid fortune, who in my name killed and robbed the Indios." But Nicolaus needed the experienced Limpias, and he, in turn, needed Federmann to find the golden lands. Federmann was willing to put aside their differences, but Limpias still harbored a deep-seeded hatred of all Germans, including his commander.

At first it was easy for Nicolaus and his troops to follow Hohermuth's trail of death and destruction, a path which led them to the valley of the Tocuyo River. It was along this river that the Federmann expedition was surprised to find a band of Spanish soldiers under the command of Juan Fernández de Alderete, an officer who had led a rebellion against Governor Jerónimo Dortal in the Paria region. Alderete and his men, all of whom looked as if they were near death, were searching for the naturally rich lands of the valley of Meta, a region they had heard about from survivors of the Diego de Ordaz expedition.

In May 1530, Diego de Ordaz, a conquistador who had greatly enriched his purse while serving Hernán Cortés in the epic campaign that toppled the Aztec empire, was granted the right to "discover, conquer and populate the western region of Venezuela lands between Rio Marañon (Orinoco) and Cape de Vela (of the Sail)."[30] Ordaz used his own money and a substantial loan from two prominent Italian bankers in Seville to finance his expedition. He outfitted five ships, an army of 600 conquistadors and thirty horses to find cities in South America as rich as those he had seen in Mexico.

Diego de Ordaz was ably assisted by Gil González Dávila, alcalde mayor; Jerónimo Dortal, treasurer; Juan Cortejo, captain-general; and Alonso Herrera, maestre de campo. Ordaz's flotilla departed the docks of Sanlúcar on October 20, 1531. The expedition crossed the Atlantic and made landfall some sixty miles east of the Rio Orinoco, a region now called Guiana (also spelled Guayana). A small boat carrying 13 men was dispatched to explore the area but were unable to make landfall because there was so much mud. They went on to explore some islands, which they christened San Sebastian. Afterwards, the expedition sailed upriver for a period of eight days only to discover the region was too flooded to make landfall.

It is generally believed that the two caravels belonging to the Ordaz expedition wrecked at some point, and a portion of the crew had to make do aboard the small boats. Many, however, were left behind to fend for themselves and were never heard from again. During a desperate effort to locate the larger ships of the flotilla several of the small boats were swept away, and one reportedly sank with all aboard. Rumors later circulated that some of the missing crew had rowed upriver and found sanctuary in the region known as Manoa, which some believed was the realm of El Dorado.

Meanwhile, Diego de Ordaz sailed north aboard the flagship. After probing the waters of the Gulf of Paria for 40 days, Ordaz docked at the island of Trinidad to obtain much needed freshwater and food, as well as grass for the horses. After 4 days the ship departed Trinidad and sailed toward the mainland of South America. Ordaz arrived at a channel that the Spanish captains referred to as the Dragon's Mouth, where the ship was greeted by natives aboard two canoes. The commander showed his goodwill by offering shirts made of Holland cloth and some colorful Venetian glass beads.

Shortly thereafter, Diego de Ordaz met with Antonio Sedaño, an ex-notary who amassed a fortune selling native slaves, particularly the notorious Caribs. Sedaño had been named governor of the yet to be conquered island of Trinidad. The newly appointed governor chose to settle along the mainland, where he was currently building a fortress. Sedaño viewed Ordaz as a potential threat and therefore gave the okay for one of his officers to arrest him. When the lieutenant attempted to apprehend Ordaz, Jerónimo Dortal interceded and bested the officer. On June 14, 1531, Diego de Ordaz established the settlement of San Miguel de Paria.

Nine days later, on the 23rd of June, Diego de Ordaz and 350 of his men sailed up the delta of the Río Orinoco. Prior to their departure, Alonso Herrera had been sent ahead to probe the waterway. He encountered a large native settlement along the riverbank, whose inhabitants displayed a bellicose nature. By this time Ordaz and his crew caught up with Herrera's small expeditionary force, and the reunited conquistadors continued to sail past a number of villages.

Along the region of Uyapari, Ordaz decided he would lead an expedition along a path that ran parallel to the river. Gil González Dávila was placed in charge of the ship and the 25 men who were too sick to join the shore excursion. Upon reaching Puerto Ayacucho, a distance of roughly 600 miles, Ordaz and his men, after having endured sweltering heat, numerous Indian assaults, incessant swarms of mosquitoes, and near constant sickness, were compelled to turn back upon encountering an impenetrable wall of unchecked vegetation. The expedition fell back to where the waters of the Orinoco and Meta converge. The Spaniards readily believed stories from the Caribs of vast amounts of gold located further up the Meta. Ordaz and his men made an effort to reach this region by boat but the strong current impeded their efforts.

Diego de Ordaz returned to Paria but his plans to continue searching for gold were cut short when Gil González Dávila was imprisoned by Ortiz de Matienzo. Diego was now at Cubagua with a mere thirty followers. He was also taken prisoner by Matienzo and shipped to Santo Domingo, where he was released by a sympathetic judge. Ordaz tried to put together another expedition but was denied permission. He decided to return to Spain to obtain a royal decree but died aboard ship on July 22, 1532. Some suspected that he had been poisoned by the hand of Ortiz de Matienzo.

Following the death of Diego de Ordaz, Jerónimo Dortal petitioned for the vacant governorship of Paria, an appointment which he was granted in October 1534. Eager to return to the Meta to find the golden region the Caribs had described, Dortal quickly organized his own expedition. A countless stream of misfortunes soon gave rise to a mutiny; Jerónimo Dortal was tied up and sent back to Paria with a small band of bodyguards while the rest of the weary troops sought to find the settlement of Coro. When the Federmann expedition encountered this sorry lot of Spanish stragglers in the Valley of Tocuyo, the German commander laid claim to the troops, along with all their weapons and provisions. Nicolaus sent Juan Fernández de Alderete and his Spanish officers back to Coro before setting off in search of the rich region of the Meta Valley he had heard about from survivors of the Diego de Ordaz and Jerónimo Dortal expeditions. Soon thereafter, Nicolaus Federmann happened upon the expeditionary force of Diego Martínez, who was returning from an exploration of the Guajira peninsula, and took the liberty of confiscating their supplies.

Now that he was reinforced with supplies and men, and bolstered by new reports of riches just waiting to be discovered, Federmann followed the course of a number of waterways, which led him and his men on a circuitous route to a region that seemed to be situated in the middle of nowhere. The expedition eventually managed to find the Orinoco just east of where the river is joined by its Apure tributary. Upon reaching this area of the Apure where he could have come to the rescue of the survivors of the governor's expedition, Federmann instead chose to blaze a trail with his soldiers-of fortune in his determined quest to locate kingdoms laden with precious metals and gems. Fray Pedro de Aguado, a priest who was a member of the Quesada expedition, wrote in his *Historia de Venezuela* that the German officer "left the route that led along the flank of the cordillera and deceitfully advanced in the interior of the llanos."[31]

After spending a year trekking through the llano labyrinth Federmann led his men west to the Río Meta, which they crossed, and proceeded to follow the upstream course of this tributary of the Orinoco. The onset of the rainy season forced them to make camp along the banks of the Meta, where they stayed from May to November of 1538. Over time their food supply was exhausted, and the soldiers had to survive on roots dug up from the ground and fruits plucked from the trees. The incessant rains contributed to the rotting of their clothes and saddles. The men were forced to use animal skins and horse hides to replace the articles of clothing lost to the elements. The beards and hair of the men grew long, and soon became matted from sweat and infested with lice. Chiggers, ticks, and mosquitoes proved to be a constant source of irritation. The hardships of this expedition had grown so severe that many of the men expressed their wish to return to Coro.

Unmoved by the pleas of his men, Federmann pushed his troops to the foothills where the Waipis Indians dwelled, which was the same region where Georg Hohermuth and his soldiers had camped for a long time. It was here that they found more than enough food to stifle everyone's bellyaching. Once the rains ended, Federmann led his men on a southerly course. The expedition spent the remainder of 1538 searching for a pass that would lead them over the steep slopes of the eastern Cordillera. Federmann's desperate search for Eldorado was fueled by the thought that Governor Hohermuth would be greatly angered by his departure, and the only chance he had to redeem himself would be to find the elusive path that led to fortune and glory.

Sporadic engagements with hostile natives dwindled the army down to just over 200, and this number was further reduced by the difficult climb up the mountains. They eventually reached the region where the Guayupés Indians told the explorers that the gold they sought could be found among the mountain tribes. These encouraging words were incentive enough for Federmann to alter his course to the west toward the towering peaks of the Andes—the same mountain range where the Hohermuth expedition was unable to find a suitable pass for the horses.

After crossing the Pauto River, a tributary of the Río Meta, a frustrated Federmann sent Pedro de Limpias to hunt for a route over the western end of the Andes. When Limpias returned without success, Nicolaus divided his force into three units in order to conduct an extensive search. The expeditions reunited at Aracheta, later known as San Juan de los Llanos. Based on information heard from others, Federmann hoped to locate the fabled wealth of Eldorado somewhere between the Meta and Guaviare rivers.

The expedition reached the Ariari River in February 1539, which the conquistadors followed to its mountain source. The cascading river led them to the Indian village of Pasacote, situated at the skirt of a mountain range that soared to the dizzying heights of 13,000 feet above sea-level. It was here that they found the Suma Paz, the gateway through the mountains that would lead them to the high treeless plain, or *páramo*, of the region they were seeking. This pass, however, was fraught with peril. The climb was marred by many dangerous twists and turns, and they would have to improvise their own route when the pass suddenly disappeared. Some cliffs were simply too steep and treacherous for the horses, and the soldiers had to use ropes to haul up their essential animals. Sixteen horses froze to death and seventy Indians died during this grueling climb to the highlands where the Chibcha dwelled. Federmann and his men suffered terribly from hunger and exhaustion; the famished soldiers had to feed on the carcasses of the fallen horses.

After twenty-two grueling days the conquistadors finally reached the Bogotá plateau. The march across the *páramo* was more difficult than they ever imagined. The bitter cold claimed the lives of many Indian porters. Twenty horses died on the very first day and another twenty would perish from the extreme cold before they reached a more hospitable site. The soldiers had to leave their dead comrades where they fell because the ground was too frozen to dig a grave.

Nicolaus Federmann and the survivors followed the riverbank of the Suma Paz to Pandi, where they passed over the immense natural bridge of Icononzo. They soon caught sight of a Chibcha village. The soldiers were, for the moment, unaware that they had finally found the legendary golden lands they had sought for so long. The expeditionary force had now been whittled down to 160 soldiers and 70 horses.

The weary troops were granted a much-needed rest while Pedro de Limpias set off on his horse to reconnoiter the region. Pedro hadn't traveled very far across the highland savannah before he came upon the unexpected sight of another group of encamped soldiers who were also in search of legendary native kingdoms flush with gold. Surprised to find Gonzalo Jiménez de Quesada and his soldiers from Santa Marta had beaten them to the realm of the Chibcha, Limpias introduced himself and then returned to Federmann to relay the distressing news of his encounter with a rival expedition.

2

The Conquistadors of Quito

The true names and exact dates of birth surrounding the conquistadors who sought fortune and glory in the New World, especially those who were of humble origin, are but a few of the many conundrums an historian must face when attempting to piece together an accurate account of events. Sebastián de Benalcázar is a case in point; There is evidence to suggest that his surname was Moyano while contradictory reports indicate his last name was García. The illiterate Sebastián listed the small Spanish town of Benalcázar, or Belalcázar, in Estremadura as his birthplace. The dates of his birth range from as early as 1495 to as late as 1499.

Sebastián apparently fled his hometown to avoid prosecution for his role in the death of a donkey. As the story goes, the young Sebastián, who earned his keep selling wood his father had chopped from the forest, was guiding around town his donkey loaded with wood when the beast of burden suddenly became stuck in the mud. Having trouble freeing his animal Sebastián made the fatal mistake of striking the donkey too hard on the head with his guide stick, and the exhausted beast keeled over and died.

Fearing the ire of his father and the judgment of the court, Sebastián fled to the port of Cadiz where in 1514 he boarded a ship that was part of the fleet escorting Pedro Arias de Ávila, better known as Pedrarias, the elderly and notorious noble who was the newly appointed governor of the Panamanian colony founded by Vasco Núñez de Balboa. The Pedrarias fleet carried a number of notable soldiers-of-fortune destined to leave their mark on the New World, a list that included Hernando de Soto, Diego de Almagro, and Bernal Díaz del Castillo.

The young Sebastián soon proved his worth when an expedition led by Pedrarias became hopelessly lost in the surrounding forest. A sense of desperation set in once their food supply was spent. A number of soldiers made their way to the top of the trees to see if they could ascertain a way out of the forest, but all they could see was a vast sea of trees. Fortunately, the keen eyes of Benalcázar spotted smoke emanating from a long way off, which he guided the governor and the troops towards. They found their way to the source of smoke, which was the smoldering campfire of friendly natives who informed them of the surest route back to their settlement. The native camp yielded a small amount of gold, which the governor awarded to Sebastían for having led them to safety. He declined this generous offer, stating he had simply done what was expected of him. Benalcázar added that since all had endured hardships on this expedition then all should share in the wealth. His selfless act left a favorable impression on Governor Pedrarias.

While stationed in Panama, Benalcázar heard the native tales of rich kingdoms to the south, a golden realm that Vasco Núñez de Balboa was eager to discover. He also witnessed the tragic beheading of Balboa, a death sentence imposed by a jealous Pedrarias. In 1524 Sebastían managed to further his favor with Governor Pedrarias by serving with distinction in the invasion and conquest of Nicaragua, and in 1527 he played a key role in the founding of the city of León, where he would serve for more than a year as the first alcalde.

In 1531 Sebastían accepted an offer to join forces with Francisco Pizarro and Diego de Almagro in their determined quest to locate the rich kingdom of the Incas. He was a participant in the capture of Lord Atahualpa at the city of Cajamarca in 1533, and an eyewitness to the tremendous store of gold and silver collected for the release of the ruler. Benalcázar was present when Pizarro reneged on his promise to free Atahualpa once the exorbitant ransom demand had been paid, and instead ordered the execution of the imprisoned Inca ruler. He was the recipient of a share of Lord Atahualpa's ransom, a payment that amounted to a sizable fortune.

Huascar, who lorded over Cuzco, was considered the legitimate heir to the Inca throne, but many of the generals at Quito threw their support behind Atahualpa, who was known to be the favorite son of Huayna Capac. After receiving news that his advance force had crushed the royal army and captured Huascar, as well as the city of Cuzco, Atahualpa and the large army that accompanied him decided to make camp at Cajamarca before continuing on to Cuzco to lay claim to the whole of the empire. The new emperor decided to linger longer at the hot-springs of Cajamarca when he learned from his spies that strangers from across the sea were making their way over the dramatic rise of the Andes Mountain range to meet with him.

While Francisco Pizarro set off with the bulk of the army to claim Cuzco, the wealthy capital of the Inca empire, Benalcázar was dispatched with 150 men to take command of the recently established garrison designed to protect the port of San Miguel de Paria. Pizarro also had him escort a significant portion of the accumulated treasure to San Miguel, which was quickly filling with soldiers-of-fortune who had sailed from various Spanish ports in the New World after learning of the riches of the Incas.

Shortly after reaching San Miguel, Sebastían was visited by emissaries of the Cañari tribe who informed him that an Inca general by the name of Rumiñavi had proclaimed himself ruler of Quito, a highland city that was, prior to the arrival of the Spaniards, being cultivated as a second capital to help oversee the vast and expanding empire of the Incas. The region was the homeland of the Inca ruler Huayna Capac, who planned to build another capital city that rivaled or surpassed the splendor of Cuzco. His sudden death of a mysterious illness around 1527, which was very likely the infectious smallpox disease introduced by previous Spanish incursions, left a great divide that severely weakened the empire. A civil war soon erupted between the two sons, Huascar and Atahualpa, of the late emperor.

The fierce Cañari tribes were eager to exact revenge against the Incas who had treated them cruelly, and therefore wanted the Spaniards to help them drive Rumiñavi, Atahualpa's general, out of Ecuador. They piqued Benalcázar's interest with stories of vast riches that awaited them at the kingdom of Quito. Without bothering to obtain permission from Francisco Pizarro, Benalcázar recruited 140 soldiers-of-fortune and, in early 1534, headed to Ecuador to conquer Quito, a city said to exceed the wealth of Cuzco. Guided by the Cañari emissaries, Sebastián and his troops made their way along the treacherous mountain path of the Andes to the homeland of the Cañaris where they were reinforced with three thousand warriors who pledged to help them capture the city of Quito. The conquistadors and their native allies won several pitched battles against the Inca army, but Rumiñavi was determined to deprive the enemy of a rewarding victory. The Inca general ordered the city stripped of the precious gold and silver that the Spaniards coveted and had the treasure buried in several secret locations. Once the city was cleansed of valuables, Rumiñavi had his men set fire to the city while he fled with a few faithful followers and a large share of Inca treasure.

Upon taking control of Quito on December 6, 1534, Benalcázar and his troops were terribly disappointed by the sight of charred buildings, several of which were still smoldering when they entered, and what little treasure the city had to offer. The Spanish commander dispatched expeditions to reconnoiter the region around Quito. These excursions were expected to round up any Inca forces in the area and hopefully locate the stores of treasure hidden by Rumiñavi.

While Benalcázar was busy laying claim to the city of Quito, Pedro de Alvarado, the governor of Guatemala and one of the principal figures in the Spanish conquest of the Aztec empire, was leading a large army into Ecuador to claim a share of the northern realm of the Inca empire. Alvarado

2. The Conquistadors of Quito

was marching toward Quito to begin his search for wealthy kingdoms equal to those of the Inca realm that had just been conquered by Pizarro. While Benalcázar was unaware of Alvarado's approach, the news of the legendary conquistador's plans had become known to Francisco Pizarro and his partner Diego de Almagro.

Diego de Almagro led a contingent of conquistadors to San Miguel where he planned to join forces with Sebastián de Benalcázar and his troops to confront the invading army of Pedro de Alvarado. Once at San Miguel, Almagro was deeply disturbed by the news that Benalcázar had set out for Quito without authorization. Worried that Sebastián had betrayed his and Pizarro's cause in order to reward himself with the governorship of Quito, or, in a worst-case scenario, the treacherous officer was scheming to join forces with Alvarado, Almagro rushed to follow the path blazed by the absentee commander of San Miguel. Once they caught up with him at the Ecuadorian town of Riobamba, Sebastián was able to convince Almagro that his intentions were not sinister and emphasized that he had to strike quickly in order to capture Quito and its rumored wealth for his commanders. The two officers then joined forces to defend their claim to the region.

After a perilous trek over the mountains, and dreading a confrontation with fellow Spaniards over claims to this disputed region, Pedro de Alvarado accepted a monetary offer of 100,000 pesos de oro from Diego de Almagro to relinquish the ships, weapons, and soldiers he had brought with him. Sebastián de Benalcázar was left in charge of Quito when Diego de Almagro set out to rejoin Francisco Pizarro. Sebastián utilized native laborers to rebuild the charred city, which the commander christened Villa de San Francisco de Quito. While laying the foundations for a new Christian city, Benalcázar's soldiers tore through existing temples and palaces in a frantic search for secret stores of precious metals and gems. Since the anticipated wealth of Quito continued

Portrait of Pedro de Alvarado (Library of Congress).

to elude him, Benalcázar dispatched expeditions to search the surrounding lands for the missing general Rumiñavi and the Inca treasure he had removed from the city.

An officer by the name of Luis Daza succeeded in apprehending Rumiñavi, and returned to Quito with the Inca general as well as a captured native messenger who had been sent by his chief from the nearby region of Colombia to seek help from the Incas, their allies, to wage war against an enemy tribe. This Indian was brought to Benalcázar for interrogation and was quick to say that he came from a region called Cundinamarca and that his tribe was at war with a tribe called the Chibcha. He captured the attention of the Spanish commander by declaring that this land was rich with emeralds and gold, much of which could be easily scooped from the rivers.

The Indian emissary from Cundinamarca also told Benalcázar of a highland chief who ceremoniously covered himself from head to toe in gold dust before sailing on a raft to the middle of a sacred lake where he cleansed his body in the water as an offering to the serpent god who dwelled below. The numerous priests aboard the raft followed suit by depositing offerings of gold and emeralds in the water. The elaborate ceremony concluded with observers casting numerous precious jewels and golden objects into the lake. According to some Spanish chroniclers, it was Sebastián de Benalcázar who begat the legend of El Dorado by referring to this native chief as *el indio dorado*.

The Indian messenger proceeded to tell Benalcázar that the rich realm of Cundinamarca was a mere 12 days march from Quito. He added that besides a natural abundance of gold and emeralds the region was home to many groves of cinnamon trees, a spice that was worth its weight in gold to Europeans. Benalcázar dispatched Pedro de Añasco at the head of forty horsemen and an equal number of foot soldiers to investigate the region they were told could be reached in less than a fortnight. A few days later the corpulent Captain Juan de Ampudia was sent with a company of soldiers to reinforce Añasco's mission. The conquistadors burned to the ground any village they came across and killed all the inhabitants. The transgressions of these Spaniards were soon dealt a harsh punishment; both officers and most of their men were killed during a fierce confrontation with the Yalcones.

Meanwhile, the imprisoned Rumiñavi was subjected to intense interrogation measures in an effort to learn the precise whereabouts of the Inca treasure he had hidden. Frustrated by Rumiñavi's refusal to reveal his secret hiding places, Benalcázar ordered the execution of the Inca general. Sebastián had his men continue to search the surrounding region for buried treasure, but the whereabouts of the wealth of Quito remained a mystery. The commander decided to focus his efforts on exploring the province of Popayán, a region he hoped was rich with gold, emeralds, and cinnamon.

Benalcázar rounded up several hundred Spaniards and several thousand native porters for his expedition, the latter of whom were to carry the great stores of treasure he expected to find. After overcoming some minor delays, and again without bothering to seek the approval of either Francisco Pizarro or Diego de Almagro, Sebastián set out to locate and lay claim to the lands rich with gold, emeralds, and cinnamon.

In Search of the Gilded Man

Sebastían de Benalcázar departed Quito in 1536, which was around the same time that Nicolaus Federmann was preparing to leave Coro and Gonzalo Jiménez de Quesada was planning to set out from Santa Marta in search of treasures just waiting to be discovered. Sebastían and his army marched across Ecuador to the small native settlement of Popayán, located near the Cauca River in present-day Colombia. This was a hostile region that was home to a number of tribes, a few of whom were reportedly cannibals. Some of these tribes raised crops and mined gold to trade for salt with the Chibcha nation. Benalcázar systematically and brutally conquered the scattered villages along this route. The large and vicious hunting dogs were often let loose on the natives, frequently just for sport.

Shortly after Sebastían's expeditionary force left Quito, Gonzalo Díaz de Pineda, one of Benalcázar's officers, set out from the city to investigate native tales of rich lands to the east. After several days of marching and battling hostile natives, Pineda and his men came to a valley laden with groves of cinnamon trees. Many natives of the tropics utilized the flower buds of these bushy evergreen trees they cultivated to create a refreshing, aromatic drink. Pineda was elated over the prospects of this discovery; cinnamon was one of the most sought-after spices, for it made bland foods, especially meat, more savory. Gonzalo christened the region *La Canela, the province of cinnamon.*

Pineda returned to Quito with samples of these cinnamon trees. He also brought back news from the local natives that by venturing east, "they would come to a wide spreading flat country, teeming with Indians who possess great riches, for they all wear gold ornaments, and where are no forests nor mountain ranges."[1] There was no immediate follow up expedition because Benalcázar was already on a quest to locate rich native kingdoms to conquer and pillage.

Meanwhile, Francisco Pizarro was deeply concerned over recent reports of growing unrest at Quito. He also was suspicious of the intentions of Sebastián de Benalcázar. The conqueror of Peru dispatched Lorenzo de Aldana and a company of soldiers to Quito to arrest the audacious commander and assume command of the city. Lorenzo set out to find Benalcázar shortly after he had successfully taken control of Quito. Aldana had little trouble following Sebastián's trail of death and destruction, but, try as he would, he could never catch up with him.

Toward the end of 1536, and shortly after he had established a settlement at Popayán to serve as a base of operations, Benalcázar continued to explore in a northerly direction for another sixty miles. At this point he stopped just long enough to establish an outpost that eventually evolved into the city of Cali before reversing course and returning to Quito in mid-1537. He planned to issue a report to Francisco Pizarro, his superior, regarding the lands he had explored, but kept secret his plan to return to Spain for the purpose of obtaining an appointment as Governor of Popayán.

Sebastián was surprised to learn that Francisco Pizarro, who was upset with him for setting out on another expedition without first obtaining his permission, had sent another officer to replace him as commander of Quito. He was able to reclaim his position of authority thanks to the intervention of Gaspar de Espinosa, the former governor of Panama, who was friends with and a loyal supporter of both Sebastián de Benalcázar and Francisco Pizarro.

Soon after having been reconfirmed Benalcázar organized an expedition to the Quillasinga region, which he did, as he had twice done before, without bothering to seek permission. Gonzalo Díaz de Pineda, who served as the alcalde of Quito, set out to inform Pizarro of Benalcázar's plans. Sebastián no longer could count on the protection of Gaspar de Espinosa, for the elderly conquistador had died from illness while attempting to mediate the escalating feud between Francisco Pizarro and Diego de Almagro. Benalcázar rounded up 200 foot soldiers, 100 cavalry, and a large force of natives to embark on his search for the mysterious realm of El Dorado.

In January 1538 Francisco Pizarro charged Gonzalo Díaz de Pineda with the tasks of returning to Quito and placing the disobedient Sebastián de Benalcázar under arrest, and assuming the post of lieutenant-governor of the region. Benalcázar learned of this sudden turn of events and in March of 1538 he led his troops northward to avoid facing charges of treason. Pedro de Puelles was among the many conquistadors pressed into service for this unauthorized campaign. The expedition trekked to Popayán and then Cali to collect enough men to bring his total to nearly five hundred well-armed soldiers, many of whom were veterans of the conquest of

Peru. The expedition headed eastward in the hope of finding another rich native empire to conquer, which would put Sebastián in the good graces of the Emperor.

Benalcázar returned in May 1538 to the Popayán settlement he had founded earlier. There he heard rumors of expeditions recently dispatched from Santa Marta and Coro that were also searching for the rich kingdoms he sought to discover. Sebastián rallied his troops for the resumption of his quest by declaring, "We are fit, and our band is well equipped with swift and spirited horses. Let us go to investigate these riches before some who are coming on their trail snatch them from our hand! For, as you know, expeditions and searches are under way by many other groups."[2] These inspiring words motivated his men to continue seeking the fortune and glory they so desperately craved.

The progress of Benalcázar's march was slowed by the difficult terrain and the size of the expedition, which was enlarged by a herd of pigs brought along to feed the troops. They would pass through a dense jungle region that was home to venomous snakes and man-eating crocodiles inhabiting the swamps. Fever and malaria were a constant threat to the Spaniards well-being. Sebastián led his men up the Cordillera Central, where they climbed to the elevated lands around the conical volcano of Purace. In addition to conquering the steep and snowy peaks, the conquistadors had to battle a number of hostile tribes.

The path the conquistadors followed led them to the lands inhabited by the Pijao, a truly fearsome warrior race. Benalcázar lost 20 men during a deadly confrontation with fighters who pelted them with arrows dipped in poison. At this stage of the expedition the army was reduced to 189 men. One of Sebastián's soldiers lived long enough to complain that the march forced them to face many difficulties, which he said included "bad mountains, bad roads, and bad Indians." Continuing with their quest, Pedro de Puelles would recall that they arrived at "mountain slopes with tiny villages and bad, poor people [armed] with much poison, where our men were being killed every day."[3]

After four difficult months of travel the Benalcázar expedition arrived at the valley of the upper Magdalena. As they neared the trading center of Neiva, the Spaniards were delighted to happen upon some of the gold dust that the tribes used to barter with the Chibcha, a tribe they had previously heard was endowed with an abundance of emeralds and gold. They also discovered tracks left a few months earlier by horses of the Jiménez de Quesada expedition. Benalcázar sent an officer to follow the trail, but he returned after having followed the tracks for a distance of twenty leagues. Sebastián feared that the expedition from Santa Marta had beat him to the prize they sought.

Sebastían de Benalcázar's search for a vast treasure trove of precious delights had led him to the wind-swept plains of Bogotá, where the temperatures are much milder. Here he was surprised to discover that two other expeditions had ventured to this region to claim the wealth of Eldorado.

3

The Fortune Seekers of Santa Marta

In June of 1533 Hernando Pizarro prepared to return to Spain with the obligatory royal fifth of the bountiful treasure that his older half-brother, Francisco Pizarro, had collected as ransom for the release of Atahualpa, the captured ruler of the Inca empire. The spoils of the conquest of Peru, which was swift and brutal, surpassed everyone's wildest expectations. Never had so few men conquered a kingdom that stored as much precious metals as that which belonged to the Incas. Even the relatively recent conquest of the Aztecs by Hernán Cortés and his much larger army paled in comparison to the enormous wealth that Francisco and his small band of conquistadors had laid claim to at Peru.

The royal tribute stored aboard Hernando Pizarro's ship was equivalent to 100,000 gold pesos. Nearly all of this princely sum of precious metals had been melted down and forged into bars of standard weight. However, a small array of gold and silver items deemed to exhibit the most outstanding native craftsmanship were spared from the fires of the furnace. These artifacts were shipped to the emperor so that he might have an opportunity to admire the many works of splendor that his new vassals were capable of producing.

This Spanish treasure ship made stops at several ports in the New World before setting sail across the Atlantic. One of those brief stopovers was Santa Marta, a Spanish settlement along the northern coast of Colombia. The north coast of South America was known to the Spaniards as Tierre-firme, the mainland, but rival nations commonly referred to this region as the Spanish Main. Founded in 1524, Santa Marta rested upon a small bay overlooking the Caribbean Sea, which was then known as the North Sea.

García de Lerma, the governor of Santa Marta, had been preparing an expedition to explore the path of the Magdalena River, which he hoped would lead to the Southern Sea, where Francisco Pizarro was known to be

"Hernando Pizarro Before Charles V" (from *Complete Works of William H. Prescott*, published 1912 by DeFau & Co.).

searching for a rich Indian kingdom. But when the Peruvian treasure ship stopped at Santa Marta, the colonists and Governor Lerma were instantly stricken with gold fever. Many colonists abandoned the Spanish settlement and headed off to join Pizarro's army, including the governor of Santa Marta.

3. The Fortune Seekers of Santa Marta

Hernando's ship safely reached Seville in January 1534. The unloaded gold and silver works of art were shown to Emperor Charles V, who put these magnificent items on display before they were melted and turned into coin. One of the many spectators who had an opportunity to gaze upon the splendid specimens shipped from South America and exhibited in Seville was Pedro de Cieza de León, a young Spaniard who was inspired to venture to the New World to serve as both soldier and historian.

There was a consensus, especially during the era of the Spanish exploration and conquest of the Americas, that gold abounded in regions resting closest to the sun. With this thought in mind, it was easy to conclude the nearer that land was to the equator the more likely were the chances of finding splendid fields of gold. The South American provinces of Venezuela, Colombia, Ecuador, and Peru all conveniently fell into this degree of latitude. Many of the native tribes of these regions referred to gold as the *sweat of the sun*. Since wealthy native empires had recently been discovered in Mexico and Peru it therefore seemed logical that other rich kingdoms were just waiting to be found in the tropical regions of the New World.

Pedro Fernández de Lugo was another of the many Spaniards beguiled by the thought of discovering golden kingdoms in the New World. Don Pedro was the son of Don Alonso de Lugo, the first governor of the Canary islands. The Lugo clan had amassed enormous wealth in commercial enterprises, particularly the lucrative sale of native inhabitants of the Canaries at the slave market. The family had strong ties to the Crown as evidenced by Don Alonso's appointment to the governorship of the Canary Islands, which was granted *in perpetuity*. The Canary Islands were a convenient stopping point for ships sailing to and from the Americas. Both father and son were interested in expanding the family's commercial wealth through exploitation of the rich resources that the New World promised to yield.

Shortly after he learned of Francisco Pizarro's astonishing discovery, Pedro Fernández de Lugo, the governor of the island of Tenerife, petitioned the Crown for the right to govern Santa Marta, a province that bordered to the west of the lands that had been granted to the Welsers. The wealthy Don Pedro was soon named to replace García de Lerma, who had abandoned his post, as governor of Santa Marta.

Don Pedro Fernández de Lugo and his son, Alonso Luis, had begun to think about settling in the Americas after a chance meeting with Francisco Lorenzo, a conquistador who served under the command of Rodrigo de Bastidas on an expedition that probed the coasts of Central and South America. Lorenzo told them about the settlement of Santa Marta, which had been established to exploit the rich resources of the region. He spoke of the Tairona, a tribe that possessed gold, and boasted of vast beds of luxurious pearls just waiting to be harvested.

Alonso Luis told his father, "Let Your Grace stay here warming the governor's seat in the Canaries, while I swear to get you the one in Santa Marta from the court by making the merits of my grandfather shine all over again. And do you go on getting ships together as fast as possible, and talking with people, because we will be making the acquaintance of Terra Firma in a few months, and then we'll start piling up the gold."[1]

After consenting to his son's request, Alonso Luis presented himself at the Court of Charles V and Queen Juana to request for his father the governorship of Terra Firma. He reminded officials of the great accomplishments that his grandfather, Don Javier Alonso Luis Fernández de Lugo, had made in the service of Spain. Then he spoke of the wealth of his father, who pledged to finance the expedition at his own expense. His persuasive manner succeeded in acquiring the governorship for his father. Depending on which account one subscribes to, the Governor of the Canary Islands was granted the governorship of Santa Marta in the year 1535 or 1536. Don Pedro Fernández de Lugo was granted control of the lands that stretched between Venezuela and Cabo de la Vega, which were pledged to the Welser banking firm, and to Cartagena, which fell under the jurisdiction of Pedro de Heredia.

After receiving his official grant and conducting a quick inspection of the Santa Marta region, Don Pedro Fernández de Lugo returned to Spain to recruit able-bodied men to settle the land and search for native kingdoms endowed with vast quantities of gold. Don Pedro dipped into his personal fortune to purchase 18 ships to cart the 1500 soldiers and 200 cavaliers, and store the horses, weapons, armor, and supplies he felt were needed to ensure the success of his mission. Other ships were to follow; the captains were instructed to join up with the fleet at Tenerife, where Lugo planned to acquire additional recruits and supplies. Alonso de Lugo, who served as a captain on this expedition, soon proved to be a man of questionable moral character.

"There is in Santa Marta," declared the historian López de Gómara, "much gold and copper, which they gild with certain pressed and pounded grass; they rub the copper with it, and dry it in the fire; the more grass they use, the more color it takes, and it is so fine that at first it deceived the Spaniards. There are amber, jasper, chalcedony, sapphire, emeralds, and pearls; the land is fertile, and irrigated; corn, yucca roots, yams and garlic flourish there." The chronicler added that the natives "pride themselves on having their houses well furnished with dyed or painted mats of palm or rush, and cotton hangings set with gold and baroque pearls, at which the Spaniards marveled greatly."[2] It was this sort of enticing picture that attracted many to sign on for the Lugo expedition. Among those who answered the call for soldiers-of-fortune was a middle-aged lawyer named Gonzalo Jiménez de Quesada.

The emperor and empress made it clear, as they had with previous expeditions to the New World, that no harm should come to the natives. Furthermore, it was stipulated that at least two men of the cloth were to accompany any expeditions in search of native wealth, and no Indians were to be enslaved or forced into labor. The catechism prepared by Francisco de los Cabos was to be read to any tribes encountered; asking them to accept Christ, God, and the Holy Trinity. It was the responsibility of a cleric to ask the natives, "Do you believe in the Holy Ghost and in Jesus Christ His Only Son who was born of the Virgin Mary?"[3]

Sailing without incident from Santa Cruz de Tenerife, it still took the fleet about forty days to reach the coastal settlement of Santa Marta, which the governor planned to use as a base for exploring inland. Pedro Fernández de Lugo had expected to find a flourishing town but instead found a settlement in utter disarray. The site was also equally shocking to the handful of Spanish ladies who accompanied this expedition. Don Pedro found the settlement of Santa Marta was in dire need of repair before he could even consider undertaking a search for native kingdoms as rich as that of the Incas. Santa Marta had been founded a decade earlier by the Spanish explorer Rodrigo de Bastidas, and García de Lerma, the acting governor, who arrived a few years later. According to the historian Fray Pedro Simon, Santa Marta was "one of the cities most combated by evil fortune that was to be found in all the Indies."[4] One of the first victims of this ill-fated settlement was the elder Rodrigo de Bastidas, who, in 1526, was killed by the hand of his lieutenant, Juan de Villafuerte.

Don Antonio Bezos, the interim commander, and members of the town council waited along the beach to greet the newly appointed governor and his entourage. The surviving settlers of this forsaken outpost were few in number and exhibited an unhealthy pallor. The men of Santa Marta lived in crude huts thatched with ferns, slept on hammocks, and cohabited with native women. It was learned that the colonists, who had never explored more than a hundred miles beyond their post, had to contend with a hostile tribe of cannibals, and many were weak with fever and dysentery. The welfare of the colonists was dependent entirely upon the good grace of the chief of the Bondas, who supplied them with food and clothing. The tattered cotton garments and worn sandals of these few residents were a stark contrast to the elegant attire and shiny armor of the arriving settlers.

The historian López de Gómara recorded for posterity a description of the natives of Santa Marta: "The women wear aprons about their waists, and wear their hair dressed in great plumes. They look very well in these, and taller than they are, and therefore are said to be comely and beautiful. The men go about naked, although some of them cover their privacies with pipes of gold."[5] The nearly naked tribe of the Bondas had some gold, which the newly arrived Spaniards demanded as tribute. All appeared before Governor Lugo, except for their chief, with an amount of precious metal that was much too small to satisfy the expectations of the Spaniards.

Since there was just one stone hut the new colonists had to house themselves in tents. Governor Lugo tended to the sick and ordered the immediate building of new shelters. He also needed time to build smaller vessels for exploring the surrounding region. The governor sought to restore the settlement of Santa Marta but the strength and will of the colonists were sapped by a rapidly diminishing supply of food and tropical fevers. Dysentery affected the bowels of many new settlers. They did not dare venture into the thick forest, where tribes of cannibals might pick them off with poisoned arrows so they could feast on their flesh.

Captain Bernardo de Vargas Machuca, a veteran conquistador, noted the savage nature of many tribes toward captured Spaniards in his *Milicia Indiana*, published in 1599: "They often pale them alive, as has been seen in Santa Marta, and they hang the heads at their houses and drink from their skullcaps in their great drunken festivals. They make flutes of the leg and arm bones; the great captains wear these at their necks. And where they eat human flesh, they grind the bones and drink them in chicha."[6]

The Spanish settlers would expend much time and energy digging graves for the dead. The governor soon had to contend with the grumblings of his recruits, most of whom felt they had been misled about the opportunities that awaited at Santa Marta. The most vociferous were the numerous sailors who had been pledged an allotment of gold for their services.

Eager to resolve his desperate need for food and gold, Don Pedro organized an inland expedition consisting of a thousand capable soldiers and his best officers. The governor set his sights on attacking the village of Bonda, whose chief had failed to pay him the proper respect and tribute he had expected. Unfortunately for Don Pedro and his men, the inhabitants of Bonda refused to yield to the demands of this invading force. Mounting a strong defense, the tribe killed and wounded a great many of Don Pedro's men before they could lay claim to the village, which failed to yield anything of value. Adding to Don Lugo's frustration was the tenacious effort of the natives to reclaim their village by bombarding the soldiers with arrows and loosening boulders from the nearby mountains. An angered Don Pedro had his troops set fire to the village and seven others in the neighboring valleys of Coto and Vallhermoso during their retreat to Santa Marta.

Meanwhile, the Santa Marta colony suffered terribly from attacks by the Tairona Indians, and the new governor decided to punish these natives who were determined to reclaim the land that was once theirs. The Tairona conducted trade with many of the tribes living in the mountains of Central Colombia, which very likely included the Chibcha.

Seeking to avenge what he perceived as a grave injustice perpetrated by hostile natives, the governor granted his son, Don Alonso Luis, command of a company of soldiers to attack a Tairona village situated along the side of a steep mountain. A grateful Alonso pledged to return with items of value. He ordered the burning of villages along their route. Once the fire had finished burning the troops sifted through the ashes and were rewarded with a considerable find of gold nuggets, large enough to raise their expectations. The sacking of pueblos in such manner was referred to as *ranching*, and the precious metal obtained was referred to as *ranch gold*. While the gold satisfied their lust for treasure it did not satisfy their hunger, which was great due to a lack of food. After conquering the main village of the Tairona, the conquistadors confiscated every ounce of gold they could locate, which amounted to fifteen thousand *castellanos* in jewelry and sculptures.

The conquistadors were pleasantly surprised to find a donkey that had survived an earlier Spanish shipwreck by swimming ashore. The animal was discovered along the coast by the natives and then brought to their mountain village, where he was accorded the name of Marcobaré, the same name as their Tairona chief. It was Sargento Mayor Salinas who took possession of the rescued donkey.

Don Alonso grew so rapacious in his desire for gold that he suddenly did not wish to share any current or potential wealth with his father. He discussed with the captains his inclination to head to Spain instead of Santa Marta, in an effort to receive his own governorship of these rich lands. Alonso failed to take into account that he was trespassing on lands awarded to the Welsers, a region presently overseen by Nicolas Federmann, their agent in the New World.

The governor's son pressed on in the hope of finding more gold to hoard and natives to enslave. The conquistadors used the cover of darkness to conceal their movements from the natives. Despite their cautious approach, Alonso and his men walked into an ambush. They happened upon a well-placed cord strung to gourds and bones, and when the soldiers bumped into them the clattering sound alerted concealed warriors who swiftly pounced on them in a most terrifying manner. Though caught off guard, the Spaniards managed to prevail, despite suffering a few initial losses.

Don Alonso returned to Santa Marta with a great many chained Indians and a large quantity of gold. He sought to conceal much of the collected treasure from his father, as well as his scheme to return to Spain to procure his own governorship of the region. However, rumors quickly spread through Santa Marta about Alonso's audacious plan. The governor, who desperately needed gold to pay his men and settle the debts he had incurred, confronted his son about this treacherous plan. The heated discussion ended with the father instructing his son to distribute amongst the sailors the gold he had returned with to satisfy their pecuniary anxieties.

The day after the governor and his son had quarreled it was discovered that Don Alonso secretly had all the gold collected on his expedition loaded onto a seized ship and quickly set sail for Spain. He left nothing for his father nor the men who had helped him acquire this treasure. A ship was quickly dispatched in pursuit of Alonso, but he managed to elude it, and arrived in Spain a month before his father's emissary. When documents were produced that proved his treachery, Don Alonso was arrested and sent to prison. Somehow, he contrived to obtain his liberty, either by bribery or some other odious means.

The church bells of Santa Marta tolled continually for the dead. An epidemic had spread through the settlement shortly after the return of Don Alonso's expedition. Don Fernandez ordered the bells to be silenced; the chimes were disheartening to the sick and dying settlers. Soon there were not enough healthy men to dig the many graves, which meant the weakened colonists had to resort to digging mass graves that held the bodies of as many as twenty. A number of survivors boarded available boats in the hope of finding sanctuary at Cartagena or anywhere other than Santa Marta.

An Unexpected Choice

Eager to locate the fabled riches that would bring prosperity to his Santa Marta colony Governor Lugo decided the time had come to dispatch an expedition to ascend the Magdalena River to where native villages with bountiful offerings of precious metals and gems were just waiting to be found. Pedro Fernández de Lugo financed this expedition with money he borrowed from merchants at Hispaniola and the Welser firm. This latter group of investors also financed an expedition from Venezuela that was embarked on a similar quest. The Santa Marta settlement suddenly came alive as settlers busied themselves preparing ships, polishing weapons and armor, harnessing horses, and rounding up supplies and food items for the upcoming expedition.

One fine morning in April 1536, the governor addressed the troops that had assembled at the main plaza of Santa Marta: "I, Don Pedro Fernández de Lugo, Legate of the Canary Islands and perpetual Governor of Santa Marta and its provinces, for his majesty, name as my Lieutenant-general the Lawyer, Jiménez de Quesada. I name him General both of the Infantry and of the Cavalry of the Army, that is ready to set out on the discovery of the great Rio Grande de Magdalena."[7]

3. The Fortune Seekers of Santa Marta

Many were surprised by Governor Lugo's choice to lead such a large and ambitious expedition, especially the overlooked captains. The erudite Gonzalo Jiménez de Quesada was quite popular with the men but his training was as a lawyer and not as a military commander. There were, however, a few lawyers who had previously distinguished themselves in the ongoing conquest of the New World; Gaspar de Espinosa played an important role in the conquest and settlement of the western region of Panama, and Nuño de Guzmán led a very bloody campaign to subjugate a northwestern province of Mexico. Even Hernán Cortés, the conqueror of Mexico and considered by many to be the greatest conquistador of all, had some legal training.

Depending on which account one reads, Gonzalo Jiménez de Quesada was born either in 1495, 1497 or 1499. We do know that he was the eldest child of Gonzalo Jiménez, a prominent lawyer, and Isabel de Quesada, the daughter of a wealthy merchant of cloth-dyes. The family relocated at the cosmopolitan city of Granada during Gonzalo's formative years. Situated along the southern coast of Spain, Granada was the last stronghold of the Moors in Spain until it surrendered in 1492 to the Christian army led by the pious King Ferdinand and Queen Isabella.

Committed to follow in the footsteps of his licentiate father, Gonzalo Jiménez, the young Quesada studied to become a lawyer. He was still attending the University of Salamanca when a youthful Charles arrived from Flanders in 1517 to inherit the title of Carlos I, King of Spain. Soon thereafter, Gonzalo earned his degree in law, presumably at Salamanca University, and then went to work in his father's law firm at the Andalusian city of Córdoba. He also worked in the supreme court of Granada.

Listed among this roster of recruits who signed on for Pedro de Lugo's expedition to the New World was the name of Gonzalo Jiménez de Quesada, who, without hesitation, quit his law practice for an appointment offered by Don Pedro as chief magistrate

Gonzalo Jiménez de Quesada, from Herrera's "Historia De Las Indias." Published 1922 for *The Conquest of New Granada.*

and second-in-command of the colony of Santa Marta. Quesada decided to abandon the practice of law after having lost a major lawsuit, a verdict which adversely affected the finances of his mother's side of the family. The suit involved a court case against the dyers of the city for false claims they allegedly made about their dyes. Gonzalo served as the defending lawyer, which found him arguing the case against his own father. Losing this decision sullied the young lawyer's reputation and damaged his name within the family, for his mother's side was heavily involved with the dealings of the defendants.

After this humiliating incident, the despondent lawyer hoped to redeem himself by joining an expedition to the New World. Gonzalo Jiménez de Quesada stated that the organizer of the expedition to Santa Marta had come to town "with a drummer on the one hand and a friar or two who later joined under the pretext of converting the Indians on the other, and they went about promising riches and turning the heads of ignorant people."[8] Gonzalo Jiménez headed to Santa Marta in the company of his brothers Hernando and Francisco. Gonzalo saw this as a splendid opportunity to find fortune and glory, an effort that eventually earned him the nickname of *El Conquistador*.

The expedition that was to set out from Santa Marta to locate the wellspring of the Rio Grande de Magdalena and the rumored golden kingdoms of the interior was divided into two groups. Quesada was to personally lead 620 foot soldiers and 85 cavaliers overland for roughly 40 leagues while an additional force of 200 soldiers under the command of Ortun Velásquez de Velasco sailed aboard six newly built brigantines. Besides the soldiers, these ships carried the bulk of the provisions that otherwise would have unduly burdened Quesada's troops. The rendezvous point was slated for the Indian trading center called Tamalameque, which had been discovered five years earlier by the Dalfinger expedition and rested about 40 leagues away at the mouth of the Sompallón River. From there the combined Spanish force would seek out the source of the Magdalena, Colombia's primary river.

Unseasoned in military affairs, Jiménez de Quesada made sure to surround himself with officers who had experience in such matters. Juan de Junco had seen service in campaigns in Italy and Hungary, as well as having been a member of Sebastian Cabot's journey up the River Plate; and Gonzalo Suárez Rendón, who served in the army of Charles V in the hard fought battle of Pavia, which led to the capture of Francis I, king of France. Juan San Martín, Pedro Valenzuela, Lázaro Fonte, Juan de Madrid, and Antonio de Lebrija were among the officers who played prominent roles on this campaign. In the event of his death, Juan de Junco was to replace Quesada as commander of the expedition. The next officer in line of succession was Gonzalo Rendón. Gonzalo's brother, Hermán Quesada (or Hermán Pérez de Quesada), was appointed chief magistrate.

Captains Antonio Diaz Cardozo, Luis de Manjarrés, and Juan Céspedes were named as commanders of the flotilla. Quesada appointed Gonzalo Garcia Zorro and Anton de Olalla as ensigns. The expedition included several priests and monks, all of whom were on a dual spiritual mission of tending to the eternal souls of the Spanish soldiers and converting to Christianity the heathen hordes who inhabited this godforsaken land. These men of the cloth included Padre Domingo de Las Casas and Padre Anton Lescano.

Amidst much fanfare, General Gonzalo Jiménez de Quesada marched his troops out of Santa Marta on April 5, 1536, though some accounts list April 6 as the day of departure. The expedition was accompanied by royal notaries and a royal treasurer, all of whom were responsible for keeping track of the enormous wealth they expected to find on this venture, one-fifth of which rightfully belonged to the Spanish Crown. There were 85 magnificently caparisoned horses and an untold number of donkeys carrying food and supplies calculated to support them until they rendezvoused with the ships. Marcobaré, the rescued donkey, strode alongside the cavalry. Juan de Castellanos, an accompanying conquistador who chronicled the expedition in his *History of New Granada*, wrote that Quesada was encouraged and guided by "vague rumors and faint echoes of a report,"[9] which probably was a reference to the Chibcha natives of the Andean plateau. Hundreds of conscripted Indians were brought along to serve both as guides and porters for the long journey.

The well provisioned supporting flotilla, however, was not quite ready to depart. The governor urged them to leave as quickly as possible and make haste to join up with Quesada, but 20 days would pass before the ships, which now totaled seven, set sail. Meanwhile, fever and hunger claimed the lives of many settlers, and a despondent Governor Lugo began entertaining thoughts of abandoning Santa Marta and joining up with Quesada.

A Perilous March

Instead of taking the direct southern route toward the Magdalena River, which was known to have numerous swamps and streams, Quesada decided to lead his troops on a path he hoped would contain fewer obstacles. The alternate course he followed would prove to be a much longer route to their intended destination. The Spaniards marched along the coast, a route consisting of a barren one hundred-mile stretch of sandy soil punctuated with patches of scrub and cactus. They quickly discovered that there was a scarcity of edible food and potable water in this desert province of Chimila. The expedition pressed on but soon became bogged down in torrential downpours, which meant all had to slog their way through a muddy morass in soaking wet clothes. The heavy rains of the season formed stagnant pools of water that served as breeding grounds for swarms of bloodsucking mosquitoes. The rains would give way to a torrid sun that caused the ground to steam and the soldiers to sweat.

The Quesada expedition eventually reached a small river that the men would christen the Rancheria before agreeing that it would be in their best interest to follow its inland course. This route brought them to barren foothills that had to be crossed before reaching the César River, so named for Captain Francisco César who discovered the river in 1534 and whose decomposing corpse was later found beneath a ceiba tree resting along the edge of the river. Quesada's troops had to cross the same crocodile infested swamp of Zapatosa that the Dalfinger expedition previously crossed.

Almost from the moment they set off on this newly charted course, Quesada and his men had to vigorously defend themselves from fierce guerrilla style attacks of the natives. Six years earlier, the Chimili tribe had a run in with the German expedition led by Ambrosious Dalfinger that trespassed upon their land, and therefore were determined to drive off this latest incursion. The pulse of the Spaniards quickened once it was learned that this tribe had in their arsenal the one weapon that struck a chord of terror in the mind of even the stoutest conquistador—arrows dipped in poison. According to the historian Oviedo, the natives used the poisonous red fruit of the manzanilla, a form of chamomile, which they mixed with the venom of various poisonous creatures to create a curare. There were many South American tribes that used a poisonous concoction to catch fish, hunt animals, or fell an enemy, and each tribe had their own special recipe that combined the poisonous secretions of select creatures and plants.

The New World explorers had learned from experience that anyone struck by an arrow dipped in curare had little hope of surviving once the poison entered the bloodstream. Drastic lifesaving measures, such as cutting away chunks of skin around the wound or cauterizing the injury with hot irons, were often administered, though usually without success. Quesada and his troops wisely swapped their cumbersome metal armor for the more effective quilted armor of the Indians, which helped reduce their losses. The horses, the expedition's most valuable resources, were easy targets for these deadly projectiles, which meant that their riders had to make sure they were as adequately armored as the troops. Even the large hunting dogs that accompanied the expedition were fitted with quilted coats.

Hostile natives were not the only threat to life and limb; marshes and swamps were home to deadly snakes and the much feared alligators or crocodiles, beasts that could devour the strongest of men with relative ease. The torrential rains compounded the miseries of the troops by turning the landscape into a nearly impenetrable sea of mud. Unable to rest on the ground, the men climbed trees and strapped themselves to limbs in order to avoid falling and drowning while they slept. Their pack animals frequently sank in the mangrove swamps and the soldiers had to expend precious time and energy unburdening them of the heavy weight they carried. The dense jungle foliage that the explorers had to cut a swath through was home to predatory jaguars, the swift and powerful beasts both feared and revered by the natives. The men also had to keep their eyes peeled for poisonous snakes that could strike without warning.

The timing of this venture played a significant role in the difficulties associated with the journey. Quesada and his men had left Santa Marta during the rainy season, a wet period that dampened their clothes, provisions, and spirit. Powerful thunderstorms and their accompanying bolts of lightning were frightening to both man and beast; the conquistadors had to calm their terrified horses. Many of the men were stricken with malaria, the victims suffering recurring and alternating bouts of chills and fevers that were often a prelude to death. Short of food, the men had to hunt for berries, herbs, and other edible items to sustain them on the march. Soldiers weakened by exhaustion, hunger, and illness desperately struggled to keep up with the group for fear that they would become the next victim of natives or jaguars who preyed upon stragglers. The puma, another breed of large cat, also stalked the Spaniards, patiently waiting to pounce on any soldier who fell behind. Each day the ranks of the Spaniards lessened, and the troops would halt just long enough to dig shallow graves for their fallen comrades.

The Spaniards continued to the lands of the hostile and impoverished Chiriguana, a tribe that remembered with enmity the trespasses of the same German led expedition that passed over the lands of the Chimila Indians. The expedition occasionally came upon a native village, which the famished soldiers quickly relieved of food. Small tribes often took flight when they learned of the approach of these strange men. The famished Spaniards would deplete the tribe's reserves of food items before resuming their search. A simple fare of corn, yucca roots, beans, and nuts were now more desirable than gold. The march across these arid lands took the expedition about a week to complete.

Fearing to cross the Ariguaní River—drowning and alligators being their primary concerns—the conquistadors constructed a makeshift bridge tied together with cut vines, which were twisted into ropes, so they could continue their journey to the main river, where they hoped to meet up with the supply ships. The crossing of such bodies of water was a precarious

"Zaparo Hunting Costume" (from *Exploration of the Valley of the Amazons*, published 1854 under Direction of Navy Department for the U.S. House of Representatives).

proposition; Juan Lorenzo, an exceptionally good swimmer, was wading a stretch of water to cut down a tree to be used for the building of a bridge. As he began to swim back he felt himself caught in the tight grip of a gator. He cried out for help, but his screams were silenced once he was dragged under the water. Those who rushed to his rescue saw only a spreading pool of blood. The horses were able to wade safely across the dangerous river thanks to the soldiers who scared away the alligators by beating the water with poles.

The expedition soon reached a lake where the adventurers could see the large village of Tamalameque, which was surrounded entirely by water. Their only access to this native town was to head across a causeway that passed over the lake. The scene was somewhat reminiscent of Hernán Cortés's account of the Aztec island city of Tenochtitlán, though on a much smaller scale. The respective expeditions of Alonso de Lugo and Ambrosius Dalfinger had passed this way but neither dared risk entering Tamalameque. Extreme hunger compelled Quesada to entertain such an effort.

The region had been pillaged on two separate occasions by different European expeditions, both emanating from Santa Marta. Nicholas Federmann had passed this way a few weeks before, and Ambrosius Dalfinger had explored the region four years earlier. The natives were determined to prevent another such disruption to their way of life. This was a fight that Quesada and his men had expected and were determined to win. As the conquistadors attempted to pass the causeway a number of warriors aboard canoes launched an assault. The Spaniards vigorously defended themselves; their faithful dogs jumped into the water and savagely attacked the natives. A great many warriors died during this confrontation. Quesada's troops rushed the city, which sent the inhabitants into a state of panic— they fled their homes leaving behind food and supplies that the conquerors claimed for themselves. Quesada and his victorious troops settled into Tamalameque, the principal town of the Pacabuey Indians, on July 28, 1536. The Spaniards spent the next twenty days feasting on native cuisine, tending to their wounds, and repairing damaged weapons and armor. They happened to notice that there were a great many baskets, stored at the village, all of which were filled with cakes of salt.

It was at Tamalameque, which rests near the right bank of the Magdalena River in the province of Sompallón, that Quesada and his soldiers expected to find the ships carrying their comrades and sorely needed supplies waiting for them. Believing that the boats had been delayed, the commander dispatched small parties to hunt for food. Unfortunately, they were unable to catch enough game to adequately feed so many. Having quickly exhausted the native's rations, the famished soldiers were compelled to subsist on a meager diet of frogs, lizards, snakes and any other edible foods.

The Spaniards waited twenty days for the overdue ships, during which many passed the time digging graves for the nearly 100 men who had succumbed to illness and fatigue. Their difficulties were further compounded by the fact that the rainy season had caused the Magdalena to overflow its banks.

Quesada soon tired of waiting for the supply ships and marched his troops to the village of Chiriguana. There they met several Spaniards who had spent five years in the jungle after deserting the expedition led by Ambrosius Dalfinger. They offered their services as guides for the Quesada expedition. Unfortunately, these new guides proved to be completely inept; the expedition wandered aimlessly for a dozen days, which probably explains why these men had spent five years wandering in the forest. The guides led Quesada and his men away from the course of the Magdalena and into the murky swamps formed by the periodic overflow of the river. Eventually, they managed to locate Tamalameque, the town Quesada had already located on his own.

The commander led his men along the banks of the Magdelena wherever possible. The healthier of the group had to cut a swath through the dense jungle vegetation with machetes and swords. One Spaniard fell victim to the sharp teeth and claws of a jaguar, and another lost his life to the powerful jaws of a crocodile. The expeditionary force trudged on while suffering terribly from hunger and thirst. Every day saw more men sicken and die. Juan de Castellanos, who was in the company of the Spanish commander, wrote, "Quesada saw his numerous troops diminished by fevers and sores from the plagues of travel, ticks, bats, mosquitoes, serpents, crocodiles, tigers [jaguars], hunger, calamities, and miseries with other ills which pass description."[10]

Vampire bats were an especially unnerving experience for the conquistadors; these creatures of the night flew out of their daylight shelters in great numbers to feast on the blood of other creatures. These vampire bats, which were attracted to the exposed body parts of sleeping soldiers, used their razor-sharp teeth to make a small incision from which they quickly and quietly lapped the blood of their unsuspecting victim, taking just enough to leave the soldier in a weakened state when he awoke. The horses also fell victim to the insatiable thirst of the vampire bats.

The native attendants and guides perished at an even faster rate, a loss that burdened the soldiers with additional baggage. Some of the extra weight was distributed amongst the horses, but the Spaniards took care not to overload their valuable mounts. The adventurers also had to endure the unrelenting assaults of black flies and worms that burrowed into their skin. Quesada's force of more than 700 men was pared to 209 by the end of the fourth month. The clergy on this expedition spent most of their time tending to the sick and listening to the confessions of the dying. All hope of survival faded with each passing day.

A Series of Unfortunate Events

With his provisions nearly depleted and his men weakened by hunger and fatigue, Jíménez de Quesada dispatched a scouting party led by Captain Juan de San Martín to locate the missing ships. Meanwhile, the commander kept his men busy building canoes capable of transporting them down the Magdalena, a nearly mile-wide river with a frighteningly swift and powerful current. Shortly after the canoes were fit for launching, which was 20 days after their arrival at Tamalameque, the Spaniards were elated to receive a message from San Martín informing them that he had located the spot where the ships were supposed to meet them.

Quesada ordered his men to break camp and march to the mouth of the Opón River, a tributary of the Magdalena, where San Martín was waiting for them. They soon located Captain San Martín and after much rejoicing, the reunited Spaniards resumed their march. The conquistadors crossed the César River in canoes collected by San Martín and his men, after which they entered the land of Sampollón. There were dense forests to pass through and deep chasms to cross, the latter required the building of bridges. The expedition located a suitable spot along the river to wait for the ships. Each passing day saw more men succumb to sickness, hunger, and fatigue. The commander dispatched San Martín downstream to locate the long overdue ships.

Captain San Martín and his small company of Spaniards and natives soon found what they were looking for: Juan Gallegos and two badly battered vessels had made it to the rendezvous point, where they unloaded moldy bread, a few kegs of wine, and some linen, the latter of which was used to make bandages. These were the supply ships dispatched by Governor Fernández de Lugo after he learned of the disaster that befell Quesada's ships. The commander suddenly found himself reinforced with 200 more men in need of food. Unbeknownst to the members of this expedition, Don Pedro de Lugo passed away shortly after these boats set sail. This meant there would be no additional reinforcements or provisions from Santa Marta.

As mentioned previously, the ships that were to join up with the inland expedition did not set sail until Ash Wednesday, which was nearly three weeks after Quesada and his troops had departed Santa Marta. On the first night the flotilla anchored in a cove while the officers formulated their last-minute plans. The ships set sail early the next morning, which was

Maundy Thursday, upon the deep-blue Caribbean Sea. Good Friday proved a pleasant day for sailing. Saturday, however, displayed ominous signs of foul weather headed their way; turbulent waters increased in intensity, and soon the ships found it difficult to keep from crashing into one another. To avoid a collision, the boats steered apart and soon lost sight of one another.

The seafaring expedition reached the mouth of the Magdalena River but could not penetrate the rush of water where the river meets the sea. The mighty flood, which was caused by the seasonal melting of the inland mountains, swept large trunks of trees that could tear the hulls of the brigantines with ease. The heavy rains further dampened their efforts. Gale force winds gave rise to powerful waves that swept away nearly everything aboard the boats, which included the supplies and rations that Quesada and his men depended upon for their survival. All of the ships were suddenly in danger of becoming lost at sea. The boat captained by Diego de Urbina managed to maneuver close to the coast, but a brigantine which attempted to follow his lead hit a sandbar and was quickly smashed to pieces by an onslaught of crashing waves. The men aboard sought to tread water, but all were soon sucked under to a watery grave.

Another brigantine suffered a similar fate. Its main mast cracked under the force of the wind and the men aboard desperately struggled to prevent its collapse. The ship managed to make it across the sand bar, but a strong gust of wind swept the ship uncontrollably toward the shore where it crashed with tremendous force. The battered and soaked crew that managed to survive this terrible ordeal rested along the shore while contemplating their next move. Some of the survivors of these shipwrecks trekked through the jungle and eventually found their way to Cartagena, a small Spanish settlement founded in 1532. Another group of survivors who swam ashore had the grave misfortune of falling into the hands of the fearsome Caribs, and all were brutally butchered and served as food for the tribe.

The swift and terrible storm swept Urbina's boat some eight leagues past the mouth of the Magdalena where an enormous wave lifted the boat into the air and threw it against a large rock along the bank. The proud but weary crew could do little to change their predicament. They were fortunate to wreck near a friendly tribe and the survivors were able to reach Cartagena.

Two other damaged ships were swept out to sea, but miraculously managed to dock safely at Cartagena. The crew was relatively unharmed, but their entire cargo was lost—all of which had been thrown overboard to help their damaged ships remain afloat. They were soon greeted by some of Diego de Urbina's men, who had been escorted to Cartagena by peaceful natives.

Another two ships avoided the impact of the powerful hurricane thanks to the slowness of their sailing speed. Unaware of what had befallen their shipmates, these two vessels entered one of the mouths of the river. At the village of Malambo they patiently waited for ships that would never arrive. After several days had passed, a brave shipmate volunteered to return to Santa Marta to inform Governor Lugo of their dire situation. Before he was able to find his way back, and prior to the return of the men from Cartagena, the Governor had already sent another ship filled with supplies to aid the expedition. Unfortunately, this ship was destroyed by foul weather and rough seas; only 15 of the crew made it ashore to tell the tale of their horrific ordeal.

Meanwhile, three messengers from Cartagena arrived at Santa Marta to inform Governor Lugo of the havoc that a hurricane had caused to his ships. Around the same time the intrepid messenger from Malambo arrived to inform the governor that two ships were anchored at the river, and were in desperate need of reinforcements and supplies if they were to continue the search for the Quesada expedition. These reports coincided with the arrival of a member of Quesada's expedition who had volunteered to inform the governor of the precarious predicament of the explorers and their immediate need for supplies and reinforcements.

Governor Lugo was informed that several men at Cartagena were too terrified to sail again to the mouth of the Magdalena and decided instead to make their way to Peru to join up with Francisco Pizarro. Included in this group of discouraged explorers was captain Diego de Urbina, who served with distinction during the turbulent rebellion of the Pizarro brothers.

To aid Quesada and his troops, as well as the men stranded at Malambo, Governor Lugo ordered the repair and fitting of three brigantines stranded along the beach. Juan Gallegos, a lawyer, was appointed as captain of this rescue mission. Gallegos recruited around 200 men for his mission, which included some who had returned from Cartagena and a handful of men who had served under Urbina. Santa Marta lost nearly every able-bodied man to this cause. The governor sent one of his officers, Luis de Manjarrés, to Santo Domingo to replenish supplies that had been lost. Unfortunately, upon his arrival the officer was arrested on charges stemming from bad debts and a jilted lover. Governor Lugo had given serious consideration to abandoning Santa Marta and relocating either at Cartagena or joining the Quesada expedition, but death robbed him of these plans.

When Gallegos and his crew finally reached the mouth of the Magdalena they were confronted with a difficult journey upriver; the men had to fight against the strong current of the river, and contend with armadas of canoes carrying armed warriors who contested the Spaniards efforts to pass through their lands with a hailstorm of arrows. The deadly discharge of Spanish firearms kept the persistent warriors from boarding the boats. Realizing that this was a battle they could not win, the natives retreated, leaving in their wake a number of dead warriors and demolished canoes. To advance upriver, the soldiers would have to rely either on the strength of men to row the boats with oars, or cables that were used by men ashore to pull the ships. Though the goal was to link up with Quesada, the members of the expedition were often distracted by promising paths along the way, which they followed to see if they led to any inland civilizations.

After learning of a native settlement up ahead, Quesada took three canoes and seven soldiers, one of whom was his brother, Hernán Pérez de Quesada, and proceeded to the village under cover of darkness. Luckily for them, the inhabitants had abandoned their pueblo after sighting the Spanish boats earlier in the day. Even though there was no gold or other valuables for them to claim, Quesada and his men were thankful that the natives had left behind a fair quantity of maize and several canoes. Word of their discovery was sent back to the main force, which arrived six days later. The Spaniards learned from some captured natives that this village, which consisted of thirty huts and situated where the port of Barranca Bermeja now stands, was called La Tora. Quesada spent three months at La Tora so that his men could rest their weary bones and fill their bellies with manioc and maize from the nearby fields. While at this village, Quesada and his men found several superior linen mantles, which convinced them that perhaps they were on track to finding a rich kingdom.

The rivers Magdalena, Opón, and Carrare all converged at La Tora. During their extended stay at this village, several soldiers who sought to quench their thirst became fodder for opportunistic crocodiles lurking along the riverbanks. Such a fate awaited Juan Luengo, an unsuspecting conquistador who, despite the best efforts of comrades who rushed to his aid, was dragged to a watery demise by an awaiting reptile. To avoid losing any more men to the powerful jaws of these stealth creatures the commander ordered his troops to stop going near the river.

In another man-eating predator related incident, Juan Serrano was mauled by a jaguar while he slept in his hammock. Fortunately, a number of comrades heard him cry out: "Help, friends, a tiger is carrying me off; for God's sake help."[11] The rapid approach of men with blazing torches frightened the beast into dropping his prey and fleeing to the safety of the woods. The lacerated and bloodied Serrano was brought back to camp and tended to, after which he was returned to his hammock, which had been raised for his protection. Unaware that the jaguar was watching their every move, the predator returned once everyone had left and quietly dragged Serrano, whose screams were muffled by the steady patter of a heavy rain, into the woods where it feasted on his flesh. The men who went to check on Serrano the following morning discovered an empty and blood-soaked hammock. They followed the trail of blood but never found any sign of their comrade's remains.

Shortly thereafter, the supply ships joined up with Quesada's camp. The arrival of Gallegos and his supplies helped to restore the health and spirit of the expeditionary force. Quesada's men satisfied their bellies with the small store of bread and drowned their sorrows in the barrels of wine unloaded from the boats. There was also a supply of linen, which the soldiers used to bind their wounds. The ships also carried letters from families and friends at Santa Marta, which warmed the hearts of the survivors.

The rejuvenated soldiers felt they were ready to resume their search for riches, but their cautious commander refused to depart until all had rested for a period of a week. Quesada dispatched scouts to learn the course of the river and the lay of the land. To give thanks to the Almighty for guiding their way to one another, an altar was fashioned along the banks of the Magdalena for Father Antonio de Lescano to say morning Mass. All knelt on the moist grass with their weapons in hand, a surreal scene highlighted by a backdrop of swirling vapors of rising steam and dew drops descending from leaves high above.

A Sense of Urgency

The two lawyers, Gonzalo Jiménez de Quesada and Juan Gallegos, agreed it was in their mutual interest to continue their quest. The boats were to head upstream while Quesada would lead his troops by land. There were no Indian trails to follow, for the natives of this region traveled by canoe along the river. Captain Jerónimo de Inzá stood at the head of small company of soldiers who blazed a trail for the army to follow. To open a path in this dense forest entwined with thick vegetation the soldiers wielded mattocks, axes, and cane-knives (machetes) to clear the jungle growth, which proved to be a slow and grueling process. The thick canopy of the forest blotted out much of the sunlight; their eyes slowly adjusted to the murky mist, but the night was encased in total darkness accept for the flittering lights of fireflies and phosphorescent eyes of animals lurking about, many of which were ferocious pumas, jaguars, snakes, and gators.

Hunger once again was the bane of the Spaniards. When the food ran out the famished troops were forced to eat the horses that had died, which were quickly cut up, cooked, and consumed. Several men died after gorging on berries that were poisonous. Captured anteaters, bats, snakes, lizards, frogs, and dug up roots were additional sources of sustenance for Quesada and his men. Some of the troops gnawed on the boiled leather of their harnesses and scabbards. Men in a weakened state who fell behind were left to fend for themselves, many of whom were killed by natives who were tracking the expedition.

Some of the soldiers fled to escape this arduous journey, a number sufficient enough to compel Quesada to force a halt to such desertions. The commander also sought to prevent his famished troops from killing the horses to satisfy their ravenous hunger by declaring anyone who killed a horse would be put to death for endangering the mission. The execution of one soldier for such a deed proved sufficient to end any further violent acts against the horses.

There are also tales of soldiers resorting to cannibalism to stave off their hunger; such men feasting on the bodies of dead comrades and native porters. Soldiers in a weakened state shuddered at the very thought that soon they might become food for their companions. Many began to fear their comrades as much, if not more, than the carnivorous beasts of the jungle. "Every night the river carried off a corpse or two or three, cast into the water to prevent alarming the timid and arouse the incipient cannibalism of the most unscrupulous."[12] After eight months it seemed as if all were fated to die in the jungle. At this juncture the expedition had followed the inland path of the Magdalena for roughly 300 miles.

While the majority of the troops were granted a much-needed period of rest, Quesada dispatched a small exploratory expedition to search for native kingdoms teeming with precious metals and gems. The commander secretly hoped to locate a province that would provide him with enough fortune and glory to permit him to cut ties with Governor Lugo and have himself proclaimed a governor. The scouting party explored for thirteen days without sighting anything of value, after which they returned to camp to issue a report that sank the hearts of every man. Quesada remained hopeful and sent out scouts to find and explore alternate routes. A trail explored by Albarracín and Antonio Díaz Cardoso led to the knowledge that natives in the region of Sompallón made salt "from human urine and palm dust" and formed it into cakes "like lumps of sugar."[13] Their tales of gold in the province of Sompallón excited the interests of the men, especially the newly arrived troops who accompanied Gallegos.

The stout hearts of Quesada's troops were tested to the limit when their comrades began perishing at an alarming rate from starvation and sickness. The fields of corn at La Tora were strictly controlled by Quesada, who wanted to keep his men from gorging on food that their stomachs were not strong enough to handle. With nothing to show for all their intense sufferings, whispers of rebellion spread amongst the disgruntled troops.

A growing number of soldiers openly expressed a desire to return to Santa Marta and nominated Captain San Martín to present their grievances to the general. Quesada listened quietly as his captain recounted all the hardships the men had endured for the last eight months, and what little they had to show for all their agonizing efforts. Without provisions, guides, or fixed destination, the soldiers felt the time had come to cut their losses and return to Tamalameque, a fertile region where they could establish a settlement that could serve as a base for future expeditions.

Even Quesada worried they might have reached a dead end, a fear that he kept to himself. He reminded San Martín that Governor Lugo had risked all of his personal and borrowed funds on the success of this expedition, and to turn back now would assuredly result in the financial ruin of the Santa Marta colony. He pointed out that the fine linens and the small amount of gold they had procured from villages, which the natives said they obtained in trade from inland tribes, strongly suggested that they were on the right track to locating the rich civilizations they sought. Seeking to allay the concerns of his troops, Quesada told them: "The natural grief I feel, gentlemen, at the loss and death of so many friends, does not drive me to despair. Grief is part of our nature.... Those who set out for wars and conquest put themselves into close touch with death.... It would be ignoble to return with nothing done."[14] He subtly reminded them that there was little waiting for them at Santa Marta.

After he had successfully persuaded his discontented troops that to turn back now would be an act of suicide, and that it was better to trust their chances going forward, Quesada dispatched a few men in canoes upstream to explore the region ahead. They soon returned with the disparaging news that the treacherous rapids of the river made travel any further along the Magdalena an impossible task. Not one to give up, Quesada made plans to send another exploratory expedition up the Rio Opón.

Remembering the cakes of rock salt on display at Tamalameque, Quesada dispatched a small detail to locate the salt rich lands of Sompallón. Between 20 and 25 soldiers under the command of Captain Juan de San Martín and an officer named Juan de Céspedes set off in six canoes up the Rio Opón, one of the major tributaries of the Magdalena. On their second day upriver San Martín and his crew encountered a canoe with three natives aboard. The frightened Indians dove into the water and swam ashore to hide in the woods. An inspection of the canoe revealed they were transporting blocks of salt and clothing material dyed purple. The captain took this as a sign that they were finally on the brink of locating a wealthy native civilization.

Captain San Martín and his crew continued upriver for a brief distance through an untamed land inhabited by only a few primitive tribes. San Martín decided to follow a promising stream, and soon stopped to investigate three huts where cakes of salt, like the kind found aboard the canoe, were stored. The officer docked the canoes at a cluster of bushes and led his men on a march inland in an effort to locate a nearby village while three soldiers stayed behind to guard the canoes. A ten-mile trek led the scouting party out of the jungle and into a clearing where they located a path, which they chose to follow in anticipation of finding a rich native kingdom. They continued along this route for some forty miles, during which time mountains and large villages with fields of crops came into view. It was along this fertile plain that the Spaniards found a village that had salt baskets, like those seen at Tamalameque, which came from the salt mines of Zipaquirá. Fearing to risk entering with so few men, San Martín impounded some salt and fine woven garments from the abandoned huts to show his commander. Soon thereafter they happened upon a well-worn trail that appeared to be a promising path to the Chibcha empire. At this point, San Martín decided to return to the canoes.

On their way back to the boats, San Martín and his men were attacked by warriors who, in great numbers, hid behind reeds at the river's edge. This whirlwind assault of natives uttering shrill war-cries, and armed with bows and arrows, spears, and hard wood clubs called *macanas*, caught the band of soldiers off-guard. The Spaniards were saved by a powerful volley from their crossbows, which managed to fend off their assailants and allowed them to take a prisoner. The captain showed the captured Indian a small gold plate in his possession and he responded through gesture and voice that he knew where such shiny metals could be found, which was the same place where salt comes from. The Spaniards decided to retain the native, whom they named Pericón, to serve as both guide and interpreter for the expedition.

After an absence of two weeks, the scouting expedition returned to camp with Pericón, and news of promising lands up ahead. San Martín told his commander that they had located some deserted villages and a storehouse filled with cakes of salt. Quesada was elated by this report, which seemed to confirm they were on the right track to finding the riches they sought. San Martín's news also helped lift the spirits of the troops, for the Spaniards remembered hearing from local natives that where there was salt there was sure to be found gold.

Deciding it was best to investigate these findings before committing all to follow a promising route to the riches of this mysterious native kingdom, Quesada took 60 of his healthiest men and headed overland the following morning to see if they could learn from local tribes of a trail or discover on their own a pass to the elusive region. They followed the left bank of the Opón river, which had flooded due to the steady rains. A small team of *macheteros* opened a path along the land while the boats slowly made headway against the currents of the river.

3. The Fortune Seekers of Santa Marta

By day, the soldiers had to wade through water up to their waists while carrying their own supplies, and at night there was no place to sleep except in the trees. A rapid rise in the river swept away their baggage, which contained their provisions, and for two days Quesada and his men were stranded on an islet until the freshet subsided. There was but a small amount of maize to ration among the men, and soon their hunger became so extreme that they killed and ate a stray dog that had followed them.

Quesada sent his officers Juan de Céspedes, Lázaro Fonte, Antón de Ollalla, and a detachment of men to explore the lands ahead, which they hoped would reveal the source of native wealth. The captive Pericón accompanied them as their interpreter. They were expected to return within twenty days. The expeditionary force followed an Indian trail that passed through a thick forest, and after a journey of 15 leagues they found themselves face to face with natives wearing elegant mantles. These friendly and courteous Indians provided the Spaniards with food.

The scouting party continued on for another 15 leagues, whereupon they reached a small village of around a dozen huts, which revealed an enticing number of golden ornaments. The frightened inhabitants abandoned their homes, but the Spaniards managed to capture a native who turned out to be the ruler, Opón, who had just tied the knot with his new wife. In an attempt to win the trust of the newly married ruler, Captains Céspedes and Fonte presented him with the standard fare of trinkets that conquistadors carried for trade with natives of the New World. Chief Opón, however, expressed little interest in the hawk bells, glass beads, knives, and other trifles they offered him.

While the weary members of this expedition rested Chief Opón secretly dispatched messages to his subjects to take up arms against the intruders. Fortunately for the Spaniards, a native woman betrayed the plans of her chief. When Opón denied there was any such plot he was knocked to the ground with a forceful blow from the flat of a soldier's sword. At this point, Chief Opón confessed his crime, and volunteered to guide them to another village he claimed had large quantities of woven cloth, salt, and gold.

The chief was rewarded for his kind gesture with the placement of a leather collar around his neck, which was attached to a rope held in the firm clasp of a cavalier. Opón and Pericón guided the scouting party up a steep trail, and after several days they broke through the boundary of the tree line and reached a flatland where there were numerous trails, all of which led to a great number of villages—each larger than the previous. It was at the village of Chipatá that the Spaniards realized the Indians of this region spoke a different language. The soldiers proceeded to raid a village that yielded a fair quantity of gold, the precious metal they had long been seeking. A number of men took this opportunity to pocket items thought to have intrinsic value. They also discovered that there was plenty of food in this region; the inhabitants planted fields of potatoes, beans, yams and yucca. Unknowingly, the Spaniards had reached the northern border of the Chibcha, or Muisca, civilization.

Nearing the end of their allotted time to reconnoiter the region, Captain Fonte and a few men remained at the village of Opón while Captain Céspedes and the rest returned to Quesada to report they had found the trail that was sure to lead them to a rich native empire. Elated by this news, the commander, along with Céspedes, San Martín, Valenzuela, Cardoso, and three soldiers made their way back to La Tora to collect the main army. Quesada returned to discover that his troops were under attack from an armada of some 500 canoes carrying an untold number of warriors bent on expelling the Spanish invaders. In the heat of battle the besieged soldiers mistook Quesada's canoe for the enemy and fired upon it. The battle-weary troops quickly realized their mistake and withheld their fire. All rejoiced at the sight of their commander, whom many feared, after an absence of almost two months, had perished in the wilderness. With renewed confidence the Spaniards found the strength to drive off the native armada.

Jiménez de Quesada was shocked to learn that 200 men had died at La Tora during his absence. This was equivalent to the number of soldiers who perished during the march from Santa Marta to La Tora. All of his men were a pitiful sight: tattered clothes, ragged beards, and unkempt hair called into question their desire to continue this quest. Quesada became ill upon his return and nearly joined the growing roster of the dead. Once recovered, the officer rallied his men to follow him to the mountains where gold and emeralds had been found.

Since the river was too shallow and the salt trail was inland, the commander had little use for the badly battered boats except to transport back to Santa Marta those too weak, sick, or discontented to continue the search for golden kingdoms. Juan Gallegos was designated to lead the ships back to Santa Marta. Gallegos pledged that he would return with reinforcements and fresh provisions. On December 28, 1537, a requisite Mass was held, after which those slated to return to Santa Marta boarded the boats and sailed away, while Quesada and his remaining soldiers-of-fortune set out to locate the bountiful lands of salt, gold, and emeralds.

Juan Gallegos and the men in his charge were led into an ambush by a native guide who betrayed their trust. Despite the express orders of their commander that none should go ashore, many could not resist their guide's assurance that it was safe to do so when the boats made a temporary stop. This was the spot where Chief Opón knew that warriors awaited their

3. The Fortune Seekers of Santa Marta

arrival. A lightening raid by concealed natives resulted in thirty soldiers taken prisoner, all of whom would later suffer horrifically at the hands of their captors. In a coordinated assault, an armada of canoes emerged from the creeks to launch an attack on the ships. A barrage of arrows fell on the boats, one of which took out an eye of Gallegos.

Only one brigantine, with the one-eyed Juan Gallegos and twenty wounded and weary Spaniards aboard, managed to reach Santa Marta. Unnerved by the painful experience of this journey, Gallegos broke the solemn promise he made to Quesada. Instead, Juan traveled to Peru where he served with distinction under Licentiate Pedro de la Gasca in the Spanish struggle to wrest control of the Inca empire from the rebellious Pizarro brothers. Jerónimo Lebrón, the interim governor, dispatched four ships stocked with food and supplies for Quesada and his troops, but they were unable to locate him.

Following the departure of Juan Gallegos, Quesada led his 173 foot soldiers and 27 cavaliers up the flooded banks of the river toward the plains sighted by San Martín on his scouting expedition. They were determined to fully explore the mountainous region, an elevated area that the natives told the Spaniards was the source of all their salt and gold. Such a claim seemed

PEDRO DE LA GASCA, VICEROY OF PERU.
From a portrait in the Sacristy of the Santa Maria Magdalena at Valladolid, Spain.

FRANCISCO PIZARRO, CONQUEROR OF PERU.
From the original painting in the Palace of the Viceroys of Lima.

Pedro de la Gasca, Viceroy of Peru, and Francisco Pizarro, Conqueror of Peru (from *Complete Works of William H. Prescott*, published 1912 by DeFau & Co.).

plausible after it had been learned that the Incas, the wealthiest of the New World tribes, made their home in the mountains.

A few days later, as they marched along the banks of the river, a flash flood washed away much of their provisions and forced the Spaniards to seek shelter in the trees. Many of the men were so weak they had to rely on wooden staffs to support themselves. The men had to hunt for food, a task made more difficult by the fact that their firearms were rendered useless because the powder was soaking wet. Many crossbow strings had rotted and snapped, and those still usable had been stretched to point where they had lost much of their strength. This grim situation forced the starving Spaniards to seek out villages where they could pillage food.

After twenty days of suffering, the expedition reached the huts where Captain San Martín had discovered cakes of salt. The conquistadors feasted on the small amount of recently harvested corn and yucca roots, seasoned with salt the natives had left behind. The malnourished soldiers temporarily satisfied their ravenous appetites by cooking two stray native dogs.

Resuming their march, the Spaniards used axes, machetes, and swords to hack their way through the thick vegetation. Quesada and his men followed an Indian trail that led to the towering mountains that needed to be crossed. They had a particularly difficult time getting the horses up the steep slopes of the mountain sides; lianas were cut from the trees to make ropes to hoist the horses. The bitter cold caused the men, who were scantily clad in native attire or animal skins to replace the clothing that had rotted during their march through the harsh tropical climate, to shiver uncontrollably. Many were weakened by fever but pressed on with the aid of tree branches or their swords, which served as crutches. Even Quesada was not immune from the ravage of the spreading fever and had to be transported by litter. The heavy mist reduced their visibility to less than two yards in any direction. The expedition was fortunate to suffer during this perilous climb the loss of just one horse that slipped and tumbled down the mountain.

After much effort, the exhausted conquistadors finally reached the village where Lázaro Fonte patiently awaited his commander's return. Preparations began in earnest for the final leg to the glorious rewards that awaited at the great plateau. Quesada assembled his troops, a muster which revealed that of the nearly one thousand men who had joined this expedition, only 180 were still alive. The commander was thankful that most of the horses had survived and were relatively healthy, for soon there was plenty of grass to graze.

Quesada and his troops arrived at the Grita valley, a broad plain punctuated with native huts. Smoke signals were employed by natives of this region to announce the arrival of these strangers. Once on the plain, Quesada and his men were attacked by a large force of warriors. The fierce struggle raged all day and well into the night before the Spaniards fled to more open ground. The natives followed close on the heels of the retreating soldiers but were repulsed by the charge of the cavalry. This victory left the path clear for the expedition. Compared to other conquistadors, Quesada was less brutal toward the natives and was willing to opt for diplomacy over force to gain his objective. He tried his best to keep other soldiers from committing atrocities—nonetheless, cruelties still occurred.

Taking a page from the lawyerly Hernán Cortés, who chose to cut ties with his benefactor Diego Velázquez, the governor of Cuba, Jiménez de Quesada resigned from the post that Governor Don Pedro Fernández de Lugo had entrusted to him. According to Bishop Piedrahita, who inherited Quesada's confidential papers: "He asked that by election of the camp, a certain general be chosen whom all must obey, since they had reached the turning point which admitted of their doing so without failing in their duty as faithful vassals of His Majesty. He would be the first to abide by the choice they made, and would obey the chosen one as his chief and follow him on the march unto death itself."[15] The entire camp threw their support behind Quesada as their leader.

Shortly after crossing the Saravita river, which was named the Suárez after the horse of Gonzalo Suárez Rendón drowned, Quesada and his men came to a deserted village where they received an offering of freshly killed deer. The conquistadors captured several natives, all of whom were compelled to carry their supplies. The expedition marched past the large town of Moniquirá and followed the flow of its river, which guided them to Tinjacá, where they were able to obtain more gold and emeralds.

4

Into the Golden Realm of the Chibcha

Quesada and his troops found their way to the plateau of Cundinamarca, the heartland of the Chibcha empire, which rested in the mountainous region of present-day Central Colombia. The Chibcha were really the Muisca, or Muysca, but European conquerors and contemporary historians chose to confer upon them the name of Chibcha because the patron deity of Musica laborers and merchants was called Chibchachum. The Chibcha worshipped several gods but their primary god was Bochica, a deity who shared many of the god-like traits associated with Quetzalcoatl of Mexico and Viracocha of Peru. It was believed that Bochica had leveled mountains to provide a place for the Chibcha to live. His grateful followers would periodically raid other tribes for the sole purpose of capturing handsome boys who were to be sacrificed to him.

Once the plateau of Cundinamarca had come into view, Quesada turned to his men and declared: "Brave Spaniards and my comrades, the time has arrived when the chain of hardships with which you have been fettered in these imprisoning mountains has been broken, and you see before you, in the broad spaces of this surrounding country, the well-merited reward of your efforts; the multitude of natives, the neatness and order of their persons, offer clear evidence of the benign influences they enjoy; the land, less cautious than its inhabitants, gives open sign of rich treasures in the shape of copious lodes upon which our hopes feed."[1] These inspiring words motivated Quesada's men to continue the search for the fortune and glory they so greatly desired.

Just as Hernán Cortés had done in his celebrated conquest of Mexico, Quesada planned to lay claim to the region by winning the confidence of the natives. He was prepared to use force if necessary, but for now he was determined to keep the peace. His men were instructed not to harm the natives by either insult or injury.

4. Into the Golden Realm of the Chibcha

The Spanish expedition had reached the realm of Bogotá, a southern area inhabited by numerous tribes, each ruled by a chief who paid homage to one almighty lord known as the Zipa. The Chibcha realm that extended to the north as far as Somondoco was known as Junza. Their chieftain, who was referred to as the Zoque, lorded over a region rich with emeralds.

The Chibcha society, which had an estimated population of 500,000 distributed amongst 42 settlements along the fertile basins of the Bogotá and Sogamoso rivers at the time of the conquest, was not quite as advanced as the Inca culture; they had no stone structures or paved roads to connect their empire like those of the Incas, no pictorial writing like the Aztecs or the Maya, and never developed a calendar—though some scholars, such as Alexander von Humboldt, believed they had, but the evidence failed to support this conclusion. The Chibcha empire, however, was rich with gold and precious stones, and their towns were adequately defended by palisades. The wealth of this native society was the source of the El Dorado legend.

The Chibcha, like the Incas and other mountain dwelling tribes of South America, had developed bodies attuned to the rugged terrain and rarified air of such lofty elevations. They were generally short and broad chested and had an expanded lung capacity. The Chibcha pierced their nose septum for the wearing of pendants. Like the Inca elite, the nobles distended their earlobes in order to wear earspools, which were often made of gold. Unlike the Inca, who built their cities out of stone, these natives built their villages primarily with wood. Most buildings were painted in bright colors, and their roofs were formed from braided ichu-grass. All the homes looked the same, except for the chiefs, which were usually much larger and adorned with long, thin sheets of beaten gold that dangled over the entrance. Held in place by ropes, these golden sheets swayed and chimed with the blowing winds. Each village had numerous temples and shrines dedicated to their gods, which were maintained by a cult of priests.

With few natural resources, the isolated Chibcha had to rely on their skills to produce items they could trade for desired items possessed by neighboring tribes. Salt and emeralds were the natural wealth of the Chibchas, and these articles were traded for gold. The Chibcha also traded food items, pottery, and fabrics at various points along the Río Magdalena for fruits, grain, cotton and gold. There existed four large trade markets where tribes would meet to barter goods: Bogotá, Zipaquirá, Turmeque, and Tunja. Most of the acquired gold dust came from the tribes of the lowland regions who swapped it for much needed salt, which was formed into loaves. Quesada and his men now understood that salt served as a form of currency for the natives of this region. The gold obtained through trade was set aside for royalty and priests. The Chibcha also had copper, which some

Spaniards referred to as coarse gold, that was cast into bars, and which fooled a number of conquistadors.

As part of their coronation celebration, the newly chosen Chibcha ruler would spend several days prior to the ceremony hidden in a cave, where he was deprived of the company of women, and the partaking of salt and chili peppers. Once the cleansing period ended, the ruler was led to Lake Guatavita where he was stripped naked and covered with clay or sticky resin, after which he was blanketed from head to toe with fine-gold dust. He was then escorted onto an elaborate ceremonial barge with four lighted braziers, which burned with incense and other resins. Numerous braziers were also lit on shore, which combined to create a great cloud of smoke thick enough to obscure the light of the sun. The chief boarded the reed raft with four prominent chiefs; all five were naked except for their golden adornments of earrings, crowns, pendants, and bracelets. A pile of gold and precious emeralds were placed at the feet of the new chief of chiefs.

The ceremonial raft was propelled by rowers toward the middle of the sacred Lake Guatavita, while musicians along the shore set a reverent mood with tones emanating from a variety of native instruments, which was enhanced by the singing of songs from the congregation. Once the ceremonial barge reached the center of the lake, a flag was raised to signal the need for silence. The ruler-to-be and his attendants then threw into the lake their precious offerings to the gods. This was followed by the gilded Chibcha ruler leaping into the lake and bathing himself in the water to wash off the gold, which shimmered momentarily on the surface before slowly descending as an offering to the serpent god that dwelled at the bottom of the sacred lake. A chorus of music celebrated the inauguration of the new lord of the Chibcha. Once the anointed ruler returned to shore, the numerous onlookers who straddled the rim of the lake capped the ceremony by dumping offerings of gold, emeralds, and other precious items into the lake. This tale of a gilded ruler was a real event, but the conquistadors were unaware of the fact that this ceremony was abolished around 1500. The story, however, lived on as the legend of El Dorado.

A Plentiful Land

On March 11, 1537, the Quesada expedition reached the southern fringe of the vast highland realm inhabited by the Chibcha. It was in this region that they saw for the first time emeralds with a striking green hue that had been mined by the natives. But this luxuriant sight paled in comparison to the reported 1,173 pesos-weight of gold they were able to acquire. Hoping to rid themselves of these greedy strangers, the natives conveyed to the Spaniards that in the lands to the north they would find a large mine rich with veins of emeralds.

In an address to his troops, Quesada stated, "We are now in a settled and well-populated country. Let no one show violence to any man. We must have confidence in God, and carry matters with a light hand. Thus shall we gain the sympathy of those we meet, for after all they are men like ourselves, if perhaps not so civilized, and every man likes to be treated with civility. So will these Indians. Therefore we must not take from them that which they do not want to give. By following this plan, they will give us what we require, whereas by harsh treatment we shall force them to withhold even necessities. After all, even the ground we tread upon is theirs, by natural and divine right, and they allow us a favor to be here, and owe us nothing."[2]

It was at the town of Sorocatá that the conquistadors were introduced to potatoes, a food that was very much to their liking, which they learned came in many varieties. Because it grew underground and looked somewhat similar to the familiar truffle (turmas), the region was dubbed the *Valley of the Turmas*. The only meat available to the Chibcha were deer and a species of guinea-pig known as cavies.

Quesada and his weary troops rested a few days at Sorocatá, where they spent much of their time removing chiggers that had burrowed into their flesh, particularly their feet. These annoying mites entered through shoes and clothing whereupon they burrowed into their flesh. To relieve the burning itch that often swelled to painful extremes, especially after they laid their eggs, the native women helped them by picking out the chiggers with pins or needles. The expedition proceeded to the large village of Nemoncón, where the conquistadors were awestruck by the sight of large sheets of beaten gold dangling from wooden platforms.

On March 28, Quesada and his men reached Nemoncón, where they had an opportunity to test the mettle of the Chibcha. As many as six hundred native warriors laid an ambush by concealing themselves behind a hill, where they patiently waited to attack the much smaller force of Spaniards from the rear. The omnipotent Zipa Bogotá (Bocotá) led his warriors in this assault against the European invaders. The Chibcha ruler, who was adorned with an array of golden ornaments, was carried into battle on a gold-plated litter. The present Zipa was accompanied by the mummy of an earlier Zipa, who was also decorated with an abundance of gold jewelry. The sight of so much glittering gold helped inspire the covetous Spaniards to victory. Much to the relief of the conquistadors, their enemy was not armed with bows and arrows, which they had learned to fear because many tribes in this part of the world laced the tips of their projectiles with poison. The native warriors were armed with javelins, but they were no match for Spanish weapons and horses.

The open plains allowed the Spaniards to fully utilize the swift and sturdy might of their horses. The Chibcha had never seen an animal as large and powerful as the horse. Frightened by the deadly force of rider and horse who worked in concert, the warriors quickly fled from the field of battle. The Spaniards gave chase, mowing down many helpless warriors. The Zipa Bogotá watched from a distance as his army of warriors were thoroughly routed. The ruler was quickly carried away on his litter to avoid being captured. The victory permitted Quesada and his men to claim 600 pesos weight of gold and 145 emeralds.

While Bogotá escaped with most of the treasure to a cave in the mountains, a great many of his subjects sought sanctuary at a fortress known as Busongotá. As the Spaniards advanced on the compound a lone valiant Chibcha warrior came out to challenge a solitary Spanish soldier to combat. Captain Lázaro Fonte accepted the challenge and rode out on his horse and dragged the warrior off by the hair. Fearing that they too were about to be taken away in the same demeaning manner, the Chibcha immediately abandoned Busongotá.

The victorious Spaniards marched into the valley of Bogotá, the epicenter of the Chibcha empire. The soldiers were greatly impressed by the splendid palaces, temples, and homes, all of which were made of wood. Many of these wooden structures were painted bright red, a color derived from the berries of the Achiote (Bixa orellana) that the natives also used to paint their faces. One Spaniard, whom some historians credit as Antonio de Lebrija, remarked that their buildings, "although thatched, they could be considered as some of the finest seen anywhere in the Indies."[3] The native cuisine of potatoes, corn, and game helped restore the strength of the Spaniards who were sorely weakened by fever, malaria, and hunger. The finely woven cloths of the natives were used to make clothes to replace their tattered garments.

The Spaniards pressed on in the hope of capturing Zipa Bogotá, whom they were led to believe was the omnipotent ruler of the Chibcha. Quesada and his men began to encounter native resistance, which grew more frequent and aggressive the closer they came to their destination. The Zipa, however, had fled deep into the mountains to avoid capture.

The conquistadors continued to follow the beaten path that led to the salt-mine village of Zipaquirá. The Spaniards were relieved that the inhabitants chose to receive them in friendly manner. It was here that they saw a tremendous store of salt baskets, so many that they decided to refer to this place as the *Valley of the Villages of Salt*. The chief told them of the town of

4. Into the Golden Realm of the Chibcha

Muequetá, a place the Spaniards were led to believe was a vast storehouse of gold and emeralds.

The Chibcha did not know what to make of these strange looking men. They deserted their homes but left behind an offering of food, as well as some gold and emeralds. The Indians of the region thought of the strangers as children of the sun and took to calling them *usachies,* meaning sun moon. The Spaniards were without the benefit of a reliable interpreter, and therefore had to rely on sign language in order to communicate their needs and desires. Quesada sought to find out where the treasures of this land were located. Native rulers were quick to learn that they could rid themselves of European intruders by simply telling them what they wanted to hear, regardless if it was true or not.

Many native tribes along the way believed that the bearded Spaniards were gods who came to feast on human flesh. Some parents took the drastic step of throwing their children at them as an offering of food. Pericón, the native guide and interpreter, did his best to convince the Chibcha that the Spaniards had come to their land in the spirit of friendship. However, not everyone believed that these strangers had come in peace.

Quesada and his troops reached Guacheta, an impressively large town consisting of some two thousand homes. The inhabitants had abandoned their village but left behind an old man who was tied to a stake near a fire, which the Spaniards concluded was an offering of human flesh. When the conquistadors ignored their elderly human oblation, the natives guessed that the strangers preferred more tender flesh. They responded by sending some of their children as a replacement offering. When the invaders ignored this gift, the natives decided to send a male and female adult along with a deer that had just been killed. Noticing that the conquistadors ate the deer and not the members of their tribe, the Chibcha realized that the strangers were not man-eaters and decided it was safe to come out of hiding. The natives soon learned that gold and emeralds made a much better offering for satisfying the rapacious appetite of the Spaniards.

Quesada and his troops departed Guacheta and soon reached the splendid lands of Lenguazaque, a region where they were able to acquire more precious gold and emeralds, along with a healthy offering of native cuisine. The Spaniards advanced on the large village of Cajicá, where the ruler Bogotá had taken shelter after his earlier battle with this invading force. An eight-day siege saw the town fall into the hands of the conquistadors. Bogotá once again evaded capture, but Quesada managed to apprehend the ruler's wooden litter that was sheathed in gold. Despite the fact that no other treasure was found at Cajicá, all were convinced they were on the right track to Eldorado.

While encamped at Cajicá, Quesada learned that the nearby ruler of Chía had anticipated the coming of the conquistadors and therefore took steps to hide all the emeralds and gold prior to abandoning his village. To make sure the whereabouts of his treasure trove remained a secret, the native slaves who carted and buried the valuable haul were slain by the trusted officials who accompanied them. When these assassins returned to tell the ruler they had accomplished their mission, the chief rewarded them by chopping off their heads, thereby ensuring they could never reveal to the Spaniards where his treasure was buried. Like the buried riches of the ruler of Bogotá, the hidden treasure of Chía has remained a secret.

Eager for another splendid haul of treasure, the Spaniards hastened their pace toward the large village of Chía, which, as expected, they found entirely deserted. The Spaniards remained at Chía through Easter searching in vain for the precious stones and metals that had been hidden by the tribe.

Resuming their quest to locate native treasures, Quesada and his men passed a number of villages along the path of the elevated plains of the Cordillera Central, the highest range of the Colombian Andes, which led to the Chibcha capital of Muequetá. The Spaniards pressed on to the valley of Suesca where they were warmly received at the town. The conquistadors proceeded to Cocunubá, which led to the discovery of a salt factory that obtained its supply from nearby saline wells.

During their extended stay at Muequetá, Jiménez de Quesada dispatched scouting parties to reconnoiter the plateau. Juan de San Martín and Juan de Céspedes led a group of soldiers westward, a path that lead them to the region ruled by the Panches, a fierce tribe of cannibals who were sworn enemies of the Chibcha. Five thousand warriors launched an attack, but the Spaniards prevailed thanks, in part, to the swift and deadly charge of the cavaliers. The officers were grateful that only ten soldiers and six horses suffered serious injuries, and all survived after their wounds were cauterized.

While the scouting expedition was still away, Quesada learned from some interrogated natives that the emerald mines were located to the west, somewhere near the lands of the Panches. The commander sent one of his captains, Pedro Valenzuela, and a small company of men to follow the route that the tortured chief said would lead to the mines. He headed eastward toward the Somondoco region, where the chief claimed they would find the source of their green emeralds. The expeditionary force made camp the first night beside a lake, unaware that they were resting at the revered Lake Guatavita, the same body of water where the Chibcha once performed their sacred golden ceremony to celebrate the crowning of a new ruler.

After breaking camp at Lake Guatavita the scouting party continued past the village of Choconta, a fortified town that stood at the furthest fringe of Bogotá's realm. During this grueling trek some forty soldiers became seriously ill after eating berries not fit for human consumption. After much effort, Pedro Valenzuela and his men finally located the emerald mines at Somondoco and labored to remove some precious samples to bring back to their commander.

The Spaniards would kidnap a number of women to serve them in various ways, which, more often than not, included satisfying their lascivious needs. Many of the native woman managed to escape sexual servitude by placing an hallucinogenic herb known as tectec, derived from flowery plants belonging to the genus Datura, into the food prepared for the Spaniards. The women quietly slipped away once their captors became stark raving mad from the toxic effects of tectec. Along the way, the Spaniards encountered an Indian woman who spoke of a city called Tunja, where doors of the homes were adorned with numerous chimes made of pure gold.

On July 14, after a fortnight's absence, Valenzuela's expedition returned to the main camp to inform Quesada they had sighted a large emerald mine in the hilly region referred to as Cerro Negro, adding they had seen natives from the Somondoco tribe work the mine. The Spaniards had expected to find mines similar to those dug to find gold, but they soon discovered that these emeralds were extracted in a very different manner. Besides the news of precious emeralds, which certainly lifted the spirits of the troops, Valenzuela reported he had seen a sweeping grassy plain that stretched as far as he could see.

Quesada seemed much more interested in the grassy fields than the rich emerald mine. He had heard stories from the natives of a rich land called Meta that existed just over the mountains. Convinced he was on the verge of discovering the wealth of Meta, Quesada sent Juan de San Martín and several soldiers to locate a pass that would lead to this region. They were to search for no more than 10 days at which point San Martín and his men were expected to return to camp.

A Chibcha guide led Martín and his men to the raging waters of the Lengupá River. The captain dispatched a message to Quesada stating it was not possible to reach the Llanos by the route he had undertaken, but he was prepared to take an alternate route from Sogamoso that the natives had suggested. They followed the path of the river, which eventually brought them to a large grassy plain. Their march was made even more difficult by the steady rains, which turned the ground into a vast sea of mud. When the food ran out the soldiers were forced to eat roots and grubs to survive. The expedition saw no signs of gold or emeralds; the only thing found worth seeing was an Indian maiden "so beautiful and modest and so well-behaved that she would have competed with Spanish women, who were adorned with these qualities."[4] As instructed, San Martín ordered his men to turn around and march back to camp once the designated 10 day period had lapsed. Meanwhile, Quesada, who was concerned about the health of San Martín and his troops, and even more about the horses, dispatched a search party. All were soon reunited at the main camp.

In the interval, another scouting expedition under the command of Hernando Vanegas returned with some gold they had stripped from a temple they happened upon in the woods. He also brought back an Indian who volunteered to lead them to a city of extraordinary wealth. Quesada learned from this native that they were very near the large settlement of Hunsa, which was the village ruled by the *Zaque*, the second most powerful chief of the Chibcha nation. Hunsa is the ancient name of the town the conquistadors knew as Tunja, a city Georg Hohermuth had heard about but was never able to locate. Shortly thereafter, Quesada and his men advanced on the town of Tunja to lay claim to its many splendid treasures.

The Spaniards suffered terribly from the severe cold of the region where the town of Tunja stood. The conquistadors had expected a confrontation and therefore were surprised to be greeted by a group of elderly dignitaries who brought them gifts and directed them to a nearby camp to rest. Quesada suspected they were merely buying time to hide their valuables and decided to have his men advance at once on the ruler's palace at Tunja. His suspicions were confirmed when the soldiers had to fight their way to the gate of the town.

Jiménez de Quesada selected a force of his fifty fittest soldiers, divided equally between cavalry and infantry, to launch a surprise raid on Tunja. The village was stormed, and the Spaniards quickly forced their way into the town. This time the Spaniards arrived before the natives had a chance to abandon their town and stash their treasure. The soldiers were encouraged by the sight of Indians with gold ornaments dangling from their pierced nose septum, and elated to see members of royalty wearing gold breast plates. They were also delighted to see that almost every house was adorned with hanging sheets of beaten gold, which emitted a pleasant tinkling tone as they gently swayed in the breeze. The Spaniards noticed that each home contained varying amounts of emeralds, beads, and cotton cloths.

While mounted on his horse, Quesada fought his way to the large wooden palace that was the home of the Zaque. Once at the gate of the palace, the commander was told he could meet with the ruler, but he would have to enter on foot. The compliant Quesada dismounted and entered the palace, which was painted bright red, with six soldiers to meet with the chief, who was bedecked with gold. Quesada read aloud an abbreviated version of the *Requirement*, which was translated as best they could to the Zaque. The ruler, an elderly man who had grown fat off the privileges of his status, listened as Quesada demanded that he submit to Spanish rule

4. Into the Golden Realm of the Chibcha   93

and accept Christianity as his true faith. The Zaque asked that he be given time to consult with his council; Quesada consented to his request, and the Tunja ruler reciprocated by providing the invading soldiers with comfortable quarters for rest.

Quesada departed the palace but made sure to leave behind a few men to gauge the council's attitude. These soldiers, however, found themselves forcibly evicted from the palace, and the gate was immediately brought down behind them. Captain Antón de Olaya rode up on his horse and used his sword to cut the ropes that latched the gate. The horsemen then charged into the compound. The Zaque and his warriors put up a valiant fight, but Quesada's men unleashed the full fury of their pent-up frustrations upon the natives. Though greatly outnumbered, the Spaniards prevailed thanks to the fear instilled by the horse. Olaya seized the elderly and corpulent ruler and made him his prisoner. Fifty Spaniards had succeeded in taking the city without suffering any serious injuries. The warriors retreated under the shadow of nightfall. They returned at dawn in an effort to rescue their chief but were thoroughly repulsed.

The subjugation of the Chibcha empire was not as difficult as other conquests undertaken in the New World. Unlike the Incas, the Chibcha did not have a large unified army to protect their realm. Instead they fought in small bands with clubs and javelins that were effective primarily for close range confrontations. These weapons were clearly no match for the hardened Toledo steel swords and the lightning charge of the cavalry. Only two Spaniards died during the conquest: One was killed by the Chibcha and the other, Juan Gordo (Fat John), who was accused of stealing a pile of blankets from a native. In the latter case, the offending soldier had secretly left camp to fill his stomach on the flesh of a horse that had just died. The sight of Juan Gordo startled a native passing by, who dropped the blankets he was carrying and took flight. Gordo would claim he believed the Indian was offering him the blankets, all of which he took back to camp. When the frightened Indian returned and saw that everyone of his blankets were gone he complained to Quesada. After investigating the matter, the captain-general decided to sentence Gordo to death by hanging. There were numerous pleas for clemency from the priests and soldiers, but they merely fell on deaf ears. Juan Gordo was executed as an example to others; a reminder that the slightest selfish act of just one man could place all in peril. The lawyerly Quesada saw this as a way to impress upon the natives that he was fully committed to keeping the peace.

The conquistadors decided to celebrate their victory by cutting down the hanging gold plates, known as *chaquales*. They went from one home to another gathering gold and emeralds, and even robbed a sacred mummy of its jewels. The Spaniards busied themselves stripping the town of treasure and piling it in the courtyard alongside the tribute paid from the neighboring tribes. The accumulated Tunja treasure amounted to 136,500 pesos of fine gold, 14,000 pesos of low-grade gold, 18,000 pesos of silver, a vast quantity of objects made of gold mixed with copper, and nearly 300 hundred emeralds. This was a hefty haul, especially when considering the fact that the Tunjans had managed to smuggle much of their gold and emeralds out of the city.

By October, Gonzalo Jiménez de Quesada and his troops had laid claim to nearly 200,000 pesos (roughly 200 pounds) of fine gold, a nearly equivalent amount of low-grade gold, and more than 1,800 emeralds of varying size and quality. The Spaniards were convinced they had found a region that was every bit as rich as the Inca empire. The division of treasure was determined by Quesada and the royal inspector. The royal fifth of slightly more than 38,000 pesos of fine gold, nearly 7,300 pesos of lesser grade gold, and 360 precious emeralds were set aside for the Spanish Crown. "Each share of the treasure, it was determined, would be worth 510 pesos of fine gold, 576 of low-grade gold, and five emeralds."[5] Quesada insisted on allocating a share to repair *La Mayor* and *La Merced*, the ruined churches of Santa Marta.

It was agreed that the governor of Santa Marta would receive ten shares of the treasure. The commander awarded himself nine shares, while the captains received four, the sergeant major three, and the lieutenants two. Cavalry lieutenants were awarded three shares, horse soldiers and clerics two, soldiers with firearms one and a half, and infantrymen one share. Nothing was set aside for the families of the 500 men who perished on this expedition, but Fray Domingo de las Casas requested from the soldiers a stipend to establish a chaplaincy, and to say continual masses for the souls of their fallen comrades. To the credit of Quesada's men, they contributed of their own free-will to Domingo's appeal. Since they had not shared in the perils of this expedition, the relief force commanded by Diego Hernandez Gallego were excluded from any claim to the treasure. When he learned of Don Pedro de Lugo's death, Quesada laid claim to the shares set aside for the governor.

Lázaro Fonte, an officer who was a vocal critic of Jiménez de Quesada, openly declared he was going to report the commander for concealing treasure, particularly emeralds, from the grand total of fortune, a fifth of which belonged to the king. Quesada avenged this slight upon his honor by having a man testify that Fonte had agreed to buy some emeralds from him, but the officer reneged on the deal without paying for or returning the precious stones. Depending on which account one subscribes to, the accuser was either a Spaniard or an Indian, and may have been in league with Quesada. Lázaro demanded the right to personally appeal to the king after Quesada sentenced him to death for plotting to swindle the seller. Appeals from the soldiers and officers convinced the commander to commute the sentence to exile in the hostile realm of the Pasca Indians, which many felt was simply an alternate death sentence. Captain Fonte was escorted to a native town and then abandoned. He was spared from a sacrificial death by an Indian maiden who had fallen for him. She convinced the chief that this Spaniard had been abandoned after he had opposed his comrades plan to sack and burn their village. Lázaro was eventually accepted as a member of the tribe.

Though delighted with the large pile of treasure collected so far, Quesada still wanted much more. The Spaniards saw that the Chibcha were excellent goldsmiths, and greatly admired their ability to beat gold into very thin sheets. They also marveled at their finely crafted gold bracelets, pins, and the detailed cast figures of various creatures, which included birds and frogs. Quesada and his men were amazed by the sight of gold tweezers used to remove facial hair and the gold jewelry inserted into their nose septum, as well as the discovery of gold masks that covered the faces of their sacred mummies. The Spaniards were impressed that the Chibcha forged small, thin plates of gold, which were used as a means of exchange. The conquistadors would soon discover that they had been fooled by some of these golden objects. Many of the items were formed into what is known as tunjos—anthropomorphic figures cast from copper and thinly coated with gold. The Chibcha had a copper mine and used this metal to fill in for the gold they lacked.

Quesada decided to take a page from the successful tactic Hernán Cortés used with the Aztec ruler Montezuma and Francisco Pizarro employed with the Inca lord Atahualpa; he held the corpulent ruler of Tunja hostage as leverage for obtaining even more food and treasure. What the Spaniards did not yet know was that there were no gold mines in the region controlled by the Chibcha. To obtain the gold they relished for its natural beauty, the Chibcha had to acquire this scarce metal from other tribes by trading their salt and cotton cloth, commodities they had in abundance. The chief, however, refused to comply with Quesada's demands, which forced the commander to drop his ransom scheme. The only words the chief spoke to Quesada were, "My body is in your hand, do with it what you choose, but no one shall command my will."[6] The elderly chief was set free but died shortly after his release.

Some eighty chained natives were forced to bear the heavy burden of the expedition's baggage when the Spaniards set off in search of other rich cities to plunder. They soon learned, much to their disappointment, that there were no gold mines and the gold of the Chibcha was mostly acquired through trade with tribes that inhabited the valley. The residents of the scattered villages were alerted of the approach of the conquistadors and quickly fled with most of their valuables.

Temple of the Sun

After having won an extremely difficult victory over a confederacy of Chibcha tribes led by a chief named Tundama, which rewarded the expedition with additional treasure, Quesada learned of another wealthy ruler named Sugamuxi, whom the Spaniards called Sogamoso. The soldiers would learn that Sogamoso, who lorded over Iraca, was looked upon as the religious leader of the Chibcha and recognized as the third most important ruler of the empire. Quesada was told that Iraca was located a few days to the northeast of Tunja. The commander also heard the tale of a magnificent temple dedicated to the Sun in the valley of Neiva said to be supported by pillars made of solid gold. Quesada was told that this town was the religious center of the Chibcha empire, and there stood their most sacred temple, the floors of which were carpeted with golden threads, and its walls reportedly lined with enormous sheets of gold. Located to the southeast, the rich province of Neiva was said to have many goldmines.

Gonzalo Jiménez de Quesada left his brother, Hernán Pérez de Quesada, in charge of the troops at Tunja while he set out with 20 cavalry and 30 infantry to find the treasures that awaited at Iraca and the valley of Neiva. The expeditionary force had to cross a vast plateau which stood at the frigid height of 12,000 feet above sea level. From there they would plunge into the steamy lowland region where the golden temple was said to be located. After overcoming several native attempts to stop them Quesada and his men managed to reach the rich plain of Iraca. Warriors from Sogamoso tried to repel them but they were quickly dispersed by the charge of the cavalry. The victorious Spaniards entered the town shortly after sundown.

The natives had learned of the conquistadors' approach and having heard of their insatiable lust for golden items they removed and hid as much gold and other valuable pieces as they could. However, the natives left untouched the many precious items that adorned their temple in the belief that the invaders would respect the sanctity of this holy temple. They had greatly underestimated the covetous nature of these men.

During the still of the night a soldier by the name of Sanchez and another called Rodriguez took it upon themselves to enter the holy temple dedicated to the god Remichinchagua. The light of their pine torches allowed them to gaze upon the numerous golden items that glowed richly under the flickering light. They saw mummies of the Chibcha elite, all of whom were decorated in gold and emeralds. The elated soldiers rested their torches on the floor so their hands would be free to pluck the treasure from the temple. The floor matting, which was made of esparto grass, caught fire and the flames quickly spread to the wood walls. It is reported that the fire which engulfed the sacred temple burned uncontrollably for five days. The Spaniards managed to salvage 40 thousand pesos of gold from the inferno.

The following day, Quesada learned that the richest region of all was the realm of Bogotá, lord of Cundinamarca, to whom all the other tribes regularly paid tribute. Realizing he had been duped Quesada, prepared to return to the region to punish the ruler. Bogotá, however, had gone into hiding in the remote hills of his province. The Spaniards continued to search for the buried treasure of Bogotá but never found what they were looking for. The prevailing rumor was that the immense treasure of gold and emeralds had been thrown into the lakes. Bogotá had hid his valuables so well that its location still remains a mystery.

As the Spaniards prepared for their return to Tunja, an Indian was spotted swimming across the three-quarter mile wide Magdalena River with a bundle upon his head. Once out of the water, the native strode into the Spanish camp to reveal that the parcel he carried contained a number of heart-shaped plates of gold, which were an offering to the Spaniards. All of the conquistadors suffered from fatigue and many were sick with fever, but the gold acquired on this expedition certainly revived their spirits.

With all the loot they had sacked from Iraca, the weary soldiers struggled for nearly a week to reach the village of Pasca; the rank and file was further thinned by the loss of six comrades. All were disappointed to learn they had missed an opportunity to capture the Zipa of Bogotá, the richest and most powerful of the Chibcha chiefs. Quesada would complain: "He has put his gold and treasure in some safe place and not with himself, so that it has not appeared up to the present; and it is said to consist of innumerable riches!"[7] Quesada appeased his troops by allotting shares of their collected loot once the obligatory royal fifth was set aside.

While his men rested at Pasca, Quesada sent a message to Hernán, his brother, to march the soldiers under his command to Bogotá, where he would meet them. The commander led his men back to Bogotá where he hoped to capture the elusive Zipa. The element of surprise was foiled by the natives' clever system of communicating over long distances; smoke signals warned that the Spaniards were headed toward Bogotá, which provided the Zipa ample time to retreat to his mountain stronghold with his family and his most loyal officials.

The conquistadors easily took the town by force, but were disappointed to learn there was less gold and emeralds than they had expected. Inside Bogotá's palace was a solitary golden vessel filled with gold dust, which Quesada estimated the value at one thousand ducats.

Unable to locate the chief, the Spaniards interrogated a number of captured natives to learn where the ruler was hiding. Once he was informed of the Zipa's whereabouts Quesada launched a night raid to apprehend the chief. Unfortunately, in their haste to gain control of the stronghold the Spaniards wounded the elderly Zipa, whom they failed to recognize in the dark, as he attempted to flee with his loyal subjects. The chief was carried by several of his subjects to the nearby woods but died a few days later from the bolt of a crossbow that had punctured his shoulder. Quesada then led his men back to Tunja, which he used as a base for launching raids on other towns. The commander planned to establish a settlement and place his brother in charge, while he returned to Spain with the royal fifth to help secure his claim as governor of this region.

Meanwhile, the Chibcha chose a warrior named Sagipa (a.k.a. Sacresaxigua) as their new ruler. Sagipa's first order was to rally his people to resist the Spaniards while he sought shelter in the mountains. Quesada turned his attention to the capture of Sagipa. The chief managed to elude the conquistadors for some time, but he was eventually captured by a dozen soldiers armed with crossbows.

The new Zipa agreed to end all hostilities and pledged to become a vassal of Spain in exchange for the Spaniards aid in fighting a rival to the throne, a chief named Chía who lorded over the Panches, a tribe currently threatening their western borders. Quesada agreed on the condition that he revealed the location of Bogotá's hidden treasure. Sagipa showed his appreciation by presenting the Spanish commander with offerings of plumes and shells.

In keeping with his part of the bargain, Quesada led an expedition against the dreaded Panches, a tribe that dwelled deep in the forest. Quesada left his brother in charge while he accompanied Sagipa with a small company of cavalry and infantry who marched alongside Sagipa's warriors to confront the Panches. The Spaniards learned first-hand that this tribe was more fierce than the Chibcha. From their fortress among the rocks, an elevated position which nullified the use of the cavalry, the warriors wielded an array of weapons, including poison darts, an arsenal they used with deadly accuracy to seriously wound ten soldiers. The Spaniards were able to turn the tide by drawing the warriors out of their stronghold and into a ravine where the armed horsemen patiently awaited. The surprised natives suffered heavy losses from the piercing lances and slashing swords of the horsemen before retreating to higher ground. The next morning the Panches sued for peace.

Quesada soon learned that chief Chía, and not Sagipa, was the rightful heir to Bogotá's empire. The Spanish commander demanded that the pretender to the throne tell him where the treasure of the previous Zipa was buried, but Sagipa told him he did not know where it was hidden. Quesada refused to believe him and rushed to put the ruler on trial. Sagípa was charged with usurpation of Chibcha authority and of knowingly keeping the royal treasure hidden from the Spaniards. The chief informed them through interpreters "he had none of the gold or jewels of that Bogotá: what he had was maize and manioc, and he knew nothing of the gold of Bogotá or of the many other things demanded of him."[8]

Sagipa was fettered and kept under constant guard. The ruler was found guilty by a jury of his Spanish oppressors and sentenced to be tortured until he revealed the hiding place of the treasure they sought. The infliction of pain did not stop until Sagipa agreed to provide them with a significant amount of gold.

Quesada told the imprisoned chief: "Know, my dear Señor Sacresaxigua, that I will treat you with all courtesy, like the great lord that you are, if, relieving me of having to take more strenuous measures, you turn over to me all the gold of Thysquesuzha, the king of Bogotá, for since his property is that of a rebellious vassal, it belongs by right to the king of Spain. For you must know that the Pope, that sovereign monarch who through God's might has supreme authority over all the men and kingdoms of the earth, saw fit to give the king of Spain this new world that his heirs might succeed to it, in order that the barbaric peoples who inhabit it and live so blindly in their idolatries might be instructed and indoctrinated in our holy Catholic faith, recognizing only one God, Author of everything created...."[9]

To which Sagipa replied: "If what Your Grace desires is Thysquesuzha's gold, I will order it gathered for you this very moment. And within forty days Your Grace will have this room filled with gold to half its height. And then, is it not true that Your Grace will let me out of this imprisonment and return me a free man to the hills, that, at liberty, I may see my own town and be happy?"[10]

Sagipa promised to persuade the other Chibcha chiefs to deliver their supply of gold to the Spaniards. Quesada wished to ransom Sagipa in the same manner that Francisco Pizarro had done with Atahualpa, hoping they could extort enough gold to fill a large native hut. Sagipa said it would take a full forty days and there must be no interference from his captors. He also stipulated that the conquistadors were to be barred from entering the room during this collection period. Quesada agreed to these terms. Native couriers were dispatched in great numbers.

Convinced that the Spaniards would never set him free, the cunning Sagipa devised a scheme that would deprive the conquistadors of the precious gold they craved. Day by day, a steady stream of natives arrived bearing a heavy weight of gold cast by hand in various forms; particularly cups, jewelry, and items fashioned in the likeness of animals and deities.

The person who carried the gold was accompanied by 36 native servants swathed in cotton cloaks. Quesada and his men could see bits of treasure bulging out of the sacks and could hear from outside the clanging of the deposited treasure.

Once the agreed upon forty days had arrived an eager Quesada entered the cell only to find that it was empty. The enraged commander turned to the fettered chief and yelled, "Great villain, deceitful dog, filthy liar! Where is the gold the Indians brought? Is not your life forfeit for this promise?"[11] The natives had fooled the Spaniards by having the bearer of gold empty the treasure while the attendants picked up one piece and concealed it in a sack, which was smuggled out beneath their cotton cloak. With the exception of Sagipa's escape, this carefully orchestrated scheme had gone exactly as planned.

A greatly angered Quesada ordered Sagipa flogged, and several others who were believed to have participated in this ruse were tortured, and then hanged. Sagipa's torture continued until he promised to lead them to the treasure hidden by the deceased ruler of Bogotá. Sagipa told Quesada: "if you will remove these shackles, allow me to go with a good detachment of troops to search for the treasure myself—for I suspect where it might be–I shall bring it to you."[12]

The chains that bound Sagipa were removed and replaced with a thick rope that hung around his neck. He was to lead captains San Martín, Suarez, and a company of soldiers to a mountain stronghold where the elusive treasure of the previous Zipa was supposedly stored. The ruler led them on a circuitous route through the hills until he arrived at a steep precipice. Suddenly, Sagipa raced toward the edge of the cliff in an attempt to end his life and consequently deprive the Spaniards of the treasure they desired. The soldiers managed to pull the chief back before he could execute his plan. He was brought back to the village and remained in prison for five months. Sagipa was subjected to repeated rounds of intense torture, which included the burning of his feet with horseshoes heated until fiery red. Despite the agony of this ordeal, the ruler refused to reveal the location of the treasure. The infliction of pain continued until the chief died. Gonzalo Jiménez de Quesada would later face an inquiry into his role in the wrongful death of Sagipa.

Quesada spent the end of 1537 and the beginning of 1538 mounting various expeditions in search of more precious gold. The Spaniards fought a difficult battle with the natives of Duitama, who had assembled a mighty force of twelve thousand warriors. The Duitama were clever enough to dig pits that disabled several Spanish horses. Quesada was knocked from his horse during the heat of battle but was rescued by his men before the natives could finish him off with thrusts of their sharp lances. The Spaniards eventually prevailed, which allowed them to resume their quest to discover more gold. The conquistadors, however, were greatly disappointed to find that the inhabitants had abandoned their town, taking with them all of their gold and emeralds. Quesada and his expeditionary force returned to Bogotá in February 1538 to rejoin their comrades. There they divided up the treasure, making sure to set aside the obligatory royal fifth.

Gonzalo Jiménez de Quesada would soon hear a tale heard by a great many New World explorers: "When the camp was in the valley of Bogotá, we had news of a tribe of women who live on their own with no Indian men among them; because of which we called them Amazons. Those who told us about them said that these women became pregnant from certain slaves whom they purchase. If they give birth to a son they send him to his father; but if it is a daughter they rear her to augment their republic.... And if they were very rich in gold ... of the same gold of this land or that of Tunja."[13] The Amazon queen was called Jarativa.

Gonzalo dispatched his brother to locate and conquer the Amazons, but the Spanish force he commanded found it difficult to penetrate the heavily forested hills. Even the natives feared to venture too far into the dense forest, for they were afraid of losing their bearings due to a lack of penetrating light, or forfeiting their lives to hostile tribes inhabiting the jungle. Hernán returned to Bogotá on May 12, 1538, to report that he was convinced they fell just a few days' short of reaching their objective.

In August of 1538 Gonzalo Jiménez de Quesada claimed the vast and rich realm of the Chibcha for Spain, Emperor Charles V, and, of course, himself. He put the Indians to work building a Catholic church at the Chibcha capital of Muequetá, a town the Spaniards renamed Santa Fé de Bogotá, and later known simply as Bogotá—the capital of present-day Colombia. Quesada christened the plateau he explored as the New Kingdom of Granada, in honor of the city that was his home. Santa Fé de Bogotá began as twelve huts, the sites of which were selected by the commander, to honor the memory of the twelve apostles. These structures were built of cane, straw, and clay by the natives of this region. The roofs of these dozen huts were thatched with palm-leaves or reeds. A spot between the huts was designated for the building of a modest church, the very site where the cathedral of Bogotá now stands. Quesada rewarded his men with an additional division of gold and emeralds.

Quesada was planning a return to Santa Marta where he hoped to sail to Spain with the sizable royal fifth of gold and emeralds collected, and request an official appointment as governor of the New Kingdom of Granada. Knowing that his own army had dwindled significantly, Quesada also wished to obtain Spanish reinforcements to aid in his conquest of other rich lands. His ambitious plans, however, were interrupted by news of yet another golden temple, which was said to be located along the western bank of the Río Magdalena. The natives called this place Menza, which sounded very much like the rich but ever elusive province of Meta. He led his men back to Bogotá to prepare for an expedition to locate Menza and the sacred House of the Sun, where he hoped to find a treasure trove of gold similar to what had been found at the temple they had accidentally burned down. But this plan was put on hold when an Indian strode into camp with news that another Spanish expedition was nearby.

5

Unexpected Encounters

Initially, Quesada had his doubts about the native's report that other men like him had reached the Magdalena Valley, but his drawings that bore the likeness of horses and pigs, neither of which were indigenous to the Americas, convinced him of the need to dispatch his brother Hernán with a detail of twelve soldiers to investigate this matter.

Hernán and his squad reached the Magdalena Valley and soon discovered that the native had spoken the truth about the arrival of other Spaniards. Unsure of this situation, Quesada and his men captured two of Sebastián de Benalcázar's soldiers while they were leisurely fishing, and proceeded to interrogate them about their commander and what exactly were his intentions in this distant land. It was learned that Sebastián and his troops had reached Neiva, a Chibcha trading village, during the early part of 1539.

Though disappointed to discover that another Spanish expedition had reached Cundinamarca before him, Sebastián de Benalcázar met with Hernán Pérez de Quesada the next day to state that he was in search of the realm of El Dorado. Hernán informed Sebastián that his brother had already conquered and settled the region, which was home to the legendary gilded ruler. After an exchange of pleasantries and gifts Hernán suggested they should all march to Bogotá to meet with Gonzalo Jiménez de Quesada. This cordial meeting concluded with an agreement that the Spanish commander from Quito would meet with the Spanish commander from Santa Marta. Hernán and his men returned to Bogotá to inform his brother that Benalcázar was eager to see him.

Benalcázar and his men crossed the Magdalena and a week later they arrived at Bogotá, where they were warmly received by Gonzalo Jiménez de Quesada and his troops. There have been many claims that both armies were nearly the same in number, and there are some accounts that contend they were the same in size—166 conquistadors to be exact. Sebastián had less than fifty men with him at the moment; the bulk of his army had remained at the four settlements he founded along the way, and the majority were stationed at Popayán. Benalcázar, however, was unaware of the fact that he held a tremendous advantage in firepower. Quesada's soldiers no longer had powder to fire their arquebuses, and the men who wielded the crossbow had used up most of their bolts. What he could count on, however, was the loyalty of his men.

In the meantime, Nicolaus Federmann and his troops reached the Chibcha village of Neiva, roughly 150 miles south of Bogotá. The exiled Captain Lázaro Fonte, who was keeping company with the native girl who saved his life, was informed by an Indian that there were other men like him who had reached the plateau of Cundinamarca. Fonte was inclined to believe them, especially after he spoke of animals that resembled horses and pigs. Hoping to return to the good graces of his commander, Lázaro Fonte sent word of this German led expedition to Quesada written in red ochre on a piece of deerskin, which was speedily carried by a native runner. The letter reached Quesada six days after his brother met with Sebastián de Benalcázar. Fonte's note stated: "My Lord. I have certain news that a band of Spaniards are at hand. They are coming up from the llanos. They are close by and will arrive here (at Pasca) tomorrow. Let your Excellency determine quickly what measure to take."[1]

The lack of information regarding the size and strength of the advancing expeditions was worrisome, so Quesada led a group of cavaliers eastward to assess the situation. As they neared Pasca the commander dispatched a soldier with a horse and weapons to Lázaro Fonte, who rushed to the aid of Quesada. Gonzalo welcomed him with open arms and renewed favor.

Later on, Quesada met up with Pedro de Limpias, a veteran soldier who led the advance force of men under the command of Nicolaus Federmann. Shortly thereafter, the German commander and his main force reached Pasca where he exchanged messages with the Spanish commander. Many of Gonzalo's officers were shocked by the sorrowful state of Federmann's soldiers, and saddened to learn that so many had perished after setting out from Coro. News of the arrival of this expedition was sent immediately to Quesada, and once received he set out to meet with his rival explorer. The Spanish officer showed his German counterpart every possible courtesy, and provided Federmann and his men with a bountiful supply of food and native cloths to replace their tattered attire.

Once all were ready, the expeditionary force from Coro was escorted to Quesada's camp at Bogotá where several days of feasting and games were enjoyed by all. During their private discussions Quesada and Federmann felt they were kindred spirits, and the two commanders became fast friends. A message soon arrived informing Quesada that Sebastián Benalcázar and his troops, who were better attired and armed, were a mere league from Bogotá.

In February 1539, the three expeditions established separate camps, each just a few miles from the other, while they sought to iron out their claims in a cordial manner. Benalcázar sent secret messages to Quesada requesting that the Spanish commanders unite their armies against the German commander from Venezuela, but Gonzalo wished to solve their disputes amicably. Quesada managed to calm the steadily mounting tensions with a tentative offer to Federmann of a share of the treasure his expedition had already collected.

The three armies spent several days feasting while their respective commanders cordially discussed their unique predicament. This spirit of cooperation was enhanced by the realization that after such a long and arduous search there was little incentive to return to their old posts. Benalcázar knew he would face the ire of Francisco Pizarro. Federmann and Quesada were equally wary of a return to their benefactors after such a lengthy absence.

Quesada told the other commanders that the Chibcha had no gold of their own, explaining that all they possessed was acquired through trade with other tribes. The precious gold obtained from Cundinamarca amounted to approximately 500,000 pesos de oro. The royal fifth had already been set aside for the Crown by the time the two other expeditions had arrived. While it was known that the gold of the Chibcha was imported, the conquistadors hoped to add to this tally by dredging Lake Guatavita to salvage precious items the Chibcha had offered to their gods.

The lawyerly Gonzalo Jiménez de Quesada drew up agreements whereby a truce was recognized by all three parties. Quesada used his legal training to first broker a deal with Federmann and then with Benalcázar, the latter pact was signed on March 7, 1539. The three commanders agreed to travel together to Spain, and to abide by the decision of the Council of the Indies. Quesada used a portion of his gold to buy what little Federmann still possessed, which included the expedition's horses, and some roosters and hens. For the sum of 10,000 gold pesos the German commander turned over his Spanish troops to Quesada, who were to remain behind to help settle the land. Benalcázar was in a better position to profit from the sale of his weapons, supplies, slaves, and soldiers to the Spanish commander. A few days later Quesada reached a similar arrangement with Sebastián Benalcázar.

The three commanders agreed to found a Spanish city at this very site; expanded plans were drawn up for the founding of Santa Fé de Bogotá on April 19, 1539. Benalcázar sold his pigs and horses to Quesada, which were for the benefit of the planned colony. While the foundations of the town were being laid, a number of men were busy building a boat at the port of Tocaima, which would transport the three commanders to Cartagena, where they would prepare for their voyage to Spain. Before his departure, Gonzalo ordered the founding of additional towns at Tunja and Velez.

Without bothering to seek permission from his commander, Francisco Pizarro, Sebastián de Benalcázar agreed to return to Spain with Quesada to request a commission as governor. Nicolaus Federmann also pledged to abide by the decision of the Council of the Indies. Gonzalo appointed his brother, Hernan Pérez de Quesada, as Alguacil Mayor of the conquered region during his absence. Jerónimo de la Inzá, Juan de Arrévalo, Juan de San Martín, Juan de Céspedes, Antonio Diaz Cardoso, Baltazar Maldonado, Lázaro Fonte were all rewarded with prominent positions in the governing of Bogotá. The priest Juan Rellejo and his assistant Fray Vincente, both members of the Federmann expedition, consecrated the church christened La Concepcíon de Nuestra Senora.

All three captains agreed to return to Spain as a group to state their cases before the Emperor and the Council of the Indies, the governing bodies that would decide which party had a rightful claim to the contested Chibcha kingdom. Quesada felt confident that his knowledge as a lawyer, the fact that he had arrived first at this wealthy New World province, and the opulent royal fifth offering would earn him the coveted appointment as governor and adelantado of the region.

Once all was in order, the thee commanders assembled their troops to express their appreciation for the numerous travails they had endured together in order to reap the rewards of the legendary wealth of Eldorado. Quesada, Federmann, and Benalcázar then proceeded to Tocaima, where a ship awaited them. The officers were accompanied by a large contingent of soldiers who wished to bid them a fond farewell.

Seeking the King's Favor

To a slowly fading chorus of *vivas* sounded by the men who remained behind, Gonzalo Jiménez de Quesada, Sebastián de Benalcázar, and Nicolaus Federmann set sail in May 1539 along the Magdalena to the port of Cartagena. Prior to his departure, Quesada divided up the estimated 20 million ducats in gold and emeralds confiscated from the natives. He cautioned his men not to squander their shares gambling on games of dice and cards. Quesada would use a portion of his funds to purchase a stylish wardrobe to wear at the Royal Court.

The voyage down the Magdalena proved more precarious than anticipated; the swift current swept them to a native town resting above rapids too dangerous for their vessel. Quesada and his companions felt compelled to go ashore to unload all the stores and supplies, and raise their empty boat. The adventurers proceeded through the thick foliage along the river's edge until they passed the rapids, at which point they carefully lowered their boat with the aid of ropes back onto the Magdalena to resume their voyage. The conquistadors soon found themselves under constant attack from warriors aboard armadas of canoes, but the soldiers had sufficient firepower to repulse these assaults.

At the village of Malabo, the voyagers again disembarked, leaving behind their boat to follow an Indian trail through a heavily forested region. A number of conflicts slowed their pace, but on June 20, 1539, the three commanders finally reached the fortress of Cartagena de las Indias, where they made preparations for their long voyage to Spain. Everyone was surprised to see Quesada, for he had been gone for three years and many believed he had perished during his search for a passage to the South Sea. All of Cartagena was abuzz with excitement after hearing that the wealth of Bogatá eclipsed the riches of both Mexico and Peru. All three commanders found themselves constantly besieged by men requesting to join their return expedition.

During their stay at Cartagena, Quesada, Benalcázar, and Federmann met with judge Juan de Santa Cruz to offer testimony as to why each felt he had the better claim to the province of New Granada. While awaiting a ship that would take them to Castile, Quesada found himself embroiled in a lawsuit brought by Diego Hernandez Gallego regarding the first flotilla of ships sent up the Magdalena to join his expedition, a mission that was unsuccessful.

Pedro de Puelles, who had accompanied the three commanders to Cartagena, provided testimony about the "fine gold and gold dust from mines" in the regions they had explored. Puelles returned to the city of Quito prior to Gonzalo Pizarro's arrival near the end of 1540. Pedro would inform Pizarro about the rich lands he had explored with Sebastián de Benalcázar.

Quesada's concerns about facing the ire of Pedro Fernández de Lugo, Governor of Santa Marta, a settlement not far from Cartagena, for not following his explicit orders were allayed by the news that he had died three years earlier. The acting Governor at Santa Marta, Jerónimo Lebrón, learned of his return and demanded that he present himself at once to give a full account of his expedition. Not wishing to jeopardize his claims to the riches of the Chibcha to the judgment of an acting governor, Quesada decided instead to return to Spain to provide the Emperor with a detailed report of his many discoveries, and to personally present his Highness with the royal fifth, an abundant offering of gold and emeralds which served as proof of his many splendid claims. On July 8, 1539, the three commanders departed Cartagena and sailed for Cuba. Following a brief stopover at Jamaica, Quesada, Benalcázar, and Federmann reached Cuba on August 28, 1539, where they were welcomed by Governor Gonzalo de Guzmán.

This trio of commanding officers returned home during a time when Spain was beginning to reap the rewards of the magnificent treasures shipped from the New World. Hernán Cortés had sent back a large portion of the accumulated wealth of the Aztecs, which was soon surpassed by the vast riches shipped to Spain by Francisco Pizarro following his conquest of the Incan empire.

Nicolaus Federmann made the overland trek to meet with Balthasar Welser before making his way to Ghent. The returning commander was convinced that a grateful Welser firm would award him the governorship of Venezuela, but instead he found himself accused by his employer of having lined his pockets with wealth that belonged to the company. The Welsers wanted a full account of his activities in the New World, especially the riches he had acquired. Nicolaus refused to comply with this request. He was arrested by a Welser agent at the city of Ghent on the charge that he had defrauded the firm of gold and emeralds. Federmann's house in Ghent was seized and all his possessions were confiscated.

A despondent Federmann languished for several months in a prison cell at Antwerp before his case was heard by the Council of Flanders. Nicolaus was able to raise the 8,000 ducats needed to bail him out of Antwerp prison, but the Welsers used their influence to sway Flemish officials to delay his release until he handed over an emerald estimated at a value of 100,000 ducats, and 15,000 ducats in gold, which the Welsers claimed had been given to him by Jiménez de Quesada. Federmann denied having any such valuables, which resulted in the continuation of his imprisonment and the impounding of all his possessions. The imprisoned officer countered that the Welser firm was guilty of improper practices in the New World.

On September 22, 1540, the president of the Council of Flanders met with Nicolaus Federmann at Antwerp prison to inquire if the commander could prove his claim that the Welsers were guilty of fraudulent activity in South America. If he was unable to prove this assertion, then he would suffer a beating at the hand of a member of the Welser firm. Nicolaus agreed to these terms.

Federmann's plight came to the attention of Emperor Charles V, who ordered the prisoner to be immediately transported to Spain. Despite the protests of Flemish authorities, the Council of the Indies declared that the suit between the Welser firm and Nicolaus Federmann fell under their purview. Nicolaus reached Madrid in February 1541. Nicolaus stood before the court on August 1541 and freely admitted that he had made erroneous charge against the Welsers in order to procure his release from the jail in Flanders. While under house arrest in Valladolid, Nicolaus was able to transfer funds from his land holdings in Bogotá, which was part of the monetary deal he had made with Gonzalo Jiménez de Quesada.

Weakened by the long and arduous search for Eldorado and depressed by the unexpected reversal of fortune upon his return, Federmann's health continued to worsen during his two years of confinement. He penned from his notes and recollections his first trip through Venezuela, titled *Charming and Agreeable Account of the First Trip of Nicholas Federmann the Younger, of Ulm, to the Indies in the Ocean Sea, and of All That Happened in That Country until His Return to Spain*, which he gave to his sister Elizabeth to have published. In this account, Federmann wrote of his encounter at a region inhabited by dwarves, claiming they were but four palms tall. The legal dispute continued until Nicolaus Federmann unexpectedly passed away on either the 21st or 22nd of February 1542.

While Nicolaus Federmann and Sebastián de Benalcázar made their way to Madrid to meet with the emperor, Quesada decided to stopover in Lisbon. There he met with Hernando Pizarro, who had served his half-brother, Francisco, with distinction in the bloody conquest of the vast and rich empire of the Incas. Finding they enjoyed each other's company, these two gentleman passed many an hour gambling and attending social gatherings, traits that seemed out of character for Quesada. By early 1540 he arrived in the city of Seville, where he prepared for his journey to meet with the emperor at Madrid. The commander was encouraged to learn that his deeds were known to many, and felt confident that he would be rewarded in a manner equal to Hernán Cortés and Francisco Pizarro, the respective conquerors of Mexico and Peru.

Prior to being received at court, a document attesting to the numerous tribulations Quesada had endured in his lengthy campaign to increase the land holdings and wealth of Spain was submitted to Emperor Charles V. This statement was signed by a number of prominent officials and nobles; a list that included the Cardinal Archbishop of Seville, the Bishop of Lugo, and the Count of Osorno. This document testified that Quesada was a true Christian, adding that he had conquered these vast and rich lands of the New World with a minimum loss of life to the natives or the soldiers who followed him. The great feats of the Spanish commander were offered in contrast to the dubious deeds of Alonso de Lugo, who had turned his back on any claims to Santa Marta after he had so callously stolen from and deserted his father. All of the signers proclaimed their support for Quesada as the best man to govern the lands he had conquered and settled. They closed by reminding the emperor that the settlers had already sent a petition requesting that Gonzalo Jiménez de Quesada be named as their governor.

While the records fail to support his ever appearing at the proceedings, Quesada would face bitter disappointment at the Spanish court: he had brought back 21 bars of gold valued at 11,000 pesos de oro, as well as nine boxes filled with hundreds of emeralds—a bountiful offering that he was sure would secure him accolades of royal grants and titles, especially the governorship of Santa Marta now that Pedro Fernández de Lugo was dead. Instead, Quesada had to defend himself against charges of inflicting extreme torture upon Sagipa, which resulted in the premature death of the ruler. He was also accused of not reporting the full amount of treasure collected, which was viewed as a blatant attempt to defraud the Crown.

Quesada had the misfortune to return during the period when Emperor Charles was mourning the passing of Empress Isabel, a loss that weighed heavily on decisions made at the royal court. He had also returned at a time when public opinion concerning the cruel treatment of New World natives by the conquistadors was being challenged by Bartolomé de las Casas. Gonzalo was held responsible for the death of the chief of Bogotá and consequently forbidden to hold any position of importance for a period of five years. Gonzalo would fight the charges—the legal wrangling continued until 1545, a time when he finally succeeded in clearing his name.

Alonso Fernández de Lugo, the unscrupulous son who had purloined more than his fair share of inheritance, would claim the rights to Santa Marta and New Granada on the grounds that Quesada had conquered these lands while in the service of Pedro Fernández de Lugo, his deceased father. The crafty Alonso had used the golden haul he swindled from his father to grease the palms of many influential diplomats. He had also advanced his position at the Spanish Court through marriage to Doña Beatriz Neroña de Mendoza, a relative of the influential Mendoza family. Her sister, Dona Maria de los Cobos, was the wife of the personal secretary of Emperor Charles V. The well-connected sisters made sure that Don Alonso was shielded from any claims against his hereditary rights to lands and titles held by his father. Quesada attempted to buy Don Alonso's release of his claim to the land but his offer was summarily rebuffed.

Suddenly, it seemed that everyone who had a complaint against Quesada, no matter how trivial, found cause to file a grievance against him. Lawsuits were filed by Pedro Briceño, the treasurer of Santa Marta and the new governor of the settlement, and Jerónimo Lebrón, who sought 5,300 pesos of gold and a share of the emeralds. The commander was also assailed by allegations that he had a Jewish heritage. Quesada had to focus much of his time, energy, and finances defending his good name.

5. Unexpected Encounters

When not petitioning the royal court for the governorship of the lands he had discovered and settled, Quesada spent a portion of his gold on gambling and the company of women. Gonzalo would go into hiding after learning that a judge had ordered the local constable to arrest him. A town crier proclaimed that Quesada must make his presence known in Santa Marta within nine days. When Quesada failed to show himself, he was officially declared a rebel. He was also ordered to present himself before the *Audiencia*. The charges against him included cruelty toward Indians, stealing the lands and possessions of the natives, pocketing gold and emeralds that should have been included in the inventory which determined the royal fifth, and stealing the one-tenth share of treasure earmarked for Don Pedro Fernández de Lugo. Quesada was also charged with cruelty toward his own men, especially Juan Gordo, the soldier he hanged, and Lázaro Fonte, the officer he banished. These charges issued by the *Residencia* were made public. Court officials also declared that he must respond to these charges within three days. Quesada's failure to comply with their request was viewed as an admission of guilt.

The most egregious charges against Quesada were leveled by the king's prosecutor: "I, Licentiate Francisco de los Cobos, your prosecutor, state that Licentiate Gonzalo Jiménez, Lieutenant Governor who was in the New Kingdom of Granada, and Hernán Pérez de Quesada, brother of the aforesaid Counsellor Jiménez, during the time they were in the said governorship, did and committed many and grave crimes to the disservice of God and Your Majesty, and injuries to the natives of that territory, committing thefts, burnings, acts of force, death, and other injuries in order to rob them of their property. I ask and implore that Your Majesty order that most severe penalties imposed upon the said Counsellor Jiménez and Hernán Pérez de Quesada which by their aforesaid crimes they have incurred; and that these be imposed upon each of them, their goods and persons alike, that it may be an example to them and to others, and I swear to God in due form that I neither state nor ask the aforesaid maliciously."[2]

Gonzalo's dream of being named governor of Santa Marta were dashed when Emperor Charles V ruled in favor of Alonso de Lugo. Don Alonso was awarded the governorship of Santa Marta more for the fact that he had an abundance of gold and his marriage to a woman of high social standing than being the son of the deceased Governor Fernández de Lugo. Adding insult to injury, Don Alonso was also granted the right to govern Bogotá and the New Kingdom of Granada.

Fearing that incarceration was imminent, Quesada fled to France, which prompted immediate calls for his arrest as a fugitive from justice. Queen Juana sanctioned this decree by ordering his imprisonment. Quesada's absence did not deter his being tried and convicted by the Court of the Council of Indies for the wrongful death of the native ruler of Bogotá. It was judged that the Spanish commander was to be banished for five years from his homeland and ordered to pay a fine of one thousand ducats.

A despondent Quesada would spend nearly nine years migrating across Europe in an effort to evade the charges leveled against him before he finally felt it was safe to return to Spain. Gonzalo kept himself hidden in a tavern room where he passed the time writing about his adventures in the New World. The restless fugitive eventually tired of France and made his way to Italy. He remained there for several years drowning his sorrows in wine, women, gambling, and writing his histories. Longing to return to the Iberian Peninsula, Gonzalo took up residence in Lisbon, Portugal, before making his way to Cordova, Spain. Nearly penniless and fifty years old at the time of his return from exile, Quesada's uncle, Jerónimo de Soria, offered him the directorship of the House of St. Lazarus, a leper hospital.

Quesada was apprehended and incarcerated in the Casa de la Contratacións prison in Seville until all claims against him had been satisfied. He was also ordered to pay a tax of 1,000 pesos to the Crown. Quesada's uncle helped bail him out of prison; he was fortunate to still have his personal stash of gold and emeralds, which allowed him to live rather comfortable for a time. The trial of Jiménez de Quesada came to a close in early February 1547. He was found innocent of the most serious charges but found guilty of the torture and death of Sagipa, for which he was to pay a fine of 100 ducats and stripped of his titles for a period of seven years. Quesada's lawyer managed to get the Council to reduce the monetary fine from 100 to 50 ducats, and reduced the prohibition of his titles from seven years to two.

During his brother's absence, Hernán de Quesada conducted a search for the gold and jewels that were said to rest at the bottom of Lake Guatavita, the body of water that was the source of the El Dorado legend. His efforts yielded 4,000 pesos de oro, which was hardly the treasure trove they had hoped to find. Hernán convinced himself that this lake was not the legendary place of precious offerings and therefore decided to search elsewhere. A great many men would die in vain during this search for the ceremonial gold and jewels of the Chibcha rulers.

Unlike Federmann and Quesada, Sebastián de Benalcázar was well received at court. Though he failed to receive the coveted governorship of New Granada, Sebastián was awarded the governorship of the Popayán province (Colombia) and a royal grant to market cinnamon. Upon his return to the New World, Benalcázar found himself on the wrong side of a war between the conquistadors for control of Peru. He was captured by one of Pizarro's brothers, but was spared for his past service to Francisco Pizarro and permitted to return to his province.

Sebastián's return to Popayán city, the capital of the province, was surrounded by intrigue, which climaxed with Marshal Jorge de Robledo being hanged for an act of betrayal. Robledo was the administrator of Popayán prior to Benalcázar's appointment as governor. When Sebastián went off to fight the Pizarros, Robledo once again took control of Popayán and the Marshal had no intention of relinquishing his authority. The hanging of Robledo would prove to be Benalcázar's downfall; powerful friends of the Marshal saw to it that Sebastián was recalled to Spain to stand trial. Despite his absence, Benalcázar was condemned by the Audencia to die for the murder of Marshall Robledo. Sebastián requested and was granted another hearing to exonerate himself. He ventured to Cartagena where he fell ill and soon died. His passing occurred around the time that Quesada had reached Santa Fé.

The Last German Foray

During a four year period, which began in 1541, an expedition led by Philip von Hutten followed the trail blazed by the veteran German knight Georg Hohermuth, a path which brought his conquistadors to lands past the Putumayao. Philip had previously met Nicolaus Federmann in Seville and was deeply impressed by his demeanor.

The prior year, 1540, Philip von Hutten was in Barquisimeto, Venezuela when he learned of the death of Georg Hohermuth. Hutten had previously served under Captain Lope Montalvo de Lugo, who was Hohermuth's favorite officer. Philip returned to Coro, where he was introduced to Bishop Bastidas. The bishop of Venezuela promoted Hutten to captain-general, and charged him with continuing the mission of the late Georg Hohermuth.

Riding at the head of 100 cavaliers and a near equal squad of foot soldiers, Philip von Hutten departed Coro in August 1541 to search for rumored indigenous kingdoms of untold wealth. His second in command was Bartolomé Welser the Younger, son of the prominent banker Bartolomé Welser. Pedro de Limpias, a veteran New World adventurer who had served with Nicolaus Federmann and had an ear for languages, served as Hutten's adviser. Joining them on this journey was padre Frutos de Tudela. The expedition crossed the river Opia by canoe, which landed them in the realm of the Guaypés tribe. Hutten led his troops along the base of the Andes, and soon reached San Juan de los Llanos, which he hoped was the path followed by Gonzalo Jiménez de Quesada.

Hutten's expeditionary force headed west and eventually came upon the Río Guaviare, a tributary of the Río Negro. They were now in the lands of the Uaupés, a tribe which had been hostile toward the previous expedition led by Hohermuth, but now displayed a willingness to supply Hutten and his men with much needed food. To avoid a potential mutiny of his ill and malnourished troops, Hutten dispatched Pedro de Limpias and a few of his healthier men down the Río Guaviare in search of food and the ever-elusive Eldorado. Limpias would rejoin his comrades after a fruitless three-month long adventure.

Philip von Hutten's expeditionary force made their way to a native town called Macatoa. The ruler told the German commander that "alongside a certain range of mountains which could be observed on clear days, there were vast towns of rich people who possessed enormous wealth."[3] More likely than not, the chief had merely told this tall tale to rid himself of these conquistadors who posed a threat to his village.

Hutten and his comrades reached a town inhabited by the Omaguas. It was here that the conquistadors saw a splendid house where numerous sacred objects were stored, including a golden statue of their revered goddess. Philip and his friend Arteaga attempted to seize two Indians. The natives fought back and managed to severely wound the officers. Forced to retreat to the forest, the lives of both men were saved by the medical knowledge of Diego de Montes. Once recovered, Philip von Hutten realized that the strength of his army was no match for the superior number of the Omaguas and therefore decided that he would return to Coro to recruit a larger army.

It was nearly a thousand-mile trek back to Coro, a long and difficult journey which lasted from January to May 1845. The small band of adventurers arrived at the Rio Pauto, at which point Hutten sent Bartolomé Welser and a company of 20 men on ahead to Coro to recruit others for his follow-up expedition. Included in this group was Pedro de Limpias, a veteran of a previous Federmann expedition, who harbored ill-feelings toward German authority figures, especially Bartolomé Welser. Despite Hutten's orders, Welser led his men to Cubagua only to be disappointed to see that this settlement had been ravaged by a powerful hurricane and a ruinous raid by French pirates.

Meanwhile, the Council of the Indies decided to establish a *residencia* in Coro, primarily to investigate the governorship of Philip von Hutten. Since it had been so very long since anyone had heard from Hutten it was generally believed that he had perished in the wilderness. Juan Frías, prosecutor of the supreme court in Santo Domingo, was selected to serve as governor once the investigation was completed. Juan de Carvajal was named as the new governor's lieutenant in Coro. Frías stipulated that Carvajal was to merely take charge of the settlement and not to lead any expeditions out of Coro in search of fortune and glory.

Juan de Carvajal found that the settlement of Coro was in even worse condition than he had been led to believe. Most of the colonists were away in search of natives, primarily Caribs, to sell as slaves in Santo Domingo. Deciding that Coro was not worth restoring, Carvajal chose to sail eastward along the coast in the hope of finding a more idyllic spot to establish a new colony. Upon reaching the mouth of the Río Tocuyo the Spanish commander founded a town, which he christened Nuestra Señora de la Concepción de Tocuyo.

Meanwhile at Barquisimeto, Pedro de Limpias parted company with Bartolomé Welser and made his way with five fellow Spaniards to Carvajal's camp. They were granted a pardon for deserting Philip von Hutten's company. Hutten and Welser tracked Limpias to the camp and a verbal confrontation with Carvajal ensued over this delicate matter. Cooler heads eventually prevailed, and Carvajal extended an offer to Hutten to forgo his mission and join forces with him. His proposal was to conduct an exhaustive search for the riches that were said to be found at the valley of Pamplona. Philip declined by stating that he must proceed to Coro to provide an account of his doings.

Following the next day's dinner Carvajal summoned Hutten to the camp tent and requested that the German officer place himself and his men under his command, to which Philip responded: "Señor governor, already you know that I and these gentlemen and brothers have been marching for five years in order to carryout the full discovery of this territory, where we have lost many friends, horses and clothes. And we come here ruined and poor, sick, tired and indebted; and as my followers have been friends, I would like them to go with me to the port whence we set off [Coro] and there we can recover, for there is the judge of the *Residencia*. I wish to give my testimony and give an account to his Majesty and, to the Welsers who have this government. I beg your excellency not to disturb us."[4] Carvajal replied: "I hope you will be a witness of the fact that this is the government of the Emperor. Here the Welsers are nothing, it is His Majesty who rules."[5]

This war of words between the Spanish and German commanders continued for several more minutes, but abruptly ended when Carvajal ordered Hutten and Welser to be taken to their tent and held as prisoners. Philip von Hutten responded that Juan de Carvajal had received his appointment as captain-general only because it was believed he had perished on his expedition, therefore, now that it was known he was still alive, his authority superseded the rank accorded to him.

Realizing that Philip von Hutten's words had caused a stir amongst his men, Carvajal stepped forward to seize the Germans, but Hutten and Welser drew their swords, as did the ten soldiers under their command. Carvajal chose to withdraw at which point the German officials retired to their tent. Within moments the lodgings of Hutten and Welser were surrounded by Juan de Carvajal's armed soldiers. Bartolomé Welser responded to this threat by striking at Carvajal with his lance, a thrust that killed his horse. Carvajal reached an accord with Hutten and Welser, one which permitted them to proceed to Coro. This agreement was recorded by Carvajal's notary, Juan de Villegas. Later that night, the German officers and their handful of supporters set off for Coro, which was still a march of around 100 miles. They were accompanied by Carvajal and his troops.

However, during the second night of their journey Carvajal had Hutten and Welser seized while they slept in their hammocks. The Spanish officer promptly ordered an African slave to sever their heads with a machete, an act which denied them the opportunity of receiving absolution. The cold-hearted Carvajal declared, "They can make their confession in heaven."[6] These executions brought closure to the German efforts to settle and exploit the lands in and around Venezuela. As for Juan de Carvajal, he was later put to death for his barbarous crimes against the members of the German expedition. He was publicly hanged by order of Juan Pérez de Tolosa, the newly appointed judge of the *residencia*.

Seeking Redemption

Gonzalo Jiménez de Quesada was finally granted an opportunity to meet with King Philip; Emperor Charles V had abdicated and retired to the monastery at Yuste where he advised his son who inherited the Spanish throne. Quesada used this opportunity to speak of the fabulous riches that awaited in the lands he had explored in the service of the Crown, and to request the governorship of the region. He was disappointed by the king's decision to award him the titles of Marshal of Bogotá and Adelantado of the Llanos instead of governor. He was promised the title of marquis if he succeeded in locating and settling Manoa, the supposed true realm of El Dorado. Such honors and titles fell far short of those bestowed upon Hernán Cortés and Francisco Pizarro; even Sebastián de Benalcázar had received a governorship.

Toward the end of 1549 Marshal Quesada sailed for Cartagena in the company of several Dominican and Franciscan friars as well as three judges of the *Audencia Real*. In early 1550, after an absence of more than a decade, Quesada returned to Santa Fé de Bogotá. The town had grown considerably thanks to the steady arrival of Spanish colonists seeking a better life. Besides being home to many Spanish women, Santa Fé could boast of having a surgeon, blacksmith, carpenters, tailors, and other skilled laborers who brought a much-needed touch of civilization to this remote part of the New World.

Absent from town were Gonzalo's two brothers: Governor Alonso de Lugo had run Hernán and Francisco de Quesada out of town with spurious claims. The brothers sought to right these wrongful charges by sailing to Cartagena to register formal complaints with royal officials. As they reached the dock a storm suddenly appeared while they were on deck. Both brothers were struck by a deadly bolt of lightning. Juan Floriz de Ocariz, a 17th century Spanish historian, made note of Hernán's demise: "The bolt burned his hair and beard and all the hair on his body, for he was very shaggy; and it burned all his clothing and he was left naked, and part of his clothing was left in bits no bigger than grains of salt, all burned, and likewise his entire body, apparently without a blow, and black as Negroes."[7] Separated by a vast ocean, the loss of his brothers was unbeknownst to Quesada for a very long time.

"Philip II at His Accession," by Titian, Corsini Gallery, Rome (from *Complete Works of William H. Prescott*, published 1912 by DeFau & Co.).

As for Don Alonso de Lugo, he had to make his way to the Royal Court to answer accusations of serious wrongdoings on his part. Upon his return to Spain Don Alonso was compelled to redeem himself by fighting in the king's army. He fought in campaigns at Spain, Italy, and France before death beckoned him.

Meanwhile, Gonzalo Jiménez de Quesada was awarded a coat of arms by the king, a crest which depicts a mountain emerging from the ocean, with numerous emeralds glistening atop the water. At the base of the mountain are trees placed on a field of gold, and a gold lion resting on a red field with a sword held between his paws. There also appears a castle on a blue field bordered by four gold and silver moons.

While at Santa Fé, Quesada was gladdened by the receipt of a dispatch from the king which declared he had been accorded the right to use the honorary title of Don. He still clung to the hope of being awarded the title of Marquess, but this appointment was never realized. Meanwhile, an envious rival schemed to rid himself of the popular conquistador by championing his appointment as governor of Cartagena. However, the salt air did not agree with Don Gonzalo; he suffered a malady that slowly ate away at his skin, a condition that worsened during his stay at Cartagena. He handed over the duties of governor to a subordinate before returning to Santa Fé.

Quesada's quest for finding the region which supplied the Chibcha with gold was renewed after learning that his late brother Hernán had discovered the cinnamon forests while exploring the eastern plains for the elusive City of Gold. Many of the residents of Bogotá, including Don Gonzalo, were convinced that the primary source of Chibcha gold rested along the rich plains of the Orinoco. For some reason they chose to ignore the fact that all the gold they had seen had been mined from the hills.

In February 1569, the nearly 70-year-old Don Gonzalo Jiménez de Quesada decided to lead another expedition in search of Eldorado. To ensure the success of his mission the elderly commander offered as collateral his land holdings, haciendas, slaves, and anything else of value to obtain the funds needed to properly equip his expedition. Even this was not enough, for Quesada had to turn to Don Francisco Aguilar, a wealthy mine owner who invested a substantial sum in his venture.

Quesada had little trouble recruiting officers and soldiers, many of whom were veterans of his previous campaign. His expeditionary force numbered 300 Spaniards, 1,500 native porters, and 500 black slaves. He also brought along 1,100 horses, 600 head of cattle, and 800 pigs for the settlements and forts he proposed to establish along the territory he explored. This train of livestock would significantly slow the pace of the expedition. Captain Diego Soleto, who had been a member of a previous excursion to the vast plains known as the Llanos, was selected as Quesada's guide.

Eight men of the cloth accompanied the expedition to tend to the souls of the Christian soldiers and spread the word of God amongst the heathens they would encounter. Fray Antonio de Medrano, who had spent fifteen years converting natives in the Indies, was appointed chronicler of the expedition. When Father Medrano died from fever and fatigue the role of archivist was assumed by Fray Pedro de Aguado, which served as the basis for *Historia de Venezuela*, a detailed and insightful account of the subjugation of that region.

Upon reaching the River Güejar the elderly commander instructed his troops to make camp. An accidental spark ignited an uncontrollable fire that threatened to consume all of their provisions, and their situation worsened when the blaze caused a barrel of powder to explode; a blast which resulted in the death of several Spaniards, the loss of gun powder, and the destruction of Quesada's tent. Resuming their march the soldiers saw for the first time boas, enormous snakes capable of swallowing whole animals, such as deer, a gruesome sight that surely gave the men pause to contemplate their position on the food chain in this region.

When the expedition reached the llanos, the Spaniards were disheartened by the sight of a seemingly endless sea of thick, bristly grass that towered above their heads. To clear a path for all to follow, several soldiers were charged with the grueling task of hacking through the growth. Neither man nor beast was immune from the sting of the countless mosquitoes, horseflies, wasps, and ants that were stirred to defend their turf. The men feared the infectious sting of the green mosquitoes the most, for their bite was followed by insufferable swelling, pain, and fever. The soldiers were also wary of the numerous snakes, many of which were highly venomous.

Quesada and his men soon realized there was a scarcity of edible items to replenish their dwindling provisions, which were rapidly depleted by consumption and rot. The famished soldiers dug up roots and herbs and plucked fruits in a desperate effort to satiate their ravenous hunger. Contributing to the sufferings of the soldiers were the steady rains that rotted their clothing. The growing number of sick soldiers compelled the commander to send the weakest of the lot back to Bogotá under the guidance of Captain Maldonado. Following an arduous trek of six months, the officer and a small number of survivors straggled into San Juan de los Llanos. Most of the sickly soldiers had died during the march to this Spanish outpost.

The natives burned their homes and fled with their food once they learned of the approach of the Spaniards. The soldiers had little choice but to chew palm roots to satisfy their acute hunger pangs. The starving soldiers eventually reached a village with plenty of crops, which they christened Matahambre (hunger killer). It was at this dire point that a number of soldiers began to entertain thoughts about abandoning the mission. Morale sank so low that even some officers schemed to return to Santa Fé. When the frequency of desertions posed a serious threat to the expedition Quesada decided to set an example by hanging a pair of soldiers who sought to abandon the mission. The execution did not have the effect the commander intended; many soldiers decided to take their chances in the wild, only to die of hunger or thirst or fall prey to various creatures of the region.

Two exhaustive years of exploration had failed to lead the Quesada expedition any closer to the discovery of Eldorado. Many of the horses and men had fallen ill with a strange fever that often led to their death. There were soon only 64 of the original 300 Spaniards still around to follow the lead of their commander.

Despite the desperate pleas of his men Quesada refused to even consider abandoning his quest, which provoked a plot to have him assassinated.

The plan was to kill him by plunging a knife into his heart, using a sword to behead him, or burning him alive. The murderous scheme came to the attention of the Marshal, who had the conspirators placed in chains. Realizing he had lost the confidence of his men, the commander permitted those who wished to abandon the quest to do so without repercussions. Though his ranks were further diminished after this offering, Quesada took comfort in the thought that those officers and soldiers who stayed would remain loyal to the end. Unfortunately, more were fated to perish during the months ahead.

Shortly after resuming their search for Eldorado the Spaniards encountered an army of warriors that greatly outnumbered them. Quesada led a cavalry charge that threw the native force into an utter state of confusion. The battle ended when Rodriguez Pérez de las Islas felled the ruler with a shot from his arquebus, which sent the natives into flight.

As the days passed more and more soldiers asked to return to Santa Fé, and Quesada acquiesced to their request by granting them leave. After three years of enduring severe hardships with nothing to show for his effort except bitter and sobering disappointment, the Marshal finally consented to the pleas of his remaining troops to quit this expedition. The elderly and weary commander felt he needed some time to recuperate before heading back.

Don Gonzalo made his return to Bogotá with a force that had dwindled to a mere 25 Spaniards. Only four of the 1,500 natives survived this treacherous trek, and only 18 of the herd of 1,100 horses endured this lengthy journey; all of the pigs and cattle had perished long ago. Besides being deeply in debt (he owed more than 60,000 ducats), Quesada had contracted an irritating skin disorder, which many believed to be leprosy or an irritation caused by exposure to unhygienic conditions such as lice. It is likely that Don Gonzalo suffered from espundia, a flesh-eating disease caused by a parasite carried by sand flies. The bites of the sand flies leave black spots, which last for many weeks and look eerily similar to signs of leprosy. In spite of his many failings, Quesada retained the respect of his soldiers and the admiration of the colonists.

The elderly commander returned to his dwelling in Santa Fé de Bogotá and his countryside house at Suesca, at the latter of which he sought solace in writing an account of his many adventures in the New World while in the service of Spain. The first book he wrote during this period was titled *Historical Compendium*, which covered his arrival in the New World and his journey to the realm of the Chibcha. The second book was a record of his return to Santa Fé after many years in Spain and his failed quest to locate Eldorado. Sadly, his histories were lost, but some of his writings may have been incorporated into the histories written by Hernández de Oviedo and the chronicles of other contemporary historians.

5. Unexpected Encounters

Once again, Don Gonzalo Jiménez de Quesada was called upon to lead an army of Spaniards, this time to put down an uprising led by chief Yuldama of the Gualies tribe. Yuldama sought to overthrow Spanish rule by forging a confederacy of tribes in the region who viewed this as a golden opportunity to exact a fitting revenge against the European invaders. The allied tribes launched merciless attacks on Spanish frontier settlements in the regions of Tocaima, Mariquita, and along the Magdalena River. The leader of this war party brutally murdered Francisco Jiménez and his two nephews. Yuldama also raped and abducted a half-breed woman who lived on the encomienda of Jiménez.

The *Real Audencia* commissioned the nearly eighty-year-old conquistador to raise an army to crush this native revolt and restore order to the region. Weakened by age and the ravages of his previous ordeals, Don Gonzalo had to be transported in a litter borne by several strong natives, but he was able to summon enough strength to mount his horse and lead the charge against the rebellious natives. The Spaniards showed no mercy; villages were burned to the ground and all inhabitants were slain. Quesada and his troops stayed just long enough at each village along their path to empty it of gold and all other treasures. They eventually found the murderous chief who was the reason for this excursion. The Spaniards killed the ruler, rescued the abducted woman, and set fire to the village. The confederation and the threat it posed quickly faded upon the death of Yuldama.

With their objectives attained Quesada marched his troops back to Santa Fé de Bogotá. He retired to a house at the village of Tocaima to live out his few remaining days. This location was chosen because of the milder climate and the nearby sulphur springs he hoped would comfort his worsening skin condition. When the cure he hoped for failed to materialize Quesada relocated to Mariquita, where he had a house built of stone. It was at Mariquita that the elderly Gonzalo Jiménez de Quesada passed away on February 15, 1579.

6

A Well Organized Expedition

Upon learning that Sebastián de Benalcázar had embarked on an expedition to locate Eldorado without bothering to seek his permission, Francisco Pizarro dispatched Pedro de Puelles to Quito to serve as acting governor and to bring the absentee governor to justice.

During the early part of 1541, the noted Spanish historian Gonzalo Fernández de Oviedo y Valdes had an opportunity to interview some of the veterans who had returned to Colombia and Venezuela from their respective expeditions in search of Eldorado. They told the historian that the ruler of the region "...was very great and very rich. Every morning he anoints himself with a kind of resin or gum to which the gold easily adheres, until his entire body is covered, from the soles of his feet to his head. So his looks are as resplendent as a gold object worked by the hands of a great artist."[1] Even though they were merely repeating the tale told by the natives of the region they had explored, the legend of El Dorado became firmly entrenched in the thoughts of the Spaniards.

Gold was not the only precious commodity that captured the fancy of the conquistadors: Pedro de Cieza de León, a contemporary conquistador who chronicled his travels in Peru wrote; "There is also a kind of spice, which we call cinnamon, brought from the forests to the eastward. It is a fruit, or kind of flower, which grows on the very large cinnamon trees, and there is nothing in Spain that can be compared to it, unless it be an acorn, but it is of a reddish colour inclined to black, and much larger and rounder. The taste is very pleasant, like that of real cinnamon, and it is only eaten after it has been pounded, for, if it is stewed like real cinnamon, it loses the strength of its flavour. It makes a warm cordial, as I can affirm from experience, for the natives trade with it, and use it in their illnesses, particularly for pains in the bowels and stomachs. They take it as a drink."[2]

A search for Eldorado seemed even more rewarding with the purported discovery in 1536 of La Canela, a plentiful land the natives claimed

6. A Well Organized Expedition

was home to extensive groves of cinnamon trees. Gonzalo Díaz de Pineda's tale of lands rich with cinnamon trees just to the east of Quito soon reached the ear of Francisco Pizarro. After the conquest of Peru and the feud between him and Diego Almagro, his former partner, which ended in favor of Pizarro's loyalists following the defeat and execution of Almagro, Francisco was now the supreme ruler of a vast realm of untold wealth. Eager to add to his fortune, Francisco decided to send Gonzalo Pizarro, his younger half-brother, to explore, claim and settle the region dubbed La Canela, the Land of Cinnamon. Gonzalo was appointed governor of Quito, so that the city could serve as a source of supplies and recruits for his expedition to La Canela.

Gonzalo Pizarro, who was illegitimate, was related to Francisco Pizarro, his elder half-brother, on his father's side. He came to the New World with his half-brothers Juan and Hernando to join with Francisco's quest to locate the wealth of Peru. Hernando was the only legitimate son of the Pizarro clan. Gonzalo, the youngest of the Pizarro brood, had served Francisco well during the conquest of Peru; he was an excellent horseman and a true warrior who had proven his skill and bravery in battle on more than one occasion. The young commander had dark hair, possessed a strong build, and was considered ruggedly handsome. Gonzalo was well-liked by the soldiers under his command. But on occasion, he revealed a cruel and vengeful side, traits common to the Pizarro clan. He was present during the battle of Cajamarca when the Spaniards seized Atahualpa, the Inca ruler, and effectively took control of the Inca empire. Gonzalo bravely served at Cuzco during the Inca siege to retake the city, a conflict that led to the death of his brother Juan.

Gonzalo was also instructed to hunt down Inca Manco, the clever native ruler who had escaped imprisonment and was waging a reign of terror against Spaniards who were attempting to settle the region. He would defeat the Inca forces in several pitched battles, but Manco always managed to elude capture. Gonzalo tried, without success, to find the secret hiding place of Inca Manco.

There was already bad blood between Inca Manco and Gonzalo Pizarro: "The puppet ruler of Cuzco endured numerous humiliations at the hands of his Spanish overlords. Gonzalo Pizarro, in particular, showed his lack of respect for the Inca emperor by forcing himself upon one of the ruler's favorite wives. In an effort to halt the lecherous advances of Gonzalo, Manco tried to deceive him by passing off a woman named Ynguil (flower), a concubine who bore a striking resemblance to his sister, the woman whom the Spanish officer longed for. The ruse was exposed when after Gonzalo embraced and kissed her in front of all, Ynguil screamed aloud that she did not wish to be with such a foul and vulgar person.

Gonzalo then merely took that which Manco did not wish for him to take."³

The Spanish commander was rewarded for his services with numerous land grants, including the rich silver mines of Potosi and Porco. Gonzalo, who was already wealthy from the conquest of the Incas, had several estates in Cuzco and Quito. He owned ranches and plantations that were worked by the conquered natives. Another source of funds for Gonzalo were tributes paid by the thousands of residents at the 140 towns and villages under his control.

Gonzalo Pizarro was at Los Charcas, where he was helping found the settlement of La Plata, when he was summoned to Cuzco to meet with his brother, Francisco, concerning the planned conquest of La Canela. Gonzalo, who was more comfortable in the role of soldier then administrator, returned to Cuzco and willingly accepted the challenges of his new appointments.

Francisco Pizarro entrusted to his half-brother the governorship of Quito, La Culata, and Puerto Viejo, a mountainous and coastal region that is now part of Ecuador. Gonzalo was to relieve Pedro de Puelles, who had recently been sent to replace Sebastián de Benalcázar, as governor of the province. Francisco wanted him to explore and claim the wealth said to be found at the spice rich province of La Canela and to seek out the legendary kingdom of El Dorado, both said to lie to the east of Quito.

It was easy for Gonzalo Pizarro to believe these tantalizing tales of untold wealth, for he had seen with his own eyes the stunning amount of gold and silver stored at Cuzco. He also knew that the Incas received much of their gold and silver from distant tribes required to pay tribute to the rulers of the Inca empire, and every Spaniard was aware of the fact that Atahualpa had offered to fill one room with gold and another with silver to secure his freedom. All who joined the Pizarro expedition were convinced that they would return as rich men—either from fields of cinnamon or the mines of silver and gold they discovered. The conquistadors fully expected to find stone cities along the route to La Canela as grand as those constructed at Cuzco and Quito.

Gonzalo Pizarro and his expeditionary force set off towards Quito, a distance of approximately 500 leagues. The conquistadors had to engage in several pitched battles with Indians in revolt before they reached Quito. Gonzalo and his army came under heavy attack from the natives at Huanuco. When Francisco Pizarro learned of his brother's dilemma, he dispatched a squad of soldiers under the command of Francisco de Chaves to aid his efforts.

After reaching the town of Huanaco, the Spaniards passed through Piura and Guayaquil. On December 1, 1540, the troops reached Quito,

6. A Well Organized Expedition

where Gonzalo submitted his commission as governor to Pedro de Puelles, who promptly resigned. The city had been under control of this officer sent to arrest Sebastián de Benalcázar ever since 1537.

Gonzalo was more interested in exploring than governing and within three months of reaching Quito he was organizing an expedition to explore the possibilities of finding another Peru beyond the Andes and to the east. He wrote to the King of Spain that he was eager to lead an expedition after being exposed to "the many reports which I had received in Quito and elsewhere from prominent and very aged chiefs as well as from Spaniards, whose accounts agreed with another, to the effect that the province of La Canela and Lake El Dorado were a very populous and rich land ... [from which] would be obtained great treasures...."[4]

Once satisfied that the city of Quito was functioning as his brother would deem fit, Gonzalo Pizarro was fully prepared to seek out the lands of cinnamon and the realm of El Dorado. La Canela was thought to be just over the ridge of the Andes. Cinnamon was a prized spice considered just as valuable as gold, but Gonzalo was also interested in discovering the precious gold said to be located within the realm of El Dorado. Pizarro hoped to establish a permanent and prosperous colony in both regions. As governor of Quito Gonzalo Pizarro had the authority to procure all that was necessary for his grand expedition.

Pizarro enlisted 220 soldiers, the vast majority of whom were on horseback, and conscripted a few thousand Indians to fulfill the role of porters to bear the burden of the wealth that awaited beyond the Andes. To prevent their escape, the accompanying natives were shackled until the expedition reached the forest. Pedro Cieza de León claimed that the troops were accompanied by a herd of pigs numbering 5,000. Gonzalo estimated that he spent 50,000 castellanos of his own money to equip this expedition.

One of the most prominent members of the expedition was not a soldier, but instead a 38-year-old priest named Gaspar de Carvajal. Gonzalo Pizarro invited the Dominican priest to join his expedition for the dual purposes of tending to the spiritual needs of the conquistadors and converting idolatrous natives to Christianity. Friar Carvajal hailed from Trujillo, Spain, a small town in the province of Extremadura—the same region that was home to the Pizarro brothers. Friar Carvajal, who probably reached the New World in 1537, sailed to Nombre de Dios and from there he crossed the isthmus to the town of Panama. One year later he booked passage on a ship bound for Lima, Peru. The earliest known records put Carvajal at Lima in November of 1538. Carvajal was one of the eight monks of the Order of Saint Dominic appointed to assist Friar Vincente de Valverde, the newly appointed bishop of Peru. The Dominican priest gladly agreed to join Gonzalo Pizarro's expedition in search of fortune and glory.

Orellana Offers His Services

Francisco de Orellana soon learned that Gonzalo Pizarro was planning a grand expedition to the promising regions of Eldorado and La Canela. Orellana hailed from Trujillo, the hometown of the Pizarro clan, located in the Extremadura province of Spain. He was a distant relative of the Pizarros—perhaps a cousin or nephew. He was from a respected family, and described himself as "an hidalgo of known ancestral estate."[5]

Francisco de Orellana was born in 1511, and it's generally believed that he reached the New World in 1527. The young soldier ventured to Panama where he very likely served in the conquest of Nicaragua. While in Central America Orellana served briefly under the command of Hernán Cortés. He sailed for Peru in 1535 as a member of the army led by Pedro de Alvarado, the veteran conquistador who sought to lay claim to the riches that awaited at the Inca city of Quito. He joined forces with the Pizarros and served as a captain to protect their interests at Lima and Cuzco. Francisco established a name for himself during the conflict with Manco Inca. But he paid a heavy price during his service in the army of Francisco Pizarro; at Las Salinas Orellana lost his left eye to an Indian arrow. He was fortunate to fight on the winning side during the Spanish civil war for control of the newly conquered Inca empire. Orellana was named ensign-general of an army of 700 soldiers dispatched to Cuzco by Hernando Pizarro.

Orellana was instructed to take charge of the Port of Guayaquil, a new Spanish settlement near the sea in present day Ecuador. Guayaquil had been founded by Sebastián de Benalcázar but was twice destroyed by local natives. In 1537, after having subdued the Indians of the region, which was no easy task, Orellana founded the city of Santiago de Guayaquil, so named in honor of Saint James. This new settlement provided Quito with a much-needed sea passage for carrying on trade. Francisco Pizarro rewarded Orellana for his bravery and dedicated service with a promotion to the rank of captain-general and lieutenant governor of the province he had settled.

Francisco proved himself to be a fair and competent administrator. He garnered the respect of many, including the city councilors of Santiago de Guayaquil, who, in a letter to Emperor Charles, praised Orellana as a man "capable of, and qualified for, whatever commissions and offices His Majesty might be pleased to entrust to him, be it governorship or any others whatsoever, because he is a person who would give a good account of them."[6] A man of unrelenting religious and moral convictions, Francisco executed two Spaniards for their sinful act of sodomy and confiscated all of their worldly possessions.

Orellana possessed another talent that would serve him well; he was a gifted linguist, a skill which enabled him to quickly become proficient in Quechua, the language of the Inca. Francisco made a concerted effort to learn the language of other tribes he came into contact with and kept extensive notes of the different Indian vocabularies.

Learning that Gonzalo Pizarro was planning to launch an expedition in search of the legendary Eldorado and the bountiful region of La Canela, Orellana left Puerto Viejo for Quito to offer his services to this grand expedition. He told Gonzalo, who was younger than him by around two years, "how he wished to go with him in the service of His Majesty and take his friends along and spend his personal wealth in order to better serve...."[7] Gonzalo gladly gave his consent, but stated that he was nearly ready to depart and therefore would not wait long for Orellana and his men.

Pizarro's Preparations

Gonzalo Pizarro had little trouble enlisting men at Quito who were willing to search for the wealth of El Dorado, a chief so rich that he could afford to powder his entire body with gold dust. The retelling of this legend progressed from a ruler performing this deed only at the time of his coronation to a ritual performed on a daily basis. A few volunteers were veterans of the conquest of the Aztecs in Mexico, an empire that controlled a vast amount of wealth. This was in addition to the Spaniards who had seen first-hand the even greater riches of the Inca realm.

Pizarro gathered intelligence from local and nearby natives, much of which seemed to confirm that La Canela and the lands of El Dorado were both real and abundantly rich with natural wealth. The tales of El Dorado and La Canela were substantiated by the words of "prominent and very aged chiefs."[8]

Pedro de Cieza de León, a 16th Spanish century adventurer who penned a classic account of the discovery and conquest of Peru, mentions that several Spanish officers had heard similar tales from the natives after their return from a scouting mission which passed over the Andes: "They had returned without a full exploration of a region of which they had heard great things ... for the Indians said that further on, if they advanced, they would come to a wide spreading flat country teeming with Indians who possess great riches, for they all wear gold ornaments, and there were no forests or mountains. When this news spread in Quito, everyone wanted to take part in the expedition."[9]

Gonzalo Pizarro sent a letter to the king of Spain which explained that these reports were the reason for his need to launch an expedition. "I became fascinated, and decided to go and conquer and explore it, both to serve your Majesty and in order to broaden and increase Your Majesty's realms and royal patrimony. I had been made to believe from these provinces would be obtained great treasures whereby Your Majesty would be served and aided in meeting the great expenses with which Your Majesty is faced every day in his realms. In my zeal and eagerness to do this, I spent more than fifty thousand castellanos which I paid out in advances to the men whom I took with me, both on foot and on horse."[10]

Pizarro expected to find at Eldorado a truly magnificent city composed of stone buildings equal to, or exceeding, the combined wealth of all the Incan cities. He hoped to find temples sheathed in gold, much like he had seen at Coricancha, the Temple of the Sun, located in the very heart of the city of Cuzco. The legend of Eldorado's wealth grew grander with each retelling; tales of streets paved with gems, golden gardens, and plates, drinking vessels, utensils made of precious metals, as well as gold and jewel encrusted thrones were treated as gospel. It was also believed that the people of this splendid realm were, just like the Inca, sun worshippers.

Gonzalo had little trouble rekindling the spirit of adventure in those Spaniards eager for a taste of fortune and glory. During preparations for his upcoming expedition the commander recruited another 100 soldiers at Quito, which swelled his ranks to 340, 150 of whom were cavaliers. Toribio de Ortiguera wrote that Gonzalo Pizarro set out on his expedition with 280 men and 260 horses; Cieza de León claims there were 220 Spaniards; and Oviedo states there were 230. Gonzalo made sure to enlist the services of carpenters who possessed the skills to build bridges and boats for fording the rivers they would inevitably encounter. Pizarro appointed Antonio de Ribera as master of the camp.

Pizarro rounded up 4,000 natives to serve as porters, guides, cooks, foragers of food, and whatever other role might be required for his epic quest. The majority of enslaved natives were kept shackled until it was time to depart. Some of the natives were women, who were expected to satisfy the various appetites of the Spaniards, which included both food preparation and sexual favors. Native guides familiar with the region were pressed into service. Unfortunately, the Spaniards would soon discover that these guides were not acquainted with the wilderness region.

A large herd of pigs were brought along to ensure the army was well fed. The swine were said to be several thousand in number (Cieza de León states there were 5,000 pigs while another chronicler puts the number of swine at 4,000). A great many llamas were also brought along to serve as beasts of burden for much of the baggage, and as a source of food during lean times. A select group of natives were responsible for tending to the herd of pigs and llamas. The Spaniards also brought along an ample supply of grain, salt, and wine. The expedition was accompanied by several hundred dogs trained to hunt game and track down escaped natives.

Gonzalo spared no expense in making sure his men were well equipped with provisions and armaments. As mentioned in his letter to the king, Pizarro spent more than 50,000 castellanos of his own money to equip the expedition, the majority of which he borrowed by pledging a share of the riches he was confident would be found on this expedition. Some of these funds went toward the purchase of crossbows, cannons, swords, arquebuses, and adequate ammunition. The long list of supplies included nails, rope, knives, axes, and hatchets; the latter two would prove useful in clearing paths through the dense jungle they would soon encounter.

In early February of 1541, Pizarro dispatched a scouting party to report on the route ahead. A few weeks later, after receiving favorable reports, the 35-year-old commander set out at the head of his expeditionary force to find the spice laden realm of La Canela and the legendary wealth of Eldorado. Pedro de Puelles was appointed deputy of Quito during Gonzalo's absence. Pizarro was convinced that the realm of El Dorado would be found in the mountains of the Andes. Depending on which account one trusts, the expedition departed Quito in late February or early March. They followed an eastward course and enjoyed an easy march along a paved road that led to the border of the vast Inca empire.

Orellana's Disappointment

After reaching an accord with Gonzalo Pizarro, Francisco de Orellana rushed back to Puerto Viejo to put his personal affairs in order, organize a company of conquistadors to join this venture, appoint competent and trusted officials to oversee the region during his absence, and obtain necessary provisions for the upcoming expedition. Orellana selected 23 of his best knights from Puerto Viejo and Santiago de Guayaquil, and spent 40,000 pesos of his own money to equip them with horses as well as the best armor and weaponry available. Much of his money was spent on the purchase of horses, an expensive proposition in the New World since most had to be imported from Cuba or Jamaica.

Orellana and the conquistadors who joined him on this grand adventure arrived at Quito on March 11, 1541, where they were surprised to learn that an impatient Gonzalo Pizarro and his large expeditionary force had already set out on their quest to discover gold and cinnamon. The last minute duties of office had delayed Francisco's return to Quito before Pizarro's departure. When he inquired about the route taken by Pizarro the natives warned him that an attempt to catch up with Gonzalo at this point would be foolish; their head start was too great, the mountain peaks too treacherous, and there were simply not enough of them to fend off hostile Indians. The natives warned that his small force would not strike fear into native tribes along the way in the same manner of Pizarro's imposing army, and therefore they would surely come under attack. Native ambushes were a common occurrence in this region and even if they survived these travails they would still have to contend with the cold and lack of food in such an inhospitable region. They also reminded Orellana of the difficult climb up the towering, snow capped mountains, which stood just seven miles from Quito.

Francisco was determined to join up with Pizarro and therefore ignored the dire warnings of the concerned citizens of Quito. Francisco proceeded to lead his small expeditionary force along the path blazed by the much larger expedition headed by Gonzalo Pizarro.

7

Lost in a Lost World

Into the Valley of Zumaque

Meanwhile, Gonzalo Pizarro's cavalcade encountered few difficulties during their first leg of the quest, which helped to sustain the morale of the troops. They followed a northerly paved path that passed through a distant region subjugated by the Incas and populated by tribes used to welcoming outside overlords. The advance guard was under the command of Antonio de Ribera, while the rear guard was entrusted to Cristóbal de Funes. Gonzalo led the bulk of the troops who marched in the middle of the pack. Ribera was instructed to march ahead to the town of Atunquijo, in the Quijos region, where he was to await the rest of the army.

Difficulties arose once the expedition passed the boundary of the Inca empire and set foot in the province of Quijos, where the Spaniards were almost immediately met by hostile natives. The size of the Spanish force, their superior weapons, and the swift and mighty horses proved too intimidating for the warriors, who made a hasty retreat.

While in the volcanic region of Quijos the expeditionary force experienced the terrifying tremors of a violent earthquake, the magnitude of which frightened the soldiers, natives, and horses alike. They witnessed the earth split open and swallow a number of huts at the nearby villages. This horrific event coincided with storms accompanied by bellowing thunder and blinding flashes of lightning, which were a prelude to torrential rains that continued for many days. Pizarro and his troops could not help but notice the extreme difference in the provinces of Peru and Quijos. The storms and rains continued for more than forty days, which was viewed as an ominous sign by many superstitious soldiers.

The conquistadors followed the Incan road which led from Quito to the gorge at the Machángara River. A march of seven leagues led the army to a snow-capped mountain range that needed to be crossed. The extreme elevation of the region weighed heavily on the Spaniards even before they reached the foot of the Andes; their slow pace and labored breathing were precipitated by the lack of oxygen at such a high altitude. The base of the Andes was the natural border of the Inca empire in this region. Clouds shrouded much of the surrounding terrain. Since Pizarro no longer had well-planned roads to follow, he would have to place his trust in the native guides who, unfortunately, were familiar with only a portion of the vast region ahead.

To lighten their load, the Spaniards left behind the llamas, some of the pigs, and a significant portion of their provisions, the latter of which they expected to replenish once they located native villages on the other side of the mountain range. Regrettably, they would soon discover that the next region was uninhabited. The steep and treacherous passes made for an exhausting climb over the eastern section of the Andean cordilleras that barred their way. A heavy snow fell in these high altitudes, and ice and snow made difficult footing for both man and beast. A number of men plummeted or froze to death during this difficult climb. The extreme cold, bone-chilling winds, slippery slopes, and arduous exertion contributed to the untimely death of more than 100 scantily clad natives.

After a laborious ascent of the towering peaks the expedition descended into a dense equatorial jungle that suffocated the explorers at every turn. They encountered an acute climate change following their descent of the eastern slopes of the Andes; the bitter cold was suddenly replaced by intense heat and humidity. Gonzalo Pizarro recalled: "We came to some very rugged and wooded country with great ranges out of which we were obliged to open up roads anew not only for the men but also for the horses."[1] The region was so dense with foliage that at the end of eleven months the exhausted Spaniards had barely penetrated 250 miles from Quito.

Gonzalo had made the unforgivable miscalculation of departing during the rainy season. The incessant rains dampened both the ground and the mood of the troops, and made it extremely difficult for man and beast to maintain a firm foothold in the soaked soil. The accompanying thunder and lightning proved very frightening to the soldiers, natives, and horses. The swamps of the lowlands claimed a heavy toll; some members of the expeditionary force caught malaria while others drowned. Their clothes began to rot from the dampness and humidity, and their food began to spoil. To make their way through this difficult terrain the Spaniards had to use axes and machetes to hack their own path for approximately 100 miles before finally reaching the verdant valley of Zumaque (a.k.a. Zumaco or Sumaco).

Pizarro sent scouts and natives ahead to find and clear a path through the thick tangle of brush and briers of the forest. The Spaniards were disappointed to discover that this land was uninhabited. This barren region offered little to replenish their dangerously low supply of food, which now had to be carefully rationed. Around 60 leagues east of Quito, the expedition reached a dense jungle divided by waters which give rise to the Napo River. It was here that Pizarro hoped to locate the cinnamon groves he had heard about.

The Spanish adventurers passed as quickly as possible through this difficult terrain until they reached the province of Sumaco, where they found a village of the same name located at the foot of a volcano. Fortunately for Gonzalo and his men, they were able to obtain much needed food. Because of the heat and humidity, which quickly wears away at fabrics, the natives of the Sumaco region were naked, except for the woman, who wore a small cloth to cover their privates. The expedition was forced to remain at Sumaco for two months because of the heavy rains which continued every day.

The Spaniards had entered regions the Incas were familiar with through trade among tribes who possessed the colorful feathers they used in their ceremonial dress. Since the region was too remote and wild to tame, and inhabited by fierce tribes, some of whom practiced cannibalism, the Incas refrained from conquering these distant lands. The long pause at the valley of Zumaco offered the time needed to rest the weary legs of the horses and soldiers, and provided Pizarro an opportunity to ascertain which direction would lead to the cinnamon groves. Along the valley the Spaniards stripped the cultivated fields of the local inhabitants to feed themselves and to restock their dwindling supplies for the long journey ahead.

Orellana's Odyssey

Meanwhile, Francisco de Orellana chose to ignore the advice of the natives of Quito and set off in the company of his volunteers to hook up with Pizarro and his troops. Gonzalo's path of death and destruction certainly made it easy for this small band of soldiers-of-fortune to follow. However, Orellana soon discovered there was merit to the warnings of the natives. Pizarro and his large army had stripped the land bare of food and in the process angered the natives who, on several occasions, would vent their rage on Francisco and his men. When the Indians saw that this band of conquistadors were few in number, they did not hesitate to launch an assault to retaliate for past abuses and ward off the possibilities of further misdeeds. Hostile encounters occurred on several occasions, but Orellana and his small band of followers managed to fend off their attackers.

Deprived of the opportunity to replenish their food, the meager provisions Orellana and his men had brought with them were soon exhausted. What little nature offered in the way of sustenance had already been claimed by Pizarro's large expeditionary force. The entire group was weakened by extended spells of hunger by the time they reached the Zumaque Valley. They also suffered the loss of most of their clothing and bedding as well as their horses—only three horses were fated to survive this harrowing journey.

After several weeks Orellana and his fellow conquistadors reached the Zumaque Valley, just shy of where Gonzalo Pizarro and his troops were currently camped. At this point, however, Francisco and his men were too weak from hunger and exhaustion to continue their quest. Desperate for food and water, Orellana dispatched scouts to find Pizarro's camp to inform the governor of their dire predicament.

Orellana's emissaries managed to locate the camp of Gonzalo Pizarro. The commander immediately ordered Antonio de Ribera, the camp master, to send aid to Orellana and his men. Ribera dispatched Captain Sancho de Carvajal and several soldiers with a quantity of food and water sufficient to renew their strength for the final leg to the Spanish camp. Captain Carvajal and his troops were shocked to see that Orellana and his men possessed little else besides their swords, shields, and the will to survive. The famished soldiers who hailed from Puerto Viejo and Santiago de Guayaquil were delighted to see Carvajal and the sustenance he brought to quell their debilitating hunger pangs.

Once their ravenous hunger had been calmed, Orellana and his equally ragged and emaciated conquistadors followed Captain Carvajal to Pizarro's camp at Zumaque. They soon joined up with the expedition at a settlement called Quema, which was located in the province of Motín. Francisco was welcomed with open arms by Gonzalo, who was so impressed with his devoted efforts that he immediately appointed him lieutenant-general, which meant he was now second-in-command of the expedition.

Into the Land of Cinnamon

Gonzalo Pizarro called a meeting of his officers to discuss their next course of action. Up to this point, the expedition had ventured nearly a hundred leagues, much of which was across a dense and steamy jungle they had been forced to hack their way through. The expedition was now bogged down by steady rains that seemed to grow heavier with each passing day. The ground had become so saturated that it was nearly impossible to walk.

To compound their dismal predicament, their clothing had begun to rot and what little food was still on-hand quickly spoiled.

While the majority of the men rested at Zumaque, where the city of Avila was later founded, the restless commander led a force of approximately eighty soldiers armed with crossbows and match-locks in search of the valley where cinnamon trees could be found or a path that might lead to the province of Eldorado. Their pace was greatly slowed by the fact that they had to travel on foot; the drenched ground and dense woods made for terrain far too difficult for the horses to trod. All of the horses remained at camp while Pizarro and his expeditionary force sought to blaze a new path.

Native guides from Zumaque led the Spaniards to a region so thick with vegetation that they had to use hatchets to clear a trail. Unbeknownst to Pizarro and his men, they were led astray by native guides who purposely kept them from villages which could supply them with sustenance. Since they were unable to locate residences in this remote region they could raid for food the Spaniards had to rely on their guides to locate edible herbs, fruits, and roots. Seventy days would pass before Gonzalo and his men were reunited with those who remained at the camp.

According to Pedro de Cieza de León, the conquistadors resumed their search for treasure by following "…a route in the direction of sunrise, having local Indians with them as guides. They started and marched for several days through dense and rugged forest country until they came to where the trees they call canelos grow."[2] Pizarro noted, "we endured great hardships and spells of hunger on account of the roughness of the country and the dissension among the guides, in consequence of which hardships a few Spaniards died."[3]

While they managed to find clusters of cinnamon trees the Spaniards were greatly disappointed to discover that these trees, which grew wild, were few in number and their cinnamon was hardly the best quality. These groves of precious flower buds and bark were not nearly as great as they had been led to believe, and even if they had met their expectations the remoteness of the region meant it was simply not worth colonizing.

Gonzalo Pizarro would later state in his report to the king of Spain, "…we found the trees which bear cinnamon, which is in the form of flower buds, a sample of which I am sending to Your Majesty; and the leaf has the same flavor, and neither the bark nor the rest [of the tree] has any flavor whatsoever; and these [trees] were in some mountainsides very rugged, unsettled and uninhabitable; and some of the trees were small and others somewhat larger in circumference, and they stood at long stretches from one another. It is a land and a commodity by which Your Majesty can not be rendered any service or be benefited in…"[4]

Frustrated by the scarcity of cinnamon trees, Gonzalo interrogated a

136   Eldorado and the Quest for Fortune and Glory

number of local natives as to where he could find more cinnamon groves or other natural resources that might enrich the Spaniards, such as the opulent realm of El Dorado. The fearful Indians responded that these were the only cinnamon groves known to them and added they knew nothing about a region that was home to a kingdom teeming with gold.

Exasperated by his inability to locate the riches he sought, Gonzalo Pizarro subjected many natives to some of the cruelest forms of torture known to mankind. Convinced that the indigenous people were concealing the truth, the commander had his men construct racks made of cane. When the tied down prisoners refused to change their story, even after having been painfully stretched, the Spanish leader ordered they were to be burned alive. When the screams of these tortured souls failed to loosen the tongue of the horrified onlookers, Pizarro further vented his frustrations by throwing several Indians to his starving dogs.

Gonzalo's troops were deeply discouraged to learn that the much-touted cinnamon groves were few and of inferior quality, and it seemed highly unlikely that this rugged and unsettled terrain would ever yield a profitable crop of cinnamon for processing and shipment. Most of these

A frustrated Gonzalo Pizarro began burning natives alive to learn the whereabouts of Eldorado (Library of Congress).

soldiers-of-fortune held out hope that Eldorado would reward their toil and turmoil. Many knew that Hernán Cortés had been beset by numerous setbacks in his efforts to conquer the rich realm of the Aztecs. Even more, several in this company knew from personal experience that Francisco Pizarro had to overcome numerous hardships to claim the riches which eclipsed those claimed by Cortés. Some of the disillusioned Spaniards, however, worried that Eldorado might also prove to be a disappointment.

The expeditionary force continued until it reached the bank of a small stream of fresh water, where they decided to make camp for the night. Unfortunately, the Spaniards camped too near this freshet; the incessant rains caused a rapid rise of the stream, which quickly evolved into a raging river. Awakened suddenly from their sleep a number of groggy men nearly drowned, but all managed to reach safety. However, a significant portion of their provisions were washed away. Many members of the advance party sensed their commander was growing despondent, and that he seemed to lament having undertaken this expedition.

Wishing to avoid linking up with the main body of troops until he had some encouraging news, Pizarro led his companions to the native settlement of Capua. The adventurers followed a different route back, a northerly path that led them to the Coca River. All rejoiced over this discovery, for surely they would find villages along the banks that could provide them with much needed sustenance. The explorers soon learned that the Coca is a tributary of the Napo, which, in turn, is a tributary of the Amazon. The Spaniards followed on foot the winding route of this deep and broad river while seeking a spot that was safe to cross.

The dispirited soldiers soon saw a great many canoes manned by numerous natives navigating the river. While contemplating their next course of action, Gonzalo Pizarro and his men noticed an assembly of Indians along the opposite bank who were eying them with suspicious looks. The Spaniards beckoned the Indians to meet with them. Their peaceful manner persuaded between 15 and 20 natives, along with their chief, Delicola, to meet with Pizarro. The Spanish commander sought to win their friendship with an offering of trinkets before inquiring about Eldorado. Delicola gladly accepted Pizarro's gifts of combs and knives.

During this meeting, Delicola was informed by one of his scouts about the horrific transgressions committed by the Spaniards against a neighboring village. The chief decided not to make the same mistake and merely told the Spaniards what he expected they wanted to hear, even though it was not true. Pizarro was told that a ten-day march would lead them to a vast region rich with gold. The chief added that this was a heavily populated and settled province. Delicola merely did what many other clever chiefs found to be an effective means of ridding themselves of Spanish intruders—he fed them tales of distant rich lands which would steer the conquistadors away from his land. The ruler hoped these avaricious and barbarous men would take the bait and depart his homeland. Pizarro believed Delicola but planned to make the chief serve as both their guide to this rich realm and as a human shield to protect them during this search.

The chief entertained his guests with food and enriching tales of lands laden with gold. Here they remained for close to two months while waiting for the main force at Sumaco to join them. Delicola's plan to rid his land of these intruders, who were placing a heavy burden on his food stores, backfired shortly after the Spaniards were reunited. Frightened by the sight of so many soldiers and the stories of their cruelties, a number of natives took up arms and tried to drive off the Spaniards. Gonzalo's men easily prevailed and the commander used this unprovoked attack as an excuse to make Delicola and his subjects his prisoners, many of whom, including the chief, were placed in chains.

The spirits of the Spaniards were lifted by a tale Delicola had spun solely for their benefit. The chief led the conquistadors to a spot along the river where it was narrow enough for a bridge to be built. A number of warriors attempted to prevent their crossing, but all were forced to flee after several of their comrades were felled by powerful blasts from Spanish matchlocks. Pizarro and his troops were then free to concentrate on building their bridge.

Once the bridge was completed Pizarro and his men crossed over and marched toward Delicola's village. The Spaniards stumbled upon a few small villages along the way that yielded a meager amount of food, particularly corn, guava, and yucca. The path led them to a savanna enclosed by another dense forest. Gonzalo instructed his weary troops to make camp after which the commander sent a messenger back to Zumaque to instruct the troops left in the charge of Francisco de Orellana to make haste to Delicola's village. Once reunited, Pizarro sent the camp master and fifty soldiers to reconnoiter the region ahead.

This scouting party returned after an absence of 15 days. Pizarro wrote that the camp master "brought back a story [to the effect] that he had found a great river, that there were houses right on the edge of the water, and that on the river he had seen many Indians wearing clothes, going about in canoes, and that it seemed to him that province was a thoroughly settled one, because the Indians whom he had seen wore clothes and [were] quite civilized. And, as soon as he came with this story, I set out and came to this province that is called Omagua, passing through great marshes and crossing over many creeks."[5]

Gonzalo Pizarro and Francisco de Orellana agreed that they should concentrate their efforts on searching for the golden land, which surely had to be the sublime realm of El Dorado. They would follow by land the eastward flow of the Coca River with Delicola serving as their guide to these wealthy lands he had bragged about. The expedition traveled nearly fifty leagues without finding a way across this broad river.

The Spaniards were drawn to the steadily increasing sound of rushing water. The source of this thunderous roar revealed a spectacular waterfall they estimated at more than 1,200 feet in height. As they looked-on in awe, Pizarro and his men noticed that the water plummeted into a narrow channel barely 20 feet from one bank to the other. The bellow of this cascading falls was so great that the Spaniards first heard it from six leagues away.

Pizarro decided to construct a bridge over this chasm in order that they might continue their quest to locate Eldorado. A small band of natives on the opposite side sought to oppose the Spaniards' efforts. A well-aimed shot from a matchlock felled one of the native defenders, which, in turn, caused the others to flee in fear. Already fallen tree trunks and accessible vines were used to construct a bridge over the San Rafael gorge. One of Pizarro's soldiers made the fatal mistake of looking down while placing the first beam of the bridge—the dizzying height caused him to lose his balance and plummet to his death in the torrent of water below. The rest of the soldiers were careful not to make the same mistake as they resumed their construction. Following a strenuous effort by all, the bridge over the San Rafael gorge was completed and the men and horses proceeded to safely make their way across. The Spaniards left the bridge intact just in case they needed to return by this route.

In Need of a Boat

The other side of the river proved little different from the one they had just left. The Spaniards followed the downstream route of the Coca River, where they were still confronted with towering trees and dense vegetation barring their way. They were now deep in the rainforest surrounded by trees that soared to dizzying heights and trunks estimated as large as 96 feet in circumference. Vines and creepers hung ominously from the trees. The sun and stars, when visible, offered some sense of direction. The feet of the soldiers and the hooves of their accompanying horses were frequently entangled by roots which sprouted in this wilderness region choked with unchecked vegetation. In what proved to be a painfully slow and exhaustive process, the adventurers used their axes and machetes to hew a path through the dense growth. Their hacking away at tree limbs and creepers frequently awakened a host of ticks, jiggers, and ants; such actions also aroused venomous snakes and scorpions. Thorns and branches tore away at their clothing, which, in turn, provided openings for all manner of biting and stinging creatures.

The trail that Pizarro and his men blazed eventually deposited them onto a plain which led to the province of Guema (a.k.a. Quema). They soon arrived at a small village of the same name with few inhabitants, but endowed with a plentiful store of food, which the Spaniards helped themselves to. They pushed on to another fertile savanna that provided the expedition with additional fruits and crops. The soldiers felt quite satisfied with the array of food items they had collected for their journey, but such comforting thoughts would soon pass.

The route that the expedition followed would lead to a sparsely inhabited region. What few villages the Spaniards encountered were often abandoned by fearful natives. Heavy rains continued to plague the efforts of the Spaniards; numerous swamps and creeks along the banks of the river made for an extremely difficult march. Several soldiers and horses drowned trying to wade through the rising waters. Their clothing would rot from the heavy rains and humidity. Much energy was exerted on the building of bridges at the various locations the soldiers needed to cross.

The thousand pigs brought on this journey had been devoured or lost to the difficulties of the trek. The heat and rain spoiled much of their food, and the ensuing shortage of sustenance meant the soldiers had to rely on their Indian guides to locate edible herbs and roots. Some of these gathered items, however, were not fit for human consumption, which resulted in many Spaniards and natives becoming violently ill, and the weaker of the lot soon faced an agonizing death. The expedition had set out with nearly 1,000 dogs, the majority of which were used to keep the native slaves in line. There came a point when the conquistadors had to quell their hunger pangs by butchering for food some of their faithful dogs. By this time many of the 4,000 native porters had perished from the extreme effects of starvation, disease, and maltreatment.

The bodies of the soldiers were constantly drenched in sweat brought on by the stifling heat and humidity of the rainforest; the muggy climate caused their armor and weapons to rust. The scalp and beards of the Spaniards became infested with lice. With their clothes worn with rot, the gunpowder soaked and useless for hunting, and a great number of native porters either dead or vanished, many soldiers wondered if their miserable condition would ever improve.

The Spaniards sighted large boas, crocodiles, and caimans inhabiting the rivers, streams, and swamps of this god-forsaken region. The soldiers had to be mindful of gators basking in the warmth of the sun along the paths they followed. In addition to the oppressive heat, Pizarro and his men were plagued by swarms of mosquitoes and flies. Many natives along the river would lather their bodies with an unction that protected their exposed skin from mosquitoes and shaded them from the heat of the sun. Several river tribes painted themselves with scarlet anatto or black genipapo vegetable dyes.

The conquistadors also had to cope with vampire bats, poisonous snakes, enormous anacondas, spiders, scorpions, ants, and a host of other voracious insects dwelling in this vast and dense tropical forest. The bite of the centipede proved to be an extremely painful experience for many Spaniards. Pedro de Cieza de Léon noted in his *Travels* that there were "certain ants, as big as the beetles of Spain, which are very black and evil, and which, by merely biting a man, cause terrible pain."[6] These inch long army ants, known as tumecas, attack in droves and subdue their victims with painful stings and bites.

In spite of these numerous hardships the expeditionary force pressed on; each man trudged onward in the belief that their efforts would be richly rewarded. Pizarro and his men happened upon an occasional small village where they were able to barter for just enough corn, guava, and yucca to keep from starving to death. One such tribe welcomed the Spaniards with food and shelter, but a conflict soon erupted, and the natives were quick to abandon their own village, thereby leaving the Spaniards to fend for themselves. Pizarro dispatched scouting parties in various directions in the hope of finding a passable route that might lead to a native empire similar to the one forged by the Incas. All returned to report that the regions they explored were no less difficult—all were heavily forested and laden with treacherous lagoons and swamps.

After receiving these disappointing reports about the surrounding region, Pizarro decided to use this time to build a boat capable of carting the company across the river, which was roughly two leagues wide, to search for food and signs of rich kingdoms just waiting to be conquered. The natives helped cut timber and round up other materials used to construct this vessel. Once completed, the Spaniards resumed their quest by following the path of the river. Most of the men, the surviving horses, and other animals marched along the banks of the river. To lighten their load, the newly built barge hauled the expedition's munitions, weapons, axes, and other provisions, It also carried men who were too weak or ill to continue on foot. As mentioned previously, the majority of conscripted natives had either died or deserted at this point.

The Spaniards confiscated some 15 canoes from their native hosts and paddled about in small parties in search of food for the journey ahead. Because of the numerous native canoes massing along the river, which they estimated between 100 and 150 and manned by many armed warriors, the Spaniards feared to venture too far down river. Pizarro permitted his troops a period of rest while Don Antonio de Ribera and several soldiers ventured down river in a desperate search for food and a promising path to follow.

The scouting party led by Ribera returned to report that they had found a fairly large settlement approximately 10 leagues from their camp. Ribera told Pizarro they had spotted clothed natives living in houses along the banks near the junction of the Coca and Napo rivers. Pizarro ordered his men to break camp and make haste for the village sighted by Ribera. The Indians of this settlement received the Spaniards warmly; they gladly swapped their fish, maize, manioc (yucca), sweet potatoes, and other food items for trinkets, salt, and axes of the conquistadors. During their stay at the village the soldiers passed the time catching a variety of fish and hunting turkeys and ducks. Pizarro made the decision to remain at the village long enough to build another boat.

Further downriver the Spaniards made camp on a bluff that buffeted them from surges in the ebb and flow of the Coca River. Here they began to build another boat, one which would be larger and sturdier, to explore the river ahead. They spent most of October at this high bluff constructing a new boat. The men survived off fish caught from the river, butchered horses, and whatever edible fruits or roots they could find in their tropical surroundings.

Many of the men, including Captain Orellana, were opposed to Pizarro's plan to continue following the course of the river. Some counseled for a return to the savannas to locate native paths that would lead to either Popayán or Pasto. In spite of having already lost so much on this expedition, Pizarro chose to stay the course; in his mind there was no honor in turning back. Unable to alter Pizarro's plan, Orellana resigned himself to help with building the brigantine, and worked harder than most to make sure it was properly constructed and loaded. The compliant officer helped with rounding up expendable iron items, which were used to make nails, and supervised the Indians on the cutting of timber found in the surrounding woods. Francisco also oversaw the collection of lianas for cordage and chicle for resin.

To make the necessary nails, the Spaniards had to build a hearth to forge the iron, which was no simple task. Because of the incessant rains, the men had to construct shelters to protect the fires needed to form metal rivets. They used iron from the shoes of the horses that had been killed to feed the troops. Spanish armor, which had proved cumbersome in this torrid region, was also cast into the fires. Trees were cut into planks, though they would later discover they had used wood that was not suitably seasoned. Spanish cloaks and shirts were used to make sails, a difficult chore since many of the clothes were badly frayed from rot or torn by gnarly thickets.

"For tar for the brigantine, they used resin [chicle sap] from the trees;

for oakum, they had blankets and old shirts; and all were ready to give up their clothes, because they believed that the remedy for all their misfortunes would be the brigantine. They then completed and launched her, believing that on that day all their trouble would come to an end."[7]

The Spanish commander also helped with building the boat; he worked alongside the men, a sight which helped to boost the morale of his troops. Garcilaso de la Vega wrote in his historical account: "Gonzalo Pizarro, as became so valiant a soldier, was the first to cut the wood, forge the iron, burn the charcoal, and employ himself in any other office, so as to give an example to the rest, that no one might have any excuse for not doing the same."[8]

It took the conquistadors nearly two months to build a small boat known as a *barqueta*. The completion of the vessel was cause for much celebration among the weary soldiers, for all took tremendous pride in what they had accomplished under such trying circumstances. The carpenters had skillfully constructed a boat which measured approximately 26 feet long and 8 feet wide. When the vessel was finished and ready to be launched the Spaniards named their camp El Barco (the Boat) and christened their ship the *San Pedro*. Juan de Alcántara was placed in charge of the newly built boat.

The *San Pedro* set sail on November 9, 1541, with as many as 25 men on board who were too feeble to march alongside their comrades. The boat traveled in the company of the canoes they had recently relieved from the natives. All of their valuables were loaded on the brigantine, an inventory that included more than 100,000 pesos in gold, numerous emeralds, and other various possessions of value. Most of the heavy gear was stowed aboard the *San Pedro*, which helped lighten the load of the men who were compelled to march by land.

The strong current of the river propelled the boat downriver while the bulk of the army had to slog their way along the banks; each party maintained a watchful eye on the other to make sure that they did not become separated. Progress along the shore was slowed by the need of the Spaniards to clear a path through a wall of vegetation with their axes and native machetes, which was an exhaustive process. Those on the boat had a tough fight to keep the current from pulling them away from their fellow soldiers. Creeks and swamps along the riverbank made their march extremely difficult. Thickets and soft soil made for treacherous footing, especially for the horses. Bridges had to be constructed to get provisions and horses over more difficult bogs and creeks. There were several points where the thickness of the forest was simply too hard to penetrate. On these occasions, the entire force had to be ferried across the river, a slow and exhausting effort that took several days to complete.

The expedition followed the river for roughly 50 leagues, during the course of which they happened upon small settlements that yielded just enough maize, yucca, and guava to stave off starvation. However, the further they ventured the less they saw of native settlements. The Spaniards eventually reached an entirely uninhabited region, during which time they saw their victuals rapidly diminish with little to replace what had been consumed. They were told by the natives that a large settlement with an abundance of food could be reached by boat in as few as four days.

All clung to the hope that the rich lands that Delicola had spoken about would be revealed around the next bend of the river. The chief had told them that the place they sought would be located where the river joins an even larger river, which supposedly was only a fortnight or more journey from where they had built their boat. Delicola had told them they would find everything they needed, especially food and gold, at this rich town. But many became discouraged once several weeks had passed without any sighting of the settlement the chief claimed they would find. All of the men were exhausted and suffering from starvation. Their miserable state was compounded when Delicola and many other chained natives found an opportunity to escape into the jungle, leaving the weary Spaniards without a guide or porters to bear the burden of their heavy gear.

The expedition halted near the Napo River in December 1541. Finding themselves deep in the dense forest the Spaniards made camp along the Coca River so they might rest their weary bodies and honor the holy day of Christmas; faith offered comfort and strength to those stranded in such an uncivilized and foreboding realm. With their food exhausted, their armor rusted from the humidity, and many having fallen ill with fever, the officers and soldiers pondered what course of action to follow. The most difficult task was finding food for so many. Most of the men were compelled to chew the leather of their saddles and belts while they awaited whatever was caught in the forest—toads and snakes became part of their regular diet— or fished from the river. Gonzalo Pizarro and his followers had long passed the point of no return and to turn back now would have surely resulted in the death of all.

After ten fruitless months in search of fortune and glory, the exhausted and demoralized conquistadors had dwindled to half their original number. The jungle path was so thick that the Spaniards had barely penetrated 200 miles into the unknown. All the hogs and many of the horses had been butchered and devoured to stave off their intense hunger. Most of the natives had perished or deserted. Some froze in the mountains, some drowned in the swamps, many died from hunger, and an untold number perished at the hands of heartless Spaniards. Many of the soldiers were wounded from guerrilla style attacks by natives, most likely Cofanes

7. Lost in a Lost World 145

Pizarro's expedition arrives at the Napo River (Library of Congress).

tribesmen. A dark cloud of desperation hovered over the Spanish camp—thoughts of the elusive riches of Eldorado were replaced by the basic need to survive. Many men had died from exhaustion, malnutrition, and disease by the time Francisco de Orellana approached Gonzalo Pizarro with an offer that the commander could not refuse.

8

An Altered Course

Captain Francisco de Orellana, who had a solid grasp of the native tongues, questioned the Indian guides brought on the expedition. They confided in him that ahead lay a vast stretch of uninhabited land, and therefore they should collect as much food as possible before resuming their quest. However, there was plenty of food and many tribes to be found where the river they followed joined with another great river. Orellana told this encouraging news to Pizarro and then volunteered to take the boat and gather provisions for the continuation of their search for Eldorado. This report was delivered at a time when the troops were in dire need of food, for the small amount of edibles collected by the men fell far short of what was needed to sustain all.

According to Gonzalo Pizarro, "Orellana told me he had questioned the guides I had placed in his charge so that he might get better information about the country beyond (as he had nothing to do since I looked after all matters to do with fighting) and told me that the guides had said that the uninhabited region was a vast one and that no food whatsoever was to be had this side of a spot where another great river joined up with the one down which we were proceeding; and that from this junction, one day's journey up the other river, there was an abundant supply of food."[1]

Pizarro added that the one-eyed Orellana volunteered to go down river and would return in less than a fortnight with enough food to feed the entire expeditionary force. Gonzalo welcomed his offer and felt confident that he would return as promised with food. With his troops at the brink of starvation, Gonzalo Pizarro had little choice but to acquiesce to Orellana's plan.

Gonzalo later wrote: "I was confident Captain Orellana would do as he said because he was my lieutenant. I told him I was pleased at the idea and that he should see to it that he got back within twelve days, and in no case go beyond the junction of the rivers, but bring the food and give attention to nothing else. He answered that he would by no means go beyond what I had told him...."[2]

Pizarro further stated, "And with this confidence that I had in him, I gave him the brigantine and the canoes and sixty men, because it was reported that there were many Indians going about the river in canoes; telling him also, inasmuch as the guides had said at the beginning of the uninhabited region there were two very large rivers that could not be bridged over, to leave there four or five canoes to ferry the expeditionary force over; and he promised me that he would do so, and so departed."[3]

Elated by the prospect of finding food and fortune, Pizarro instructed Orellana to take the *barqueta*, several canoes (twenty-two according to testimony given later), and a select group of men downriver to find the hospitable place the natives had mentioned, a distance believed to be approximately 80 leagues away. Gonzalo instructed his lieutenant that once he had located said village residing at the junction of the Coro and Napo rivers, he was to unload his cargo and stock the boat with food items, after which he was expected to paddle upstream in order to distribute the victuals to the anxiously awaiting troops. Afterwards, Orellana was to transport another group of men downriver to their new campsite, a procedure which was to continue until all were safely at the new camp.

Gonzalo's trusted lieutenant and valued friend departed camp in the company of fifty-seven Spaniards and two African slaves on December 26, 1541. Also on board was Gaspar de Carvajal, a Dominican priest of the Order of Preaching Friars who, in addition to tending to the spiritual needs of the men, kept a journal of their adventure. The number of men who accompanied Orellana on this journey range from no less than 50 to as many as 60. Padre Carvajal claims there were 57 of them. However, Carvajal may have just been taking into account soldiers, and failed to include Orellana, himself, and a friar from the Order of Mercy by the name of Gonzalo de Vera. Also, there were two Negroes who served as oarsmen, but their names do not appear on any known document.

Gonzalo Pizarro clearly exaggerated his claim that Francisco de Orellana took all of the weapons—the lieutenant's explorers were armed with only three arquebuses, some gunpowder and ammunition, and five crossbows for their protection. They also made sure to carry some medical supplies that belonged to the surgeon of the expedition. The *San Pedro* also stored a large share of the company's clothing and bed linens. These materials were to be unloaded at their destination and replaced with stores of food for the return journey. The *San Pedro* was equipped with oars and a sail to expedite their journey downriver. There was very little food aboard the *barqueta*; most of the expedition's meager food supply remained with Gonzalo and his famished troops.

Pizarro and his men watched as the current swiftly swept Orellana's boat beyond their sight. Now stranded along the bank of the river, the commander and his remaining troops sought cover from the pouring rain as they anxiously awaited the return of their comrades.

A Dangerous Course

According to Carvajal, Orellana and his crew coasted very close to the riverbank, but tragedy occurred on the second day when the *San Pedro* struck a submerged tree trunk that had fallen into the river. The collision tore a gaping hole in the side planks which threatened to sink the boat. It was clear to all that immediate repairs had to be made if they wished to continue their quest. The damaged vessel was brought ashore and its large hole was quickly patched so they could resume their course downriver; this time the crew made sure to stay in the deeper middle section of the river in order to avoid a similar accident.

The river's swift current sped the boat along at such a rapid clip that the men were spared from having to operate the oars or sails. The torrential rains made the river swell and caused the current to become even more forceful, which explains why the *San Pedro* easily averaged between 20 to 25 leagues a day downriver. It took just three days for the powerful current to carry Orellana's boat the eighty leagues to where the two rivers, the Coca and Napo, merged. Unfortunately, they could not find the foretold villages which were to provide essential food for either themselves or the famished comrades who awaited their return.

A week without food caused the crew of the *San Pedro* to slip into fits of delirium. Forced to go ashore to search for food, Fray Carvajal wrote: "We reached a state of privation so great that we were eating nothing but leather, belts, and soles of shoes, cooked with certain herbs, with the result that so great was our weakness that we could not remain standing, for some on all fours and others with staff went off into the woods to search for a few roots to eat and some there were who ate certain herbs with which they were not familiar, and they were at the point of death [and] they were like mad men and did not possess sense."[4] The poor souls who ate plants that proved to be poisonous were successfully treated by consuming a small amount of medicinal oil stored on their boat. These severe privations had left Orellana and his men at the brink of succumbing to starvation.

Into the Realm of Aparia

Orellana's vessel floated eastward down the Napo, the source of which is Mount Cotopaxi, a volcano located along the eastern slopes of the Andes mountains in northern Ecuador. The Napo, which was once known as the River of the Canela, flows 550 miles southeast through the dense rainforests before becoming one of many tributaries of the mighty Amazon River. These facts were unknown to Francisco de Orellana and his entourage; what they did know was that both sides of the river were lined with an impenetrable jungle wall that extended for as far as they could see.

On New Year's Day a few Spaniards claimed they heard the faint sound of drums emanating from the jungle, while those who did not hear them thought their comrades were simply imagining such sounds. To those who believed, the rhythmic patterns offered a glimmer of hope that a village might be very near. No sounds of drums were heard for the remainder or the following day. Their failure to spot any native villages merely affirmed the thought that the others were suffering auditory hallucinations.

On January 3, while devouring the small quantity of wheat and flour that Carvajal had brought with him for ceremonial offerings, several adventurers again heard the sound of distant drums, which they estimated to be five or six leagues away. This time Captain Orellana and many of the skeptics also heard the steady, rhythmic drumming. Gladdened by the thought that they were near a village which might provide them with food, the Spaniards rowed intently while remaining alert for a potential native attack. At nightfall a few soldiers kept watch while their companions slept.

After enduring a restless night, the dawn offered the Spaniards a better opportunity to search for a native village. The pounding of drums reappeared, only this time the sound was very close. That same morning, which marked the ninth day since they had left the main force, the Spaniards passed a bend and happened upon a village. Four canoes occupied by several warriors rowed out to investigate; the natives were curious about the strange vessel and peculiar looking men with beards floating down their river. Orellana and his comrades mustered the strength to frighten the natives back to shore with a series of threatening gestures. The Spaniards soon heard the ominous sound of drums beating a frantic pattern that alerted others of their presence. The officer ordered his men to ready their weapons, an arsenal that included three arquebuses and four or five crossbows.

As Orellana and his men rowed toward the village, they saw a large number of warriors gathered to defend their homes. This village, which rested at the mouth of the Aguarico, was home to as many as 200 Indians who were members of the Aparia confederation, and lorded over by the tribal chief Aparia the Lesser. Once ashore, the famished soldiers attacked with such ferocity that the natives fled for shelter in the surrounding jungle. Luckily for Orellana and his men, the natives left behind their food. The starving adventurers helped themselves to maize, fish, peppers, yucca, sweet potatoes, and drink until their bellies became bloated. Carvajal wrote that the famished Spaniards "set about to make up for the past, because they did nothing but eat of that which the Indians had prepared for themselves and drink of their beverages, and this they did with so much eagerness that they thought that they would never satisfy themselves."[5] A few days after their arrival at Imara, seven crew members succumbed to the deprivations and illnesses they had been subjected to previously.

Once their appetites were satisfied the Spaniards began loading a large quantity of corn on their boat while they contemplated the difficult journey back to Pizarro's camp. Meanwhile, the natives cautiously returned to their village and Orellana was able to calm their fears by addressing them in a familiar tongue. Francisco, who had an ear for languages, made it a point to learn as much as he could of the various native dialects he encountered. He even kept a record of the meaning and pronunciation of native words—linguistic efforts on his part that would help soothe native ill-will on several occasions. Orellana respectfully requested an audience with their chief.

Aparia the Lesser, the ruler of this region, returned to his village the following day and Orellana expressed his goodwill toward the natives by embracing the chief and presenting him with an offering of trinkets and a Spanish costume. Pleased with these items, the ruler presented Orellana with gifts of feathers, gold ornaments, and more food. Carvajal wrote: "...and in a very short time they brought, in abundance, all that was needed, including meats, partridges, turkeys, and fish of many sorts; and after this, the Captain thanked the Chief heartily and told him to depart with God's blessing and to summon to him all the overlords of that land, of whom there were thirteen, because he wished to speak to them, all together and announce the reason for his coming...."[6]

Francisco de Orellana laid claim to the village in the name of Gonzalo Pizarro and Emperor Charles V, and formally took possession of the land by planting a cross where all could see. He christened the region Victoria. Orellana would learn that each tribe of the region had a chief, who was lorded over by a mighty chieftain of the province. While at Imara the Spaniards enjoyed bountiful dishes of fish and fowl provided by their native hosts. They even tasted monkey meat and the flesh of big game cats. During his stay at the village Orellana made a concerted effort to learn the speech of the Imara people.

Carvajal wrote that during their nearly month long stay at Imara, "The Mercy of God permitted the Indians from the districts round about that stopping-place to come in a peaceful mood, and just like friends some gave us fish in exchange for barter goods, others brought in birds and certain quantity of monkey-cat meat; and in that village this worn-out company of ours got a rest, not only those who were sick, but those who were well."[7]

8. An Altered Course

The kindness shown by the Imara people encouraged Orellana to be more respectful of the culture of other tribes he encountered along the way.

Friar Carvajal goes on to say that the meeting of local lords provided them with an intriguing story of female warriors who sounded very much like the Amazons of ancient Greek lore: "It was here that they informed us of the existence of the Amazons and the wealth farther down the river, and

Imara natives of the Amazon (Library of Congress).

the one who gave us this information was an Indian overlord known as Aparia, an old man who said he had been in that country, and he also told us about another overlord who lived at some distance from the river, far inland, who he said, possessed very great wealth in gold."[8] It was Aparia the Lesser who was the first to tell Orellana and his men of the existence a tribe of female warriors they called the Coniupuyara, or *grand mistresses*, who supposedly dwelled in the region that is now Belem, in Brazil. The chief also told them that there were a great many rich and powerful kingdoms to be found inland.

A Change of Plans

With information supplied by the natives, Orellana reckoned that the river had carried them nearly 700 miles from where they had left their comrades, and most agreed it would be near impossible to overcome the swift and strong currents of the river that had swept them this far. Travel by land seemed an equally difficult option, for the distance was nearly 3 times further than the Pizarro expedition had trekked in a year, and the terrain was extremely treacherous. Orellana and his men knew from personal experience and native confirmation that there was no food between Pizarro's camp and Imara. They could not carry enough food to last such a long journey. Many doubted that Pizarro, who expected their return in less than a fortnight, would bother waiting for them, especially since they were in such dire need of food. As one who knew the resolve of Gonzalo Pizarro, Orellana should have realized such a scenario was unlikely.

Padre Carvajal and others calculated that because of the powerful current they would only be able to row upstream three leagues a day at best. They also surmised that a return by land would take even longer than by boat. The general fear was that they would die of hunger and exhaustion long before they ever reached Pizarro's camp. Carvajal added, "We soon realized it was impossible to go back. We talked over our situation (seeing we were already nearly dead from hunger) and we chose what seemed to us the lesser of two evils ... trusting to God to get us out, to go on and follow the river: we would either die or get to see what lay along it."[9]

Meanwhile, Francisco de Orellana instructed his men to collect as much food as possible to bring back to Pizarro and the others who awaited their return. But the officer encountered resistance from several men who voiced the opinion, which was shared by most, that it was impossible to row upstream against such a swift and powerful current. Orellana was handed a petition written by the notary and signed by 49 crewmen, including Gaspar de Carvajal, whose name appeared at the top of this appeal; "We, the cavaliers and hidalgos and priests who are here with this expeditionary force with your Worship, having become aware of Your Worship's determination to go up river over the course down which we came with Your Worship, and having seen that it is an impossible thing to go back to where Your Worship left Gonzalo Pizarro, our Governor, without risking the lives of us all.... Therefore we beseech Your Worship, and we beg him and summon him, not to take us with him back up the river." The crew added, "We hereby exonerate ourselves from the charge of being traitors or even men disobedient to the service of the king in not following Your Worship on this journey."[10]

The petition also contained an overt threat of mutiny: "In the name of God and of the King ... not to enter on this so uphill journey, in which the lives of so many able-bodied men are placed in jeopardy ... and not let Your Worship take the position of ordering us to do so, for that will be furnishing an occasion for our disobeying Your Worship."[11]

After listening to their complaints, Orellana announced that he would need a night to ponder over his obligation to Pizarro and the objections of his crew. The next day Francisco replied in writing "inasmuch as it was impossible to go back up the river again, he was ready, although against his desire, to look for another route to bring them out to a port of rescue."[12]

Hoping to appease the crew and avoid risking the lives of all under his command, Orellana proposed to send volunteers back upriver in the canoes with corn to feed Pizarro's troops and carry letters informing the commander of their predicament. Francisco offered a reward of one thousand castellanos to any six men who would volunteer for this difficult task. He also pledged to provide them with the two negroes and a few Indians who would help them row back to Pizarro's camp. Only three soldiers volunteered, and even then, they had conditions; the crossbowmen were to accompany them as protection. Convinced they would be volunteering for a suicide mission, none of the crossbowmen agreed to accompany the volunteers. It was estimated that it would take forty to fifty days to make their return—all feared that Gonzalo would not wait this long and therefore such an effort to return would be in vain.

Orellana reasoned that it was best to take their chances down the uncharted river rather than risk the certain dangers that awaited upriver. Concerned that if they were lucky enough to survive this ordeal their decision not to return to camp might be construed by Spanish officials as an act of desertion, the commander thought it best to legitimize their position on paper. Orellana appointed Francisco de Isásaga as scrivener to record their actions in a legal format, which showed all were in agreement that a return journey was too perilous and that their only chance for survival was to continue downriver. Whether Francisco de Orellana and his crew deserted their mission or simply had no choice has been a constant source of debate amongst historians.

According to the historian Garcilaso de la Vega, the illegitimate son of a Spanish conquistador and an Incan princess, Hernán Sánchez de Vargas, a young soldier from Badajos, stubbornly refused to go along with Orellana's plan to continue downriver and therefore was marooned along the river bank. Left without food, Hernán would have to fend for himself amidst a vast and near impenetrable forest, and a river too wide and powerful to swim. Vargas had been abandoned to what seemed certain death.

The tale of Hernán Sánchez de Vargas being stranded by Francisco de Orellana has been noted in later retellings, but the source of this intriguing narrative is from the pen of Garcilaso de la Vega, an historian known to embellish his writings. Fray Carvajal wrote of Orellana's offer to pay a thousand gold castellanos to any man who would venture back to inform Pizarro of their pact but made no reference to Vargas being marooned. The added fact that Hernán Sánchez de Vargas does not appear on the roster of the men known to have participated in this expedition seems to confirm that Garcilaso de la Vega was not above resorting to the use of poetic license to add spice to his historical account.

Orellana had spent enough time with these natives, who were part of the Aparia confederation, to learn what to expect downstream. He was warned about the hostile realm of Machiparo, natives who certainly would not take kindly to any Spaniards trespassing on their domain. Past the lands of Machiparo was the land of the equally unfriendly Omagua.

Having learned there were many hostile tribes ahead, Orellana decided to build another boat, a sturdier craft to better accommodate the surviving troops and to store the foodstuffs obtained from the natives. Francisco and his men busied themselves with the building of a brigantine large enough to carry thirty men while the other twenty would remain aboard the older and smaller boat. It was decided that they would construct a square-rigged vessel with two masts, a difficult task since they lacked any experienced shipbuilders.

Friar Carvajal wrote of the difficulties they experienced in building a second boat: "There being no craftsmen who were expert in this or that trade, some were engaged in making charcoal in spite of their not being charcoal burners, others in cutting and bringing in wood in spite of their not being woodcutters, others making nails in spite of their not being smiths, and others in working the bellows of the forge; and ... within a few days two thousand nails of good quality were made out of the chains and horseshoes and iron materials which were found scattered among the company."[13]

Juan de Alcántara and Sebastián Rodríguez managed to make the numerous nails needed for constructing this second boat. Orellana personally thanked them for their outstanding effort in the making of some 2,000 nails over the course of 20 days, a herculean feat completed by men with no previous experience at such a task. Those who were not strong enough to cut timber either worked the bellows or carried water. Francisco supervised and pitched in wherever help was needed. After 20 days enough wood planks and nails were completed to assemble a second boat, Orellana decided they would find a new spot further downriver to build the new boat; materials for their new vessel made at Imara were stored on the *San Pedro*.

Accommodating the needs of the Spaniards placed a severe strain on the food supply and patience of their native hosts. It was very difficult for the tribe to provide food for so many men who did not help with harvesting crops and hunting game. During the latter days of their stay the Spaniards found the natives were noticeably uncooperative; with each passing day they brought less food to offer or trade with them. By month's end the Spaniards sensed they had over-stayed their welcome. The men collected as much food as they could carry before boarding their boat and canoes to resume their course downriver. On the second day of February the Spaniards departed Imara. By this time Orellana's expeditionary force had dwindled to forty-seven men.

9

The Great River

Francisco de Orellana and his company of adventurers cast off in search of the region lorded over by Aparia the Greater. Orellana also hoped to locate another chief who had extended an invitation to visit him. Twenty leagues downriver they came to the mouth of the Curaray River, home of a principal ruler of the Irimarais, the other chief whom Francisco had heard was a mighty lord. Unfortunately, the powerful current of the river prevented a meeting with this ruler. The Spaniards had counted on replenishing their supplies at the village they had been invited to visit.

The might of the river was of great concern to Orellana and his comrades, for they were entirely at the mercy of its swift current. Enormous tree trunks swept past them, and all feared their small craft might be sunk by a collision with one of these massive stems. This fear was nearly realized when their boats were almost overturned by a log jam formed by the current. The expedition passed by many burned and abandoned villages—the consequences of ongoing tribal wars. Once again Orellana and his men faced the possibility of starving to death.

They soon noticed that the current was growing steadily stronger and in the distance, they could hear a roar that grew louder and more frightening with each passing moment. They were about to discover that the mighty Napo was but a tributary to a far more powerful and larger river, for on the following day, February 11, 1542, the expedition reached a junction where the river they navigated was joined by two other large rivers. The Spaniards looked on in wonder at the breadth and might of this imposing river.

Padre Carvajal wrote: "It [the new river] did away with and completely mastered the other [Napo] river, and it seemed as if it swallowed it up within itself, because it came on with such fury and with so great an onrush that it was a thing of much awe and amazement to see such a jam of trees and dead timber as it brought along with it, such that it was enough to fill one with the greatest fear just to look at it, let alone go through it."[1] The trees in this tropical region sprout with astounding swiftness, but the thin

9. The Great River

top soil is not strong enough to support the roots and therefore numerous trees collapse from their own weight, many of which land in the river.

Never before had these Spaniards seen a river so large and forceful, and many feared that their meager little craft would be utterly destroyed by its unrelenting fury. Their sense of dread and apprehension was justified; the roar of the surging river and the vast number of trees propelled by the swift current, anyone of which could ram their vessels with enough force to cause a severe rupture, contributed to the growing fear of the crew. Since this discovery had been made on Saint Eulalia's day, the Spaniards christened the junction of these three rivers the Saint Eulalia Confluence.

While the Nile is considered the world's longest river, the Amazon dwarfs the placid Nile in the sheer volume of freshwater it carries. The Amazon starts in the snow-capped Peruvian Andes and steadily grows, thanks to its roughly 500 major tributaries, into a massive waterway that snakes through the world's largest rainforest. The Amazon is nearly 4,000 miles long and roughly 50 miles wide at certain locations. One-fifth of all the earth's freshwater flows through the Amazon, making it the world's largest repository of freshwater.

Francisco de Orellana and his comrades were not the first Europeans to lay eyes upon the Amazon River. The Spanish seafarer Vicente Yáñez Pinzón was the first to locate the mouth of the mighty river, which is 150 miles wide, during his expedition along the coast of Brazil in February of 1500. From the mouth, he sailed roughly one hundred miles inland before anchoring at the depositing waters of the Marañón River, but feared to stay long because it appeared far too treacherous. Pinzón departed after taking several natives prisoner and christening the waterway Rio Santa Maria de la Mar Dulce or more simply, Mar Dulce (Freshwater Sea). The Portuguese explorer Pedro Cabral made landfall at the southern region of Brazil a few months after the Pinzón expedition.

The Marañón was also known as the Rio Grande or, in some Portuguese accounts, the Maranhaõ. The origin of the Marañón name is uncertain; some early historians claim the first to discover this was a navigable river was a captain named Marañón around the year 1515, a possible scenario since many rivers were christened with the name of their discoverer. It was later called the Rio de Orellana, after Francisco de Orellana, but was eventually abandoned in favor of Rio de las Amazonas after hearing stories told by the explorers of their life-threatening encounter with a fierce tribe of women warriors. Even today, the Amazon is still known as the Marañón in parts of Peru, while Brazil calls a section of the river from the Iquitos to the mouth of the Rio Negro the Solimões.

The Orellana expedition cruised the Amazon at a swift and steady pace. The mighty river swept the crew to some friendly villages where the residents were willing to share or barter with the Spaniards their stores of maize, fish, turtles, monkey, cat, and partridge meat. The men saw that the natives kept large parrots in their huts, from which they plucked colorful feathers for their ornamental needs. The Indians also served them as food, a taste which the explorers learned to savor. At the end of February, they reached a large village where Orellana decided to make camp and keep himself and his men occupied with the building of a second brigantine.

Orellana and his followers continued down the Amazon, marveling at the vast jungle wall that abounded on each side of the river. The Amazonia rainforest stretched for as far as they could see; a wooded region characterized by heavy rainfall, high humidity, and sweltering temperatures. While native villages along this stretch of the river were few and far between, the Spaniards were certainly not alone.

The Spaniards saw a great many strange animals during their journey downriver, which included several species of New World monkeys. The most common are the red howlers or guaribas, a breed known to chatter quite loudly during the morning and evening hours. Other monkeys of this region include the nimble spider monkey; the tiny marmoset; the long-tail titi; and multicolored squirrel monkeys. All served as a source of food for the natives.

Additional creatures of the Amazonian rainforest include squirrels, otters, raccoons, rats, mice and two types of porcupines. The jungle is also home to five different species of armadillos, three breeds of anteaters, two varieties of sloths, small forest deer, and peccaries. The cat family species include the jaguar, puma, and ocelot. The tapir, the largest animal of the forest, makes its home along streams. While the tapir can weigh several hundred pounds it is an excellent swimmer. The capybara, the largest rodent in the world, also makes its home along the riverbanks. This creature can grow to a length of four feet and weigh as much as 110 pounds. The capybara are excellent swimmers who feed on the lush natural vegetation along the banks of the river. Other rodents are the paca, the spiny rat, and the agouti.

The Amazon region is home to an incredible array of birds: brightly colored parrots and macaws constantly fly in pairs between feeding grounds; flocks of parakeets flutter about the trees; long-legged herons wade through shallow waters in search of food; and a variety of toucans with their long, colorful bills reside in the tropical forest. The jungle is filled with the sounds of woodpeckers busy with their *rat-a-tat-tat* assault on the trunks of trees; hawks and eagles screech from their lofty heights; and doves can be heard cooing during the afternoons. A chorus of calls led by toucans, whippoorwills, and goat suckers break the silence of the night. The sighting of bats swarming the night skies, including the bloodsucking

Natives and monkeys gathering nuts in the lush Amazon rainforest (courtesy Library of Congress).

vampires, and the presence of vultures lurking about for carrion were ominous reminders to the Spaniards of the dangers of this region.

The tropical rainforest of Amazonia is also home to a host of insects and other small creatures; killer bees, army ants, scorpions, tarantulas, centipedes, ticks, flies, and mosquitoes are omnipresent. Cicadas, of which there are several species, produce a steady chorus of mating sounds. Small black flies known as *piums* can inflict a bite that will itch terribly for several days. Butterflies with extraordinarily beautiful markings offered a striking contrast to the ominous surroundings that engulfed Orellana and his men.

The Amazon River supports an abundance of underwater creatures, a list which includes electric eels, stingrays, silver carp, neon tetras, and giant catfish. The dreaded piranha inhabit various portions of the Amazon; when provoked, piranha can sever chunks of flesh with their razor-sharp teeth, and as a school they can prove deadly in a matter of minutes. The giant red fish, which can grow to 15 feet and weigh as much as 600 pounds, thrives in the waters of the Amazon. Orellana and his comrades also saw manatees (sea cows), which can reach nearly 8 feet and weigh roughly a ton. The nature of manatees, which are mammals, was a source of debate among the Catholic Spaniards who, by Church decree, were forbidden to eat meat on Fridays.

Giant river otters, caimans, crocodiles, freshwater dolphins, frogs, toads, eels, and large turtles are among the many other denizens of the Amazon. Turtle meat was a native delicacy, and a taste that Orellana and his crew grew to relish. Turtles migrate from the sea to lay their eggs along the sand bars. Caiman are found in great numbers along the waters of the Amazon, but alligators are far greater in number and much prized by the natives for their thick skin. There are toxic frogs that are deadly to the touch, the poison of which some tribes dabbed on their darts and arrows to subdue prey or enemies.

Natives catching an alligator with lasso (Library of Congress).

The Amazon is home to several varieties of poisonous snakes, but they are not as numerous as those which merely appear dangerous. Boa constrictors, which grow as long as 20 feet, are not unusual, but pose a small threat to people. In many areas, the river would overflow its banks and turn the neighboring forest into swamplands. Anacondas, some as large as 25 feet, and a very real threat to humans, are often seen floating across these swollen waters. From the comfort of their boat, the Spaniards saw giant water lilies float past them. They also viewed splendid orchids and giant moths, the latter having a wingspan of nearly a foot.

Without any villages to ransack or barter for food, the Spaniards were desperate to find ways to feed themselves. They fished and hunted, sometimes with good results, but more often than not they came away empty-handed. Despite the abundance of food that surrounded them, the conquistadors had a difficult time finding enough to satisfy their daily needs.

Orellana and his men had a hard time adapting to their jungle surroundings: they failed to learn from the natives they encountered that the surrounding jungle was home to a host of edible insects; ants, grasshoppers, wasps, and grubs were all part of the diet of the Indians along the river. Amazonian tribes also feasted on wild tubers, fruits, nuts, and honey, the latter a much sought-after delicacy. The river provided a large and varied quantity of fish, which the tribes conserved by catching only what they needed so there would be more for later. The Spaniards eventually learned that iguanas, spider monkeys, large turtles and fish were excellent sources of sustenance. However, they did their best to avoid contact with the fierce jaguars, crocodiles, anacondas, piranha, and large biting ants.

The Domain of Aparia the Greater

Prior to reaching the village of Aparia the Greater the expedition spent two weeks cruising the river, all the while engaged in a desperate search for food. They happened upon some small villages, but the natives chose to scare off the strangers with an intimidating show of force. Once again confronted with the deprivations of food and other life-threatening dangers, Orellana sent two canoes carrying eleven Spaniards on ahead to probe some islands located on the river. Tragedy nearly occurred when those aboard the canoes lost their bearings among the islands that dotted the river and found themselves separated from the main party.

Meanwhile, with the corn they had stocked at Imara nearly depleted, the men aboard the boat decided to risk a landing in order to catch some fish. Unfortunately, their boat entered an inlet that escaped the notice of the crew aboard the two canoes. They raced downriver thinking that their fellow Spaniards had sped far from their view. Orellana and his crew looked on in disbelief as their comrades passed by without noticing them.

Orellana and his crew attempted to chase after their companions but the current had swept the lighter canoes far from their field of vision. Those aboard the boats soon saw that the river split into many arms and all feared they were separated forever from their comrades. Fray Carvajal and the others offered up prayers to the Almighty. Orellana privately worried that the loss of so many men would doom their chances of surviving the perils of the hostile regions the Imara tribe had warned them about; Machiparo, Omagua, and Paguana provinces, where they anticipated unfriendly receptions.

Their prayers were answered two days later with the joyful reunion of those aboard the two lost canoes. Orellana brought everyone ashore for a period of rest, and to avoid another such mishap he ordered that henceforth the manned canoes could not distance themselves more than a crossbow shot from the brigantine. All rested for one day after having been reunited.

The following day the Spaniards headed downriver and eventually came upon a small cluster of abandoned huts where they decided to camp for the night. They soon realized this was the outskirts of a very large village. Orellana dispatched a few men in the canoes in an effort to peacefully barter for much needed food. The successful Spaniards returned with a few large turtles and some parrots; the meat of both easily satisfied everyone's appetite. However, an unrelenting assault by a swarm of blood-sucking mosquitoes forced them to move to a nearby village, which probably was the reason why the village along the river had been deserted by the natives.

The next morning the Spaniards were visited by several natives who informed them that they were now in the province of Aparia the Great, which was home to numerous settlements along the river. It had now been 19 days since they had left the village of Imara, which was in the region of Aparia the Lesser. Warmly received and cared for by the natives, Orellana and his men remained in these pleasant surroundings for three days. Francisco and his crew bade the friendly natives a fond farewell before returning to the river.

The sufferings of the Spanish explorers continued to mount as they sailed along the river, for the next several hundred leagues were devoid of villages which could provide them with food. Farther along, the river gradually revealed itself as home to a great many villages, most of which were quite small. Many of the tribes were friendly and willing to trade their food for various Spanish items. At one point, Orellana and his crew reached some villages where the inhabitants failed to notice their presence. The commander sent 20 men ashore to plead for much needed food. The

9. The Great River

natives proved friendly and provided turtles and birds in exchange for the odd Spanish trinket.

Orellana and his companions proceeded to a different village where they were met in a similarly friendly manner. The natives provided them with additional food to bring on their voyage. The Spaniards continued past several villages and on Sunday, the 26th of February, they encountered in the middle of the river a few canoes—one account puts the number at two while another states there were four such craft—manned by several natives. The Indians aboard presented the Spaniards with a gift of fish, birds, and 10 or 12 large turtles. The well-supplied canoes had been sent by the omnipotent Aparia, as news of peculiar men floating downriver had traveled quickly from village to village.

Captain Orellana made good use of his linguistic skills to converse with the natives, who were greatly impressed that he could speak their language. Francisco's efforts to learn the native speech helped them on numerous occasions to avoid misunderstandings and to soothe tensions; his natural aptitude, good memory, and perseverance helped the crew out of several tight spots. Seeing that the river split into two paths, the commander asked the natives in the canoes which course he and his men should follow. The Indians told Orellana, "Follow along where we shall go,"[2] which was a clear invitation for the Spaniards to visit their village and meet their chief.

The adventurers followed the canoes on a course which led them down a branch of the river where there stood a large village that was home to the mighty ruler of the region. Francisco and his comrades remained alert, for there was an air of defiance. Once they reached the shore where the village rested, Orellana leapt out of the boat and began conversing with the natives in their own language. The villagers were amazed that this strange looking man with lighter skin and a full beard knew their tongue. Orellana had spent his free moments at Imara learning the native dialect. The natives invited the commander and his men to visit their village. The rest of the Spaniards came ashore after the captain had impressed the tribe with his gift of gab.

Any remaining concerns of the Spaniards were laid to rest once Chief Aparia stepped forward to greet them. Orellana conversed with the supreme ruler who bore the same name as the province he lorded over. The natives proceeded to bring their guests a variety of their daily food, a cuisine which included turtles, various kinds of fish, some birds and monkeys.

With their unkempt beards and hair of varying colors, the Spaniards were certainly a curious sight to the natives. Their naturally white skin, however, was no longer a noticeable difference now that it had been burned and tanned from overexposure to the blazing sun. Their armor, most of

Native boy with his monkey (from *Exploration of the Valley of the Amazons*, published 1854 under the direction of Navy Department for the U.S. House of Representatives).

which had begun to rust, and their clothing, much of which was tattered and torn, seemed peculiar to a people accustomed to wearing little or no clothing.

Captain Orellana communicated as best he could that it was his desire to become friends of the people ruled by Aparia. He revealed to the natives that they were Christians who worshipped the one true god, and that they "were servants and vassals of the Emperor of the Christians, the great King of Spain, and [that] he was called Don Carlos...."[3]

The commander further stated that their emperor was designated as the lord of this region, and that they had been sent as emissaries to greet the inhabitants of the lands he ruled, and to reconnoiter the area and report their findings. To impress the natives that they were rightfully entitled to claim the lands where they dwelled, Orellana told them that the Spaniards were Children of the Sun. Like most conquistadors, Orellana knew from experience that many tribes of the New World revered the Sun. The tactic worked, for many of the Amazonian tribes worshipped the Sun, a supreme being they called *Chise*. From that day forth, the natives of this region showed great reverence toward the Spaniards.

Believing these strangers were indeed Children of the Sun, the natives willingly complied with their requests. Orellana further endeared himself to the natives by giving them many of the trinkets still in his possession. The natives reciprocated by clearing the entire village in order to house the Spaniards. The compliant natives told Orellana that he could remain here for as long as he wished. The Spaniards hoped to use this opportunity to build a sturdier boat for their voyage downriver.

Francisco de Orellana requested from the chief to have the neighboring overlords come pay their respects. The next day 26 chiefs met with Orellana, all of whom he gave trinkets to express his desire for friendship. The natives continued to bring food to the Spaniards; providing them with bountiful offerings of turtles, manatees, and a vast assortment of fish. Francisco and his men also feasted on roasted birds, which Carvajal said were partridges, along with cat and monkey meat. Turtles were a delicacy to the river dwellers and the Spaniards quickly developed a taste for the succulent flesh.

Carvajal made sure that Orellana lectured the natives on the virtues of Christianity. Afterwards, Francisco boldly laid claim to the region with the construction and planting of a large cross, a monument the Indians admired greatly even though its true meaning was lost on them. Meanwhile, Gaspar Carvajal attempted to convert the seemingly receptive natives by explaining the basic tenets of Christianity, and informing them it was wrong to worship pagan effigies.

The Spaniards enjoyed their stay at the village, the exception being the swarms of bloodthirsty mosquitoes. According to Carvajal, the mosquitoes were so numerous that the men had to take turns fanning one another; while one ate or worked another stood by to swat away the pesky bloodsucking insects. To counter the malaria carried by the mosquitoes, the Amazonian Indians used quinine, an ingredient found in the bark of the cinchona tree, to calm its ill effects. This effective treatment would elude European adventurers for several centuries.

It has been estimated that as many as five million Indians lived along the Amazon basin when the Spaniards first invaded the region. The rainy season runs for roughly 130 days, and annual accumulation can range from 60 to 80 inches—the ensuing runoff leads to a swelling of the rivers. Consequently, the Amazon River crosses a vast flood plain—a delta surrounded by a seemingly endless sea of trees. The natives feared to venture too far into the dense forest, for they were terrified of losing their bearing due to a lack of penetrating light or losing their lives to other tribes or creatures of the jungle.

Amazonian Indians paddled the river in dugout canoes, traditionally made of cedar wood, to fish and hunt game. The inhabitants of this region used the bow and arrow and many were adept hunters with a blowgun. Stone axes and hatchets made with turtle shells were used for clearing the land. The natives were at home on the land and water and proved themselves proficient in maneuvering their canoes. Many of the tribes planted a variety of crops, a list that included peanuts, corn, legumes, sweet potatoes, arrowroot, yams, taro, and squash. The hammock is an invention of the Amazonian tribes—its ingenious design provided the natives protection from numerous pests that roamed and slithered about the ground. Unlike the Inca realm, there were no stone masons in the lands explored by Pizarro and Orellana because there were no stones suitable for use.

Building a Better Brigantine

The ominous report of inhospitable regions further downriver convinced Orellana that he would need a bigger and sturdier boat. He decided to take advantage of native hospitality and build a better brigantine, one which could withstand the powerful current and onslaught of river debris that threatened their efforts on this mighty river. Francisco also wanted a vessel that could better shield his men from native projectiles, especially those arrows dipped in deadly poison.

Diego Mexía, a carpenter from Seville, oversaw the construction of the new boat. Though not a boat builder by trade, Mexía was a skilled woodworker and therefore was the most qualified for this position. Since there were no blacksmiths or experienced boat builders, the adventurers hoped to learn from mistakes made during the construction of their first boat. Sails were patched together from blankets. Palm leaves were used to shield the adventurers and their supplies, particularly the gun powder, from nature's elements. The Spaniards diligently worked on the construction of this new brigantine, a daunting task they managed to complete in 35 days. Diego Mexía later wrote, "[It was] a wonderful thing to see the happiness with which our comrades worked. There was no one amongst us who was accustomed to such work but, all the same, they conducted themselves as if they had been professionals."[4]

The natives fueled the strength of the Spaniards with generous offerings of food, which included manatee and turtle flesh. The well-nourished men dedicated themselves to building a better boat for the long voyage ahead. Besides food, the Indians supplied the Spaniards with cotton, tar, and resin to caulk the boats. Their task was made more difficult by swarms of mosquitoes that refused to give them a moment's rest. Several men were assigned the sole job of swatting and shooing them with fans supplied by the natives.

During the assembly of the boat, four very tall and rather elegantly attired natives, all with fine hair that hung to their waist, came to visit the Spaniards. What was unique about these tribesmen was that each was significantly taller than the tallest Christian in their group. Friar Carvajal added that they were finely adorned with much gold. These messengers brought an offering of food and greetings from an inland chief who was eager to learn more about the Spaniards. Orellana expressed his sincere thanks and reciprocated with an offering of trinkets, which the Indians found more than satisfactory. They asked to return to their chief to inform him of the kindness of the Spaniards and Orellana responded that he would be pleased if their chief came to meet with him. The messengers departed but were never seen or heard from again. The adventurers never learned the whereabouts of the province where the towering natives lived.

Orellana and his crew also had to overhaul the leaky *San Pedro*, the vessel that had transported them this far. This boat had begun to rot and therefore was repaired during this stopover. The tribes inhabiting the Amazon region knew from experience to wait until the last quarter of the moon to cut wood; trees cut down during the other quarters were prone to rot and became fodder for insects, which was the reason why the first boat had begun to decay. The natives helped with the construction of the second boat, so they surely would have advised the Spaniards as to whether or not the wood they used was properly seasoned. The newly built vessel was christened the *Victoria*.

"Such great haste was applied to the building of the brigantine," Gaspar de Carvajal noted in his journal, "that in thirty five days it was constructed and launched, caulked with cotton and tarred with pitch, all of which the Indians brought because the Captain asked for these things. Great was the joy of our companions over having accomplished that thing which they so much desired to do...."[5]

Forty-one days would pass before the construction of the new brigantine and repairs to the older boat were completed. The Spaniards did not work on Sundays and sacred holidays, which included Maundy Thursday, Good Friday, and Easter, which accounts for the discrepancy in the number of days reported by Padre Carvajal. Their unwavering faith in God lifted their spirits and provided all with hope during such desperate times. The task at hand also bound them to a routine which helped fend off feelings of despair.

Their new boat was nearly twenty-four feet long and had nine oars on each side to help speed them along the course of the river. Orellana appointed Cristóbal de Segovia, a veteran of the conquest whom Fray Carvajal referred to as simply Maldonado, as captain of the refurbished old boat while he took the command of the new boat. Alonso de Robles was named second-in-command of the expedition. In the coming months Robles was often sent ahead with a few men to probe both the river and the land.

The expedition was ready to sail on April 24, 1542. Orellana thanked his gracious hosts with gifts, which included a Spanish sword that he personally presented to the ruler. The captain and his crew had received plenty of supplies from Aparia for the journey downriver. While saddened to leave behind the food and safe haven provided by the natives, the Spaniards were certainly glad to take leave of the mosquitoes.

Divine Intervention

Leaving behind the comforts of the village ruled by Aparia the Greater, Fray Carvajal recalled, "From here on we endured more hardships and more hunger and passed through more uninhabited regions than before, because the river led from one wooded section to another wooded section and we found no place to sleep and much less could any fish be caught, so that it was necessary for us to keep to our customary fare, which consisted of herbs and every now and then a bit of roasted corn."[6]

Up to this point Orellana and his crew had yet to face a difficult native assault, but that would soon change. After a few days downriver, the Indians stopped coming to trade with the Spaniards, which led Orellana to understand that they had passed the province of Aparia, a realm which stretched for more than eighty leagues. Fearing they had now entered a hostile domain, the Spaniards quickened their pace.

One morning, shortly after their departure from a small village along the banks, the Spaniards happened upon a lone native paddling the river in his canoe. The Indian came alongside the Spanish boat and was coaxed aboard to meet with Orellana. The captain decided this native might be a useful guide, and therefore pressed him into service. After 5 days downriver, during which time their guide was unable to locate any villages, it became evident to all that the Indian knew very little about this region. The Spaniards granted the native his freedom and he quickly paddled away in his canoe.

The powerful current swept the expedition down stream; the river soon became so broad that it was nearly impossible to go ashore to replenish their dwindling food supply. The Spaniards continued in this desolate manner until May 6, at which point they stopped at an elevated spot to try their hand at catching some fish. One soldier caught a large fish with a hook, and another brought down a vulture with a well-aimed shot from his trusty crossbow. It was here that Diego Mexía, who was an excellent wood worker, but apparently an inexperienced crossbow user, took aim with his crossbow at an iguana perched on a tree limb looming over the riverbank. In his rush to shoot the iguana the Spaniard improperly loaded the crossbow. Not only did he miss the intended target but the nut to the crossbow fell into the river, a loss which rendered the weapon useless. Later that afternoon another soldier cast a line and hooked a fish. As it was being prepared for cooking the men were shocked to find the missing crossbow nut inside the stomach of the fish. Once they were able to repair the damaged weapon, many, including Father Carvajal, believed they had witnessed the divine hand of God at work on their behalf.

Orellana and his crew resumed their voyage through this remote and uninhabited region. The men saw that the river had overflowed its banks and inundated much of the land as they floated past villages abandoned due to flooding. For their safety the Spaniards slept aboard the boats, which were securely tied to trees resting along the banks. Here they were constantly harassed by mosquitoes while suffering terribly from hunger. Finding the swift current made it extremely difficult to catch fish, the frustrated crew subsisted on herbs and toasted maize.

10

An Interminable Wait

While Francisco de Orellana and his companions set off in search of food for the entire expeditionary force, Gonzalo Pizarro and his remaining army, which numbered roughly 200, awaited Orellana's return while camped near the confluence of the Napo and Coca. Fearing that inactivity could fuel desperation which, in turn, might ignite discontent, Pizarro made sure his starving soldiers stayed busy hunting and fishing for food, and building canoes and rafts to transport them along the river. They eventually constructed between 10 and 12 vessels of varying size and style.

Pizarro and his weary soldiers sought to shelter themselves as best they could from the incessant rains. When Orellana and his crew, who were instructed to come back in less than a fortnight, failed to return when expected Gonzalo and his troops were overcome with ominous thoughts; wondering if they might have been captured or killed by an overwhelming force of warriors; maybe their boat had sunk, therefore stranding ashore those who did not drown; or perhaps they had purposely deserted the mission and therefore condemned those left behind to face a harrowing existence.

With their food rations exhausted the Spaniards sought to fend off their ravenous hunger by killing and cooking what few animals they could catch in the woods. They had already consumed most of the nearly 1,000 dogs that had set out with them on this journey. As many as 100 horses had died or been killed for food. Pizarro and his men tried to find food in the surrounding jungle but experienced little success. The men had little to eat except for palm shoots and some fallen fruit. When lizards and snakes failed to quell their hunger, the soldiers began rounding up any plants and fruits they thought might be edible. The natives they had counted on were of no help, for they abandoned their villages once they learned of the Spaniards' approach, taking with them all their food and provisions. They hid in the forest that was familiar to them. Many of Pizarro's men fell sick and a great number soon died of hunger.

10. An Interminable Wait

Meanwhile, one of Pizarro's search parties managed to confiscate five native canoes. The commander decided to put these canoes to good use by dispatching Captain Alonso de Mercadillo and a dozen soldiers downstream in search of food and signs regarding the whereabouts of Orellana and his crew. Mercadillo returned after eight days with discouraging news; he reported they were unable to locate any signs of Orellana, food, nor the legendary golden kingdom.

After the Mercadillo expedition returned without success Pizarro decided to march his famished troops to the river junction. Not wanting to take a chance on missing the return of their comrades, Gonzalo had his men trek along the riverbank. Unfortunately, the Spaniards soon found themselves bogged down in an impassable swampland.

With hope fading fast, Gonzalo sent a better equipped expedition downriver in the canoes to search for answers regarding the whereabouts of the absent Orellana and his crew. This search party was led by Gonzalo Díaz de Pineda, the same Pineda who had been on an expedition in 1530 that learned of the Land of Cinnamon, news which had prompted this very expedition. The canoes continued until they came to where the Coca merged with the Rio Napo. This large river was a tributary of an even larger river later known as the Amazon. Pineda and his men continued downstream until they reached the mouth of river known as the Aguarico. Here they made landfall and located a spot where Orellana and his crew had previously camped.

Pineda spotted knife slashes on trees along the river's bank, which he viewed as signs indicating Francisco de Orellana had passed this way. He deduced that Orellana and company had either perished or continued on without any intention of returning. A native guide suggested they should head up a tributary to search for much needed food. The search party paddled roughly 30 miles up the Aguarico before happening upon an abandoned field of cassava. All paused to give thanks to the Lord above before proceeding to fill their bellies with cooked cassava. Once their appetites had been satisfied Pineda had his crew fill their canoes with as much cassava as possible for their famished comrades. They followed the current of the Aguarico to the Napo, where they rowed upriver to rejoin their fellow Spaniards.

Meanwhile, Gonzalo and his starving soldiers anxiously awaited the return of Pineda; they sought to satisfy their terrible hunger with the remaining dog and horse meat, which was seasoned with herbs and leaves taken from the forest. They also had to resort to chewing the leather of the saddles and stirrups, which was boiled for softening and then cooked. Gonzalo and most of his men survived off palm kernels and *bihao*—leaves of a plant that belongs to the banana and plantain family. The Spaniards ate any lizards they could catch and devoured various plants, some of which were poisonous. Several died and many more became violently ill. The lingering effects of starvation led to the prolonged death of many Spaniards. At night, the moans of the weak and weary were accompanied by a cacophonous chorus of strange sounds emanating from the surrounding jungle. All were near the point of death.

Gonzalo Pizarro later wrote of their interminable wait, "...eating nothing but saddles and stirrup leather, sliced, boiled, and toasted over embers, with palm shoots and fruits fallen from the trees together with toads and snakes. For we had now eaten in this wild country over one thousand dogs and more than one hundred horses, and many of us were sick, and others weak, while some had actually died there of hunger."[1]

Pizarro and his starving soldiers rejoiced when Pineda returned with a boatload of cassava. They had been gone twenty-seven days, and many at camp feared all had perished in the wild. Gonzalo decided to march his weary troops to where the Napo joins with the Amazon. They had to hack a path along the river's edge for an estimated 200 leagues, an exhaustive chore which took them nearly two months to complete. Ravenous hunger, steady rains, and extreme exhaustion were their toughest foes.

Gonzalo and his men had been told they would find much food where the rivers joined, advice which proved to be true. It was here that they ate several of their remaining horses. The expedition had reached the junction where Francisco de Orellana and his men briefly stopped. Here they saw indications that Orellana and his men had deserted them, signs which further discouraged the downtrodden troops. Pizarro decided they had little choice but to make their way back to Quito.

The Vargas Tale

According to the historian Garcilaso de la Vega, Gonzalo Díaz de Pineda happened upon a nearly naked Hernán Sánchez de Vargas where the Napo and the Coca converge, and very near where Orellana and his crew had previously camped. Vargas, who had allegedly been left behind after he refused to continue downriver with those who chose to disregard their mission, was found wandering aimlessly. Hernán looked even worse off than the weary troops who followed Gonzalo Pizarro. He was escorted back to Pizarro and then proceeded to tell a dreadful tale that confirmed Gonzalo's worst fears; Francisco de Orellana had deserted him.

Vargas told Pizarro that the brigantine had reached the juncture of the Coca and Napo in under three days. It was here that Orellana used his knife to make marks in the trees as a sign of their having made landfall. The officer and his men debated their course of action, with most arguing that the current was far too swift to row back, especially in their weakened state. It was decided that they would continue on without sending word back to Pizarro and their comrades. Hernán Sánchez de Vargas was the lone dissenter. Orellana and the others elected to leave Vargas behind to fend for himself.

This troubling tale of treachery told by Vargas surely made the blood of Pizarro and his comrades boil. Left in a remote land with few weapons to protect themselves, and little prospect of food, Gonzalo still had a hard time accepting the idea that one of his most trusted officers would betray him in such a callous manner. He wanted to believe there was another explanation, such as the explorers were slain by a hostile tribe. Gonzalo was disheartened by this news, as were his troops, but the commander did his best to lift the spirits of his men and encourage them to continue their quest. As mentioned previously, the Vargas tale was concocted by the historian Garcilaso de la Vega.

Once his men had satisfied their hunger and regained their strength, Pizarro decided he would lead his soldiers to the fields of cassava, where they would be assured of food and, hopefully, find natives who could direct them to other rich and abundant natural resources. Gonzalo ordered all aboard the canoes so that Pineda could guide them to the yucca fields. This would prove to be an extremely difficult trek for the weary conquistadors.

Sensing that his troops were near death, Pizarro took the five canoes and several soldiers downriver to search for food. One day into their search they located the place where the natives said sustenance would be found. Gonzalo returned to inform the others and hoped such news would revive their dwindling spirits. Unfortunately, he found his troops were at the brink of death, a great many resigned to the thought that their passing was near and certain. Some were so despondent that they stated they would rather die than continue such a fruitless quest. Gonzalo heard their complaints and sympathized with them, but implored his men to not give up hope.

The expedition followed the flow of the river for more than 100 miles, during which time everyone kept their eyes peeled for signs of Orellana and his men. Scouts were dispatched but no signs were discovered. Pizarro's expedition crossed the swamp, after which they marched eight days along the banks of the river, a trek which brought them to the Aguarico River. The Spaniards spent a week ferrying themselves, their few remaining animals, and gear in their canoes across this river. They found the task more difficult than envisioned; several horses drowned in the deep water, an incalculable loss to the expedition. The surviving horses were transported by raft while the Spaniards blazed a path through the dense foliage along the banks.

Following their crossing of the river the wayfarers hiked upriver for one day, at which point they arrived where Pizarro previously found food. The famished soldiers gorged on maize as well as raw and cooked yucca. Cassava can be poisonous if not cleaned and cooked properly; two members of the expedition died from eating improperly prepared cassava root and many more became violently ill. They were unable to locate the natives who had planted these crops. After their bellies were filled and their bodies rested the Spaniards gathered as much food as they could carry for the long journey back to Quito.

Pedro Cieza de León provided an insightful account of Pizarro's pitiful march along the Napo, "The Spaniards were in a very bad state. They had eaten nothing but the yucas, which brought on a flux which wore them out; besides that they all went with bare feet and legs, for they had nothing in the way of shoes, except that a few made a sort of sandal from the leather of the saddles. The road was all through forest, and full of prickly trees; so that their feet got scratched all over, and their legs were constantly pierced by the many thorns. In this condition they went on, nearly dead with hunger, naked and barefooted, covered with sores, opening the road with their swords; while it rained so that on many days they never saw the sun and could not get dry. They cursed themselves many times for having come to suffer such hardships and privations, which they could have avoided."[2]

After nine days at the cassava field, Pizarro decided they needed to leave before everyone perished in this god forsaken land. By now, all, including Gonzalo, had abandoned all hope of finding Eldorado. Pizarro was thoroughly convinced that Orellana and his men were traitors, and later wrote: "So he [Orellana] displayed towards the whole expeditionary force the greatest cruelty that ever faithless men have shown, aware that it was left so unprovided with food, and caught in such a vast uninhabited region and among such great rivers, carrying off all the arquebuses and crossbows and munitions and iron materials of the whole expeditionary force...."[3]

Upon declaring that Orellana and his men were mutineers, Pizarro decided the time had come to find their way back to Quito. A return through lands they already knew were sorely lacking in villages that could provide food or shelter was certainly not a wise choice. It was estimated they were 400 leagues from Quito, a distance which took them a year to reach when they were relatively healthy. Gonzalo rallied the hopes of his men by promising to lead them back by another route, one that hopefully would offer safe passage and bountiful offerings of food. After these encouraging words, the despondent troops placed their full faith in Pizarro's ability to lead them safely home. Those too weak to walk were tied atop the remaining horses. The Spaniards used axes, swords, and billhooks, the latter a blade curved like a sickle to clear away the brush.

The Long March Home

While Francisco de Orellana and his men were making their way down the Amazon toward the distant Atlantic, Gonzalo Pizarro and his famished and weary comrades were attempting to find their way back to civilization. Unsure of which direction to follow, Gonzalo had his men follow the upstream course of the Napo in the hope that it would lead to either a Spanish settlement or a friendly native civilization. For more than 120 miles they had to hack their way through a dense wall of vegetation. The strongest of the troops went first while the weaker tended to the needs of the weakest. Leading by example, Gonzalo cast aside the privileges of rank and labored alongside his troops, a burden he bore without complaint. He marched at the rear to help tend to the sick and boost the morale of those who had lost hope. Pizarro won the enduring devotion of his men with his words and deeds.

Pizarro and his men ventured north of the river where Orellana had chosen to abandon them. The dense vegetation forced them to expend much energy clearing a new path in their desperate effort to return to Quito. Their journey was slowed by many obstacles, which included thick foliage; large rivers and streams which had to be crossed by canoe or the building of a bridge; and treacherous swamps and marshes formed from the flooding of the river, which forced the Spaniards to wade through water that, on occasion, reached to their waist.

Starvation, however, was the Spaniards' toughest foe. They survived on a slim diet of herbs, roots, and fruits, but many were fated to die of hunger and exhaustion. The death of the dogs made the journey even more difficult, for they were deprived of the canines hunting abilities. Soldiers feasted on the flesh of their dead dogs, and when all were gone they had to rely on the meat of the horses. The more than 80 surviving horses suffered horrifically at the hands of their masters. To keep from starving, the men cut off small strips of flesh from the remaining horses and dressed their wounds with mud from the river. They also drained the blood of the horses, which was collected and mixed with herbs to make a soup they boiled and served in Spanish helmets salvaged from dead comrades.

Agustín de Zárate wrote of Pizarro's dreary march to Quito: "They chose another route at random but it was no better, keeping alive by killing and eating their remaining horses and a few greyhounds and dogs they had with them. They also ate shoots and herbs, and a vine similar to garlic in taste. A wild puma or a fowl changed hands at fifty pesos of gold, and a pelican at ten."[4]

Unsure of which route to follow, Gonzalo consulted his officers Antonio de Ribera, Sancho de Carvajal, Villegas Funis, and Juan de Acosta. A consensus was reached to send Gonzalo Díaz de Pineda upriver with his lieutenant, Diego de Bustamante, and a contingent of soldiers to probe the river for a route that might lead to villages that could provide food for the members of the expedition. Bustamante brought along the expedition's only working crossbow.

Pizarro sent Pineda on ahead with several soldiers and native paddlers aboard two canoes tied together to scout the route of the river while the main force followed on foot. Pineda would light fires to reassure Pizarro that he had not abandoned him like Orellana, and to show his commander which route to follow. This routine continued for the next 150-plus miles. At this point, hunger was still their toughest enemy.

Pineda and Bustamante soon encountered a flotilla of canoes carrying many armed warriors. As the natives, who were probably the Cofanes, launched a sudden and unprovoked attack, one warrior was instantly killed from the blast of an arquebus while another was wounded in the arm by a bolt fired from the crossbow. The Indians responded with shrill war cries and a barrage of darts, The Spaniards killed two more natives and frightened away the rest from their canoes with their skillful sword play. The soldiers were thankful that the natives left their food on the boats. Pineda and Bustamante cut crosses on the trees to let Pizarro know they had passed this way.

After eleven days had passed Pineda and Bustamante finally discovered a village where they were able to obtain a small amount of food. Pineda continued to cut marks in the trees for Pizarro's benefit. Continuing upriver the scouting expedition soon sighted a mountain range they were sure would lead to the northern realm of the Incas, which, therefore, would provide a route to the Spanish settlements of either Quito, Popayán, or Cali. The scouting expedition decided the time had come to return to report their findings to Pizarro; a day and a half voyage led to the discovery of their commander's whereabouts.

Pineda found the main army in a desperate state. Pizarro and his famished troops had continued ever so slowly on foot, the strongest went ahead to cut a path through the dense foliage. Several soldiers had died from starvation, and many more were too weak to walk and therefore had to be carried by their comrades. Few of the men had any footwear. All the dogs had been eaten except for two, and they belonged to Gonzalo Pizarro and Antonio de Ribera. A great deal of their time and energy was expended in search of food, particularly herbs, roots, and fruits wherever possible. The spirits of the soldiers were rejuvenated by the news of a village up ahead, and a possible pass that would lead them back to civilization.

Over the next stage of the march, which stretched for nearly 200 miles, a growing sense of despair set in among the members of this expedition. Unlike Orellana and his men, Pizarro and his troops did not have the good fortune of encountering tribes that offered food and shelter. Also, they were unsure of which direction to follow to Quito or any other Spanish settlement. Pizarro had considered retracing his tracks but changed his mind after noticing the jungle was quick to reclaim any land that had been disturbed. Once again, they had to continue clearing a new path. The strong led the way while the weak continued to tend to the needs of the weakest.

Pizarro did his best to help his feeble soldiers across the difficult terrain by offering words of encouragement and lending a helping hand. The sick and weak exceeded the number of healthy men; because of their consumption of improperly prepared cassava, many conquistadors were ill with dysentery. Deprived of essential minerals and fruits caused many to suffer the debilitating effects of gout and scurvy. A number of soldiers were too weak to walk and had to crawl along the ground as best they could to keep from being left behind. Those who could no longer continue walking would simply sit down and wait for death to end their miserable ordeal. The natives, who were at the very bottom of the rationed food chain, perished in great numbers.

The conquistadors followed the path blazed by Pineda and Bustamante. As they neared a village, whose inhabitants were unaware of their approach, Pizarro dispatched nineteen of his healthiest soldiers to round up food for the others. These soldiers launched a lightning raid that frightened the natives into immediately seeking safety in the surrounding jungle. The rest of the soldiers entered shortly thereafter. The Spaniards ate and rested before resuming their search for a Spanish settlement.

Incessant rainfall made the adventurers return journey even more miserable, for not only did it dampen their spirits, the rains turned the ground into near impenetrable fields of muck. The latter difficulty was greatest on the heavy hooves of the horses. Besides their clothes rotting from extreme rain and humidity, the shoes of the soldiers rapidly disintegrated from the soggy ground. All soon suffered from the lack of shoes to protect the soles of their feet. Eventually the soldiers were without a stitch of clothing. Seeking a modicum of modesty, the Spaniards covered their genitals and buttocks with leaves attached to a belt made of vines and leaves. Their nakedness exposed them to the thorns and jagged edges of vegetation that tore at their flesh.

Pizarro described their ordeal: "In the course of this uninhabited stretch of river all the remaining horses, more than eighty of them were eaten. There were many rivers and creeks of considerable size to be crossed, and there were days on this march when to get two leagues forward a dozen or more bridges had to be built. And there were days when we waded through swamps up to our knees in water, for many stretches up to our waists, and even higher...."[5]

Once all the horses had been consumed, the Spaniards resorted to chewing leather saved from the saddles. Some of the soldiers became man-eaters, feasting upon the flesh of their fallen comrades. Those who ate the flesh of a recently deceased comrade surely must have wondered how long before they would become fodder for others. These were the desperate measures of desperate men, which is why no one wished to fall behind. Many still succumbed to the terrible pangs of hunger. After eight days, the expedition reached some small villages. Through the use of sign language, the Indians made it clear there were no villages ahead.

In June 1542, Pizarro and his men stumbled upon a village at the border of the cinnamon region they had visited the previous year. Luckily, the natives proved friendly and took pity on the weary Spaniards with a bountiful offering of food. The Indians told Pizarro of a shorter route to Quito, which was different from their previous course. Gonzalo willingly took their advice. Along this path the Spaniards encountered several wide rivers that could only be crossed by building bridges.

While on watch during the building of a bridge, a task which took the Spaniards four days to complete, a comet was spotted streaking across the night sky. That night, Gonzalo Pizarro had a disturbing dream in which he envisioned a dragon attacking him and plucking out his heart, which the beast proceeded to tear to pieces with his sharp teeth. Gonzalo summoned Jerónimo de Villegas, who was an acknowledged astrologer, to interpret his dream. Villegas told him that something he held dear to his heart was no more. Later, Gonzalo would learn of the assassination of his brother, Francisco Pizarro. While Gonzalo was in search of Eldorado, the eldest of the Pizarro clan was killed by men seeking revenge for the execution of Diego de Almagro, a soldier of fortune who had been Francisco's partner during the conquest of Peru. Messengers had been sent to find Gonzalo Pizarro in the cinnamon province to bring tidings of his brother's death, but they were unable to locate him.

After an arduous march of around 300 leagues, Pizarro and his surviving soldiers emerged from the dense forest and arrived upon an open and more hospitable region. They were able to hunt game, especially deer, with their few remaining weapons. Thankfully, they had managed to salvage a small quantity of powder. The Spaniards used the skins of the felled deer to replace their impromptu coat of leaves. The exposed skin of the emaciated troops were covered with dirt and matted, tangled hair. Their insufferable march home lasted more than a year. While their dreams of fortune and glory had been dashed all were thankful to be alive, though barely.

The eighty near naked and gaunt Spaniards wobbled toward Quito, most needing the support of walking sticks or rusted swords to keep from falling. Many kissed the ground and gave thanks to God once they reached the recognizable terrain of the Quito province. Upon learning that Gonzalo Pizarro and his small band of survivors were headed their way, the citizens of Quito rounded up a dozen horses and a great quantity of food to aid them. The residents also sent clothing but could only gather enough to suit five or six men. Quito was half emptied of soldiers, valuables, and provisions by those who had chosen to support the Almagro uprising. A dozen emissaries rode out to greet Pizarro and offer their horses to the officers. They met up with Gonzalo and his comrades about 30 leagues from the city. The emissaries were shocked to see how emaciated the survivors were.

Pizarro appreciated the offerings of the delegation, but since there were only enough clothes for him and a few captains, the commander and his fellow officers declined. The historian Agustín Zárate states they refused, "to change their clothes or ride the mounts, wishing like true soldiers, to preserve equality in everything, and they entered the city of Quito one morning in the state we have mentioned, going straight to the cathedral to hear mass and give thanks to God for bringing them safely through so many dangers."[6] The proud commander chose to enter Quito on foot.

Gonzalo Pizarro and his remaining troops staggered into the city of Quito in June of 1542. The inhabitants who came out to greet them were shocked by the cadaverous and unrecognizable men who paraded into the city; all were nearly naked, their long hair and beards were matted, everyone's skin was burned from overexposure to the sun, and their shriveled flesh revealed skeletal frames. Some hobbled in with the support of another's shoulder, some used sticks or swords to brace themselves, and a few crawled along the ground. All of the llamas, pigs, and natives who accompanied the expedition had perished during their futile search. These survivors had returned after an absence of two years, during which time they trekked nearly two thousand miles without any reward except for being spared from death.

Agustín de Zárate, a Spanish official at Quito when Pizarro returned, wrote "All, the general as well as the officers and men, were nearly naked, their clothes having been rotted by the constant rain and torn besides, so that their only covering consisted of the skins of animals worn in front and behind, and a few caps of the same material.... Their swords were without sheaths, and all eaten up with rust. Their feet were bare and wounded by thorns and roots, and they were so wan and wasted that one could no longer recognize them."[7]

The townsfolk brought the returning soldiers food and clothing.

Pizarro's malnourished men could consume only a small portion, for they had to give their stomachs time to adjust to digesting larger quantities of food. A few Spaniards gorged on so much food and drink that they ruptured their shrunken stomachs, and after having endured so much starvation these hapless men died from consuming too much food.

Reflecting on the difficult journey home, Gonzalo Pizarro wrote, "At the cost of great suffering and with the loss of everything which we had taken with us, we returned to Quito with only our swords and a staff in hand. To Quito from where we turned back must have been more than 800 miles and a much greater distance by the route by which we returned."[8]

While recuperating at Quito, Gonzalo was shocked to learn there had been an uprising during his absence. He was saddened to learn that his half-brother Francisco Pizarro, the Marquis, had been murdered nearly one year earlier by soldiers who sided with the late Diego de Almagro, the loser in the civil war between the Spaniards for control of Peru. The elder Almagro was once a partner of Francisco Pizarro, but a bitter dispute between the two over the division of land, wealth, and titles led to a conflict that ended with the defeat of Almagro's army and his execution at the hands of Hernando Pizarro, another of the Pizarro brood who found fame and fortune in the New World. Don Diego de Almagro, the mestizo son of the executed ex-partner of Francisco, assumed control of the former Inca empire following the assassination of his father's celebrated partner. Gonzalo also learned that he was no longer governor of Quito, and that the Spanish Crown had appointed the Licentiate Cristóbal Vaca de Castro to govern the land that the Pizarros had conquered and settled. Governor Vaca de Castro was supported by those who remained loyal to Francisco Pizarro.

At the time, neither Gonzalo Pizarro or Francisco de Orellana knew the fate of one another. The members of the Pizarro expedition who made it back to Quito resigned themselves to the thought that Orellana and his companions had met their demise somewhere along the Marañón.

Gonzalo found it convenient to blame Orellana for the calamitous failure of his expedition. Pizarro immediately sent off a letter to Emperor Charles in which he complained of the callous and mutinous actions of Orellana: "Paying no heed to what he (Orellana) owed to the services of Your Majesty and to what it was is his duty to do as he had been told by me, his captain, and to the well-being of the expeditionary force and of the enterprise, instead of bringing the food, he went down the river without leaving any arrangements, leaving only the signs and choppings showing how they had been on land and had stopped at the junction of the rivers and at other parts, without there having come in any news of him at all up to the present time; he thus displayed toward the whole expeditionary force the greatest cruelty that ever faithless men have shown, aware that it was left so unprovided and caught in such a vast uninhabited region and among such great rivers, carrying off all the arquebuses and crossbows and munitions and iron materials of the whole expeditionary force."[9]

11

Into the Realm of Machiparo

Francisco de Orellana and his crew became concerned after a number of days passed without sighting any villages. Finally, on May 12, six days after the odd incident with the crossbow, the adventurers entered the heavily populated realm of Machiparo, a powerful ruler who lorded over many villages in a region that stretched for 200 to 300 miles along the river. Padre Gaspar de Carvajal claimed that Machiparo could quickly muster a force of fifty thousand warriors. He added that boys and young men were barred from combat, therefore his warriors ranged from 30 to 70 years in age.

Once they reached the main village of Machiparo the Spaniards were met by several canoes sent to escort them to the ruler. The soldiers went ashore cautiously, their guns and crossbows readied for a possible confrontation. "When the chief saw them to have different dress and aspects from all other people he had seen, and all bearded (for Indians are not), he revered them to some extent, and was courteous towards them."[1]

The chief permitted Orellana and his crew to stay at his village, but the soldiers quickly wore out their welcome by looting homes and capturing turtles living in the nearby lagoons. Machiparo's warriors attacked with spears and clubs while carrying shields made from the rough hides of crocodiles or manatees. The Spaniards managed to drive them off but suffered the devastating loss of two comrades and the wounding of sixteen others.

As the fleeing Spaniards approached one of the larger villages, there suddenly appeared an armada of canoes filled with warriors armed for battle, their bodies ominously decorated with greasepaint. The sound of beating drums, blaring wooden trumpets, and native war cries announced their attack. Carvajal recorded for posterity: "We saw [their] villages glimmering white. We had not proceeded far when we saw coming up the river a great many canoes, all equipped for fighting, gaily colored, and [the warriors] with their shields on, which are made out of the shell-like skins of lizards, and the hides of manatees and of tapirs, as tall as a man, for they covered them entirely. They were coming on with a great yell, playing on many drums and wooden trumpets, threatening us as if they were going to devour us."[2]

To reduce the number of sides they had to defend, and to keep from being separated during this assault, Orellana had the two boats tied together. Once in range he issued the order to open fire. Unfortunately, as the guns prepared to fire the soldiers suddenly became aware of the fact that their powder was too damp to ignite, thereby rendering these weapons useless. The blast of these cumbersome firearms were counted on to frighten off the natives. Orellana had to rely on the marksmanship of his crossbowmen to keep the warriors at bay. The crossbows were more accurate than the muskets but it could take as long as 90 seconds to properly load and set this complex device. The crossbowmen felled several natives with their volley, but the natives were quick to respond with a barrage of arrows from their less awkward bows. An exchange of arrows and bolts continued during this desperate race down river. The Spaniards' predicament grew more dire when they reached a ravine where there awaited a great many native reinforcements. The warriors were not frightened off by the weapons of the Spaniards and continued with their assault.

Orellana instructed his men to row as fast as possible for a nearby village resting along the river. The crossbowmen provided sufficient cover for all to safely make their way to shore. Half of the Spanish party followed the retreating natives to their village while the rest of the soldiers kept the armada of canoes at bay. This conflict, which was bitterly fought on both land and water, lasted for half an hour. The natives called off the assault after five or six of their own had been wounded by shots from the crossbows.

Seeing that the village was quite large, Orellana instructed Alonso de Robles to take some of his men to search the huts for food that could be stored aboard the boats. All were anxious to make their getaway before the warriors returned. The soldiers found food but were compelled to battle a number of natives who did not wish to let the Spaniards take what was rightfully theirs. Robles and his comrades killed several and wounded many natives in order to abscond with a healthy portion of fish, dried meat, and some turtles, all of which were to be stored on their newly built brigantine. Upon their return, the scouting party found Orellana and his men desperately fending off a fierce attack from warriors in canoes. Once the natives finally dispersed Robles reported that the tribe had left most of their food in the village. He also stated that there were a great many pools of water that the natives used to store and fatten their prized catch of turtles, which they estimated to number greater than one thousand.

It was Orellana's hope to secure the area in order to provide his men with much needed rest from the hardships of their perilous journey. Realizing they could not take and defend the village, he sent another officer,

Cristóbal Maldonado, and twelve soldiers to pilfer as much food as possible, especially the turtles, a meat they knew was agreeable to their tastes, to sustain them on their voyage.

Upon their return to the village Maldonado and his comrades discovered that the warriors were well prepared to protect their property. They immediately engaged the Spaniards who twice compelled the warriors to retreat. Several Indians were killed and many more were seriously wounded in these encounters. The natives returned with more warriors, but Maldonado and his men drove them off with a tenacious assault. While the natives regrouped for yet another attack, Cristóbal decided the time had come to return to the boats. Lieutenant Maldonado had survived the confrontation despite being pierced in the arm with an arrow and struck hard in the face with a stick. Several of his men were wounded by arrows, and all were thoroughly exhausted from the desperate fight to save themselves. Maldonado and his scouting party returned with a large number of natives in hot pursuit. The soldiers managed to abscond with several large turtles, which further incited the ire of the natives. Such turtles were captured alive, stored in retention ponds, fattened on maize, and later roasted; turtle eggs were considered a delicacy to the river tribes.

Meanwhile, Orellana and the remaining crew were busy sifting through another nearby village. Behind them could be heard and seen a vast number of angered natives intent on catching the turtle thieves. A sentry, Cristóbal de Aguilar, spotted the approach of the warriors and immediately sounded the alarm. He single-handedly held off many warriors. Aguilar received several blows and wounds, and he surely would have been killed if his comrades had not come to his aid in the nick of time. Aguilar and his rescuers valiant effort had given the others the time they needed to arm themselves, but not enough time to put on their armor, Orellana and the crew rushed out with their swords in hand to face an assembled force of 500 warriors attacking from two sides. The warriors protected themselves from harm with hide-skin shields, which proved too strong for the crossbow shots to penetrate. These warriors of the Machiparo realm were armed with bows and arrows, spears, and macanas, the latter was similar to a broadsword. Orellana and his men were thankful these warriors did not have poison arrows in their arsenal.

The Spaniards launched a furious attack that succeeded in killing several warriors, wounding many, and startling the remainder. This confrontation lasted for nearly two hours before the natives finally retired. Orellana, who was nearly killed by an Indian but saved by the timely intervention of a soldier who felled the warrior with a blast of his arquebus, won the respect of all with his valor in battle. Singled out for courage was Blas de Medina,

Orellana and his men battle Chief Machiparo's warriors (Library of Congress).

who rushed at the warriors with only a dagger and fought like a man possessed. Orellana sent one of his men in search of Maldonado. The missing lieutenant and his men soon returned to camp with several large, live turtles. Lacking medical supplies, the eighteen wounded Spaniards tended to their injuries as best they could. One of Maldonado's men, Pedro de Ampudia, would die eight days later from his wounds.

The soldiers soon discovered that many Indians were holed up in a wooded gully preparing for another attack. Fearing that their shouts were a prelude to a renewed assault, Orellana ordered Cristóbal Enríquez to take 15 men to flush out the warriors. The soldiers were met with fierce resistance, which resulted in one of the arquebusiers suffering a severe wound to his leg. Needing more men because the warriors numbered far too many, Enriquez sent one of the men back to inform the commander of their dire situation. Realizing the natives were not prepared to give up their claim to their village, and not wanting to risk any more lives, Orellana determined the time had come to end this conflict. He sent a message back to Enriquez advising him to slowly and carefully make his way back to camp.

Orellana addressed the men to declare the time had come for them to leave this place. He reminded them of their greater purpose, which was to explore the river for a safe passage back to civilization. The commander added that they had already seen much and surely there was much more to see and learn. Besides, what good were their daring exploits if they did not live to tell of them. All were comforted by the thought that God had seen fit to favor them on this arduous journey and surely He would continue to do so if they maintained their faith.

River Chase

Once they agreed that it was too risky to remain in this region the Spaniards boarded their boats and left that very evening. As they departed the natives came out of hiding and announced themselves with a terrifying chorus of hoops and hollers accompanied by the steady banging of drums. Orellana and his comrades estimated the enemy to be 10,000 strong. The warriors unleashed a barrage of projectiles in the direction of the fleeing Spaniards.

The natives continued to give chase throughout the ensuing night in their numerous canoes, thereby depriving the adventurers of any chance to eat or sleep. Nightfall saw the Spaniards surrounded by an armada of canoes and piroques that attacked the boats on two sides. A number of Indians tried to board the Spanish vessels. The fleeing Spaniards fought back with their weapons, killing and wounding many with shots from their arquebuses, bolts released from their crossbows, and the slashing of their swords when within close quarters. The loud blast of the arquebus frightened the natives, but despite the damage inflicted the warriors persisted in their assault.

During their desperate flight downstream the Spaniards sailed past many villages, one of which was of particular interest to Carvajal: "There was one settlement that stretched for five leagues without there intervening any space from house to house, which was a marvelous thing to behold: as

11. Into the Realm of Machiparo

we were only passing by and fleeing, we had no opportunity to learn what there was in the country inland; but, judged from its resources and appearance, it must be the most populace that has been seen, and this was just what the Indians of the province of Aparia had told us that it was, that there was a great overlord in the interior towards the south whose name was Ica, and that this latter possessed very great wealth in gold and silver; and this piece of information was considered to be very reliable and exact."[3]

The next morning the native war party was nowhere to be found. Convinced that the warriors had given up the chase, Orellana ordered his men ashore at one of the many islets situated in the middle of the river, where they hoped to dine on their catch of turtles and get some much needed rest. The hungry and weary Spaniards headed toward shore, but no sooner had they docked then the fleet of canoes reappeared and Orellana and his men were forced to return to their boats and paddle as fast as they could while being closely followed by a throng of agitated warriors.

The following morning Orellana and his comrades noticed that the natives of the violated village were reinforced by a fresh fleet of manned canoes dispatched from neighboring villages located for the next eighty leagues along the river. There were reportedly 138 very large canoes carrying an estimated total of eight thousand warriors. Weary from hunger, wounds, and rowing, the Spaniards found it was becoming nearly impossible to maintain a safe distance in their desperate race downriver.

The Machiparo warriors continued to chase the Spaniards for two days and nights, a frenetic race which prevented the Spaniards from getting any rest. Friar Carvajal provided a detailed account of this native assault in his journal: "There were among these men and the war canoes four or five sorcerers, all daubed with whitewash and with their mouths full of ashes, which they blew into the air, having in their hands a pair of aspergils, with which as they moved along they kept throwing water about the river as a form of enchantment, and after they had made one complete turn about our brigantines ... they called out to the warriors and at once they began to blow their wooden bugles and trumpets and beat their drums and with a very loud yell they attacked us."[4] This surreal encounter succeeded at instilling fear in the Spaniards.

As the natives continued their tenacious pursuit, they unleashed a barrage of projectiles aimed at the fleeing boats. Orellana and his comrades were able to fend off the attack with shots from their crossbows and arquebuses. However, the natives tricked the Spaniards into entering a narrow tributary where numerous warriors waited in ambush on both land and river. All the Spaniards surely would have met their maker at this point had it not been for the accurate shot of Hernán Gutiérrez de Celis. As the warriors aboard the canoes moved in for the kill, Celis set his sights on a native standing in a canoe, his dignified stance betrayed the fact that he was in command. The shot struck the war chief in the chest, a blow that killed him instantly.

The natives were in a state of panic and confusion over the sudden death of their leader, which provided an opportunity for Orellana and his men to escape the tributary and resume their flight downriver. The natives regrouped and once again gave chase, a pursuit that continued for two more days. The chase ended once Orellana and his men passed the boundary of Machiparo's realm. The confrontations with Machiparo's warriors resulted in the wounding of 18 Spaniards, one critically. A war of attrition clearly favored the Amazonian tribes.

12

The Amazons

Having barely escaped the wrath of Machiparo's warriors, Orellana and his weary crew entered the region lorded over by Omagua, a powerful chief who was a steadfast ally of Machiparo. Approximately nine or ten leagues from where the natives ended their pursuit, the Spaniards spotted a village ruled by a chief named Oníguayal. When the inhabitants saw the approach of the strange boats in the water, they massed in great numbers and armed themselves with shields and spears. Since the Spaniards were in dire need of food and rest from their exhaustive escape, Orellana decided they would seize the village.

The Spaniards opened fire with several arquebus and crossbow shots, which succeeded in wounding a number of natives along the shore. Once they were near the river bank several soldiers leapt out of the boats and charged with a fury that scared off the inhabitants. A fight on land provided Orellana and his men with an advantage they sorely lacked on the water. The victorious Spaniards were free to enjoy the food the villagers had left behind.

Francisco de Orellana and his comrades rested for two nights at this village, where they feasted on roasted turtles, various fruits, and biscuits made of cassava. Meanwhile, the displaced natives plotted to retake their village by seizing the Spanish boats. On the third day, while Orellana's men were busy loading their vessels with confiscated food items, the Indians launched an all-out attack from their canoes, and hurled spears at the few Spaniards on board the boats. The crossbowmen came to their rescue, killing several warriors. The remaining warriors promptly retreated.

The Spaniards resumed their course along the river and after two leagues discovered that this body of water emptied into a river that was much wider and more powerful. Orellana and his men christened this vast waterway the Trinity River, because of three islands situated at the mouth. They soon happened upon a fertile region that provided enough sustenance to support a great many settlements.

Native armed with spear (from *Exploration of the Valley of the Amazons*, published 1854 under the direction of Navy Department for the U.S. House of Representatives).

12. The Amazons

Noticing that there were villages along both banks of the river, the wary explorers sought to guard against an unexpected assault by rowing down the middle of the river. They soon discovered the river had grown so wide that if they tracked one side in search of villages, they were unable to see the banks of the opposite shore. Francisco and his men pressed on, though not without a struggle. The natives physically and verbally harassed the Spaniards, and though they may not have understood exactly what they were saying, their gestures and tone made it clear that the Spaniards were not welcome. They went ashore only when their dwindling food supply dictated the need. Orellana and his men were quick to realize that the larger villages were often the more hostile. When they tried to approach such settlements, the inhabitants were quick to assemble in a menacing manner. The only Spaniard to die during the trek through this region was Pedro de Empudia. His passing was not from a wound, but, as Carvajal states "on account of the unreasonableness and disorderly behavior which he himself indulged in."[1]

The expedition eventually happened upon a small village resting on a high bank which Orellana felt could be easily seized and used to defend against native counterassaults. The battle lasted an hour before the Spaniards were able to claim the settlement as their own. Francisco and his men entered the village and helped themselves to all of its provisions, which included a large quantity of food. The adventurers were pleasantly surprised to see finely crafted porcelain jars, plates, bowls, and vessels that were magnificently painted and glazed by the natives, all of which they claimed equaled or excelled any such items found in Europe. They also discovered intricate drawings and paintings, items the natives told them came from a tribe located further inland. The soldiers saw indications of gold and silver, as some weapons and jewelry were inlaid with these precious metals. They saw a copper hatchet similar to the kind used by the Incas of Peru. Orellana and his comrades encountered an entrance to what appeared to be a temple guarded by two giant idols carved from palm wood, each of which depicted elongated ears similar to Inca royalty at Cuzco. The Spaniards named this place Pueblo de la Loza (Porcelainville).

After expressing his appreciation over the quality of their wares, the natives told Orellana of a race of people living further inland who, like the Incas, wore disks in their ears and, just like the Incas, possessed vast sums of silver and gold. They boasted that these natives had pottery far superior to their own. There were two inland paths leading out of the village, seemingly similar to the Inca roads, which they were told led to other settlements inhabited by a great many people. Intrigued by these claims, Orellana, Robles, Maldonado, Carvajal, and several soldiers ventured into the rainforest. Carvajal recalled, "he had not gone half a league when the roads became more like royal highways and wider; and, when the Captain had perceived this, he decided to turn back, because he saw that it was not prudent to go on any farther; and so he did return to where the brigantines were, and when he got back the sun was now going down, and the Captain said to the companions that it would be well to depart at once from there because it was not wise to sleep at night in a land so thickly populated."[2]

A number of Spaniards speculated that the paved road might lead to the legendary Eldorado, but precious metals were of little concern at this point. Finding food, shelter, and safe passage were of greater importance, for what good were riches if there was nothing to spend it on. Lingering in the back of Orellana's mind was to one day return to this region if he was fortunate enough to find his way back to Spain. He made sure the boats were watched over while his men slept along a hillside in the woods.

The Spaniards inquired as to where the great river ended, but this was a question the natives were not prepared to answer. For them the waterway simply was as it had been and would always be, a river which existed without beginning or end. Orellana and his crew were beginning to believe this truly was a river that would go on forever. Five months on the water had brought them into the land of Brazil, a New World region that, according to Papal decree, fell within the domain of Portugal. The explorers feared remaining on shore where the natives greatly outnumbered them, so they seized as much food as possible and continued on to the next village.

The adventurers continued for another hundred leagues downstream, taking care to avoid any hostile contact by keeping to the middle of the river. At some points the river widened so great that it was impossible to see from one bank to the other, which accorded them the advantage of staying beyond the view of potentially unfriendly tribes. The monotony of the river was periodically broken by sudden twists and turns, only to reveal, as it had before, that the jungle stretched endlessly on each side. A curious audience of macaws, herons, eagles and other tropical birds stared at the Spaniards as they passed by in their boats. Monkeys chattered excitedly when they saw the travelers.

The repetitive scenery of the voyage was occasionally disrupted by periodic sightings of villages. The blue sky overhead was punctuated with picturesque puffs of large, low flying white clouds, which gave the Spaniards pause to be thankful it was not the rainy season. Some Spaniards talked about ending this quest and taking up permanent residence at a friendly village, for there they would have food, shelter, and female companionship. A few entertained the idea of being worshipped as a god with the claim of being a child of the sun. These plans of going native came to the forefront at the next port of call.

May 29, 1542, marked the day that the Spaniards passed the Jurua, a large tributary of the Amazon. They had now traveled an estimated 1,000 miles since departing their first camp among the Imara. Unbeknownst to Orellana and his men, they had reached the mid-point of their long river voyage. On that very day, Francisco had his boats dock at a large village, where they stayed without encountering any difficulties from the natives. It was here the Spaniards found the inhabitants so docile that they nicknamed this place Pueblo de los Bobos, or Village of the Idiots. Orellana and his men were greeted by Paguana, a mighty chief who was very accommodating.

Many of the Spaniards wished to abandon the quest and take up residence with an available native woman. Friar Carvajal wrote, "I am telling the truth when I say that there were among us a few so weary of this kind of life and of the long journey that, if their consciences had not kept them from so doing, they would not have failed to remain behind among the Indians."[3]

Perhaps modesty prevented Carvajal from mentioning the stern lecture he most surely offered to those who contemplated such action to ensure that they remained within the Christian fold. The Spaniards left Pueblo de los Bobos after taking a hefty portion of the villagers' food, as well as several women and a few young boys. Padre Carvajal claims the women were only taken "to make bread for the companions" and later granted their freedom. The conscripted lads were to serve as guides.

Once again, the Spaniards saw a number of paths which they were led to believe were links to large inland settlements. Carvajal wrote, "from this *pueblo* there were many roads running inland, with many llamas, and there seemed a good deal of silver about."[4] Orellana was wary of exploring these roads, fearing that the company would become separated or waylaid by natives along the route. Clearly, he could not afford the loss of any men in such a hostile region.

Resuming their voyage, the Spaniards passed several villages before happening upon the mouth of another river that emptied into the one they were currently cruising. They soon came upon a fertile region which sprouted a vast number of fruit bearing trees that served as sustenance for the numerous villages that could be seen along the shore. The region was so densely populated that Orellana feared going ashore, where they could be easily overwhelmed. Every day during this phase of their journey the Spaniards saw villages along the banks of the river, sightings which made it easy to conclude that further inland might lay a civilization similar to the Incas of Peru or the Aztecs of Mexico.

Orellana and his crew soon encountered a number of canoes filled with natives frantically shouting as if they were trying to chase them away. Much to the concern of the Spaniards, the flotilla of canoes began to follow them, but at all times maintained a safe distance. The wary crew made sure to further distance themselves from the seemingly hostile natives.

On the day after Whitsunday the Spaniards sighted a very large village that Carvajal estimated at more than five hundred houses with cultivated fields where custard apples, avocados and guavas were harvested. The natives gathered in great numbers and in a menacing manner along the banks to make the Spaniards understand they were not welcome. Orellana and his comrades stayed away from the place they named Pueblo Vicioso, or Viciousville.

Hostile encounters continued to plague the adventurers. On the eve of Holy Trinity, Orellana steered the boats to a village in the hope of procuring sorely needed food. The natives were unreceptive to their requests and a fight ensued when the Spaniards persisted in their demands. The town was eventually captured, and the victorious Spaniards were free to feast on the inhabitants' supply of fresh fowl.

Later that day, on the third of June, as they resumed their voyage, the Spaniards saw that this river converged with another tributary of the Amazon. Friar Carvajal wrote, "We saw the mouth of another great river on the left, which emptied into the one which we were navigating [and] the water of which was black as ink. For this reason we gave it the name of Rio Negro, which river flowed so abundantly and with such violence that for more than twenty leagues it formed a streak down through the other water, the one not mixing with the other."[5] The separation of the waters continued for many leagues before the black water of the Rio Negro was fully absorbed by the brown water of the Amazon River.

Warrior Women

The next day, which was Trinity Sunday, the explorers happened upon a hillside that served as a fishermen's quarters for a nearby village. The famished Spaniards helped themselves to the fish that had been left out to dry. After satisfying their hunger, the Spaniards turned their attention to the village, where the inhabitants had taken up defensive positions. A unique feature of this place was that the fishing area and the village were fortified by a palisade made of large timbers. A desperate fight ensued once the Spaniards broke through the wooden barricade that encircled the village. The tenacious soldiers eventually prevailed, whereupon they proceeded to stock up on food items for their voyage.

The adventurers departed the village on the fifth day of June, and later that day they stopped at a much larger settlement. "In this village there was a very large public square, and in the center of the square was a hewn tree trunk ten feet in girth, there being represented and carved out in relief [thereon] a walled city with its inclosure and with a gate. At this gate were two towers, very tall and having windows, and each tower had a door, the two facing each other, and at each door were two columns, and this entire structure that I am telling about rested upon two very fierce lions [jaguars],

Native fisherman (from *Exploration of the Valley of the Amazons*, published 1854 under the direction of Navy Department for the U.S. House of Representatives).

which turned their glances backwards as though suspicious of each other, holding between their forepaws and claws the entire structure, in the middle of which there was a round open space: in the center of this space there was a hole through which they offered and poured out *chicha* for the Sun, for this is the wine which they drink, and the Sun is the one whom they worship and consider their god."[6] Carvajal saw this spectacular piece of work as evidence that this village was part of a vast inland empire similar to the Incas. The square housed a large building that was clearly a temple built to honor their deity. Inside they found fanciful robes woven with colorful bird feathers, which the natives used during their ceremonial rituals.

When the Spaniards inquired about the carving of the walled city, the natives claimed it was a representation of the city ruled by a race of women warriors that they, and many other neighboring tribes, paid tribute to on a regular basis. They told Orellana that this tribe of women were known as the Coniupuyara, or *grand mistresses*, and they periodically paid them a large offering of colorful plumage collected from parrots and macaws, which were used to line the roofs of their homes. To the Spaniards it sounded as if they were on the verge of discovering the legendary realm of the Amazons that had been described by Herodotus. Since this was a realm where men were not permitted to enter, the all-female tribe grew their numbers by once a year visiting another village for the sole purpose of becoming impregnated by the men. The male children were either put to death or returned to their fathers, while the baby girls were raised as members of their tribe. According to Greek mythology, these fearsome female fighters would amputate their right breasts so they could draw their bows more easily.

Carvajal noted in his journal: "We obtained many intimations about these women during all the voyage and even before we left the domains of Gonzalo Pizarro the existence of a kingdom of women was regarded as certain. But we improperly called them 'Amazons' among ourselves."[7] The very thought of entering the realm of the Amazons conjured up the image of finding lands of extraordinary wealth; to Spaniards in the New World, tales of fierce warriors was an indication that the natives had something valuable they wished to keep hidden from outsiders.

The voyage downriver brought Orellana and his companions to another large village. While the natives were determined to keep the Spaniards at bay, the awesome might of the crossbow and arquebus once again tilted the balance of power. The victorious Spaniards helped themselves to the village's store of maize and some birds.

The wandering Spaniards continued on past other sizable villages where the inhabitants presented themselves in great numbers to prevent them from coming ashore. Clearly, the dubious exploits of the adventurers had preceded their arrival. At one village, the soldiers fired upon the assembled crowd, and though their blasts succeeded in felling several warriors these shots failed to disperse the crowd. Realizing that the numbers of those who opposed their coming ashore were much too great to overcome, the Spaniards wisely chose to resume their voyage along the river.

Orellana and his crew witnessed more of the same during the next leg of their voyage; they encountered other large settlements where many warriors were prepared to challenge them. At one of the villages, a number of bold natives climbed up a hillside to shout out challenges, threats and curses. Adding to their woes, further downriver the Spaniards found it increasingly difficult to reach either shore because of the powerful pull of the current and the accompanying waves.

On the seventh of June, Orellana instructed his men to make for a small ridge resting atop a hillside away from the banks of the river. They felt fortunate that the natives offered no resistance to their movements. From this elevated position, the Spaniards could see that the village was presently inhabited by only women, unaware that the men had left to hunt for food in the forest. The soldiers believed they had happened upon a village of the Coniupuyara, even though the women did not appear as fearsome as imagined. Their successful capture of the village rewarded them with a large haul of fish the inhabitants had been roasting.

Since the following day was Corpus Christi, the men requested they be allowed to remain at the village so they could celebrate this sacred day in a proper manner. Orellana was not keen on this idea, preferring the safety of the boats, but relented to their request. This plan was interrupted shortly after sunset, which was the time when the male inhabitants returned from their hunting expedition. The natives immediately took up arms in a concerted effort to reclaim their village at a time when the Spaniards were enjoying their supper. Luckily for Orellana and his men the Indians were too few in number to reclaim their village, and the soldiers were able to drive off their attackers without suffering any loss or injury.

The Spaniards proceeded to pitch camp for the night, making sure sentries were posted. Another attack occurred just around midnight. This time the inhabitants were reinforced by tribesmen from surrounding villages of the province. The warriors hurled a barrage of sharpened sticks from two directions. This sudden assault wounded two soldiers, both of whom were tended to by Fray Carvajal. The startled Spaniards met the attack and succeeded in driving the Indians back into the woods.

An irate Orellana turned cold-hearted following the wounding of his two men; a captured native had his back sliced open with the sharp blade of a Spanish sword. Francisco released him in the hope that the return of the wounded warrior would be viewed as not only a warning but also an act of mercy. Fearing that the warriors might return in even greater numbers, Orellana posted several sentries along the path to the village. All of the men donned their armor for a long night's rest, but few, if any, were able to sleep, most prayed while awaiting the light of day so they could depart this hostile tropical region.

The sleep deprived Spaniards departed at dawn's first light, but not before loading their boats with a supply of fish and fowl to feed upon. By midday they found a spot where they could safely rest. From this point on, Orellana would never again allow his men to camp in a native village. When an opportunity presented itself, the explorers would seize food by day, and eat and camp in a distant woodlands. Francisco hoped he had struck enough fear into the natives that they would not pursue him and his men downriver. The warriors still followed them but not for very long.

On the 10th of June, the stout-hearted adventurers came to the mouth of a great waterway that emptied into the river they were plying. The Spaniards named this river the Grande, but it is now known as the Madeira. On the 13th of June 1542, after having sailed past the long island of Tupinambarana, the men came upon a large settlement situated on higher ground, which from the river they could not see in its entirety. They could, however, see that the homes were very different from any they had viewed previously, which led them to the conclusion that they had entered another province.

The attention of Orellana and his crew was soon fixed upon an ominous sign: seven tall gibbets with severed human heads attached were on prominent display. This was believed to be a warning placed by the Coniupuyara, the female warriors whom the Spaniards referred to as the Amazons. The explorers assumed the rotting heads were war trophies taken from an enemy tribe, or even worse, the result of a cannibalistic feast. Cannibal tribes along the Amazon commonly placed heads of those they had eaten on the points of canes planted around the village or along the riverbank. The Indians they encountered claimed a similar fate awaited them if they dared to trespass upon the territory of the Coniupuyara. With their nerves on edge, the soldiers unleashed a round of fire from their crossbows and arquebuses. Orellana and his men grew more fearful after this gruesome sight and became ever more aggressive in their dealings with natives who displayed a fierce disposition. The Spaniards referred to this land as the Province de Picotas (Province of the Gibbets).

The following day the expedition came upon another hostile village. The men of the settlement assembled along the banks while the women and children remained in their huts. The warriors armed themselves with bows and arrows to frighten off the intruders. The Spaniards feared the arrows might be dipped in poison, but with their provisions running low they decided to risk a landing at a village located further downriver. The armed natives panicked when several Spaniards leapt out of the boats and charged directly at them, and retreated after their chief, who was betrayed by his more elegant manner of dress, was felled by a shot from a crossbow. When the warriors refused to surrender, Orellana ordered his men to set fire to the huts. The natives fled into the woods, leaving behind all of their food, which included turtles, parrots, bread, and maize. The victorious Spaniards gathered as much food as they could and found a nearby island that served as a safe haven. One soldier was wounded by an arrow, but it was not poisonous and he soon recovered.

The next morning a greatly angered Orellana punished several captured natives by summarily hanging them. He also ordered his men to burn all the homes of the settlement. A number of warriors, along with several women and children, barricaded themselves inside a large hut and refused to come out—they continued shooting arrows at the Spaniards until all were consumed by flames. Orellana and his men called this place Quemados Village, Village of the Burned People.

The discharge of arrows and spears plagued the adventurers at several locations. As they continued their voyage, the Spaniards began to worry that they had suddenly entered a region where natives used arrows dipped in poison, a concern prompted by the discovery of several arrow points covered in a sticky black substance. To allay their concerns a native woman kept aboard the brigantine was cut on the arm and the mysterious matter was rubbed into her wound. All were relieved to see that the young girl did not suffer any ill effects. However, the Spaniards remained fearful that regions ahead were inhabited by tribes of cannibals and warriors armed with poisoned arrows.

On the following Friday the Spaniards sighted along the left bank of the river a cluster of villages. They speculated that these were the outlying villages of a large inland empire. A canoe with several Indians came out to get a closer look at them. The curious natives rowed alongside the boat Orellana was aboard, but the captain, despite his linguistic skills, had a difficult time understanding their speech. The natives pointed at the beards and skin of the Spaniards and then signaled toward land, which was understood to mean that there were other Europeans who dwelled inland.

Orellana and his crew did not know at the time that the natives were probably speaking of survivors from the 1531 expedition of Captain Diego de Ordaz, who planned to found colonies along the Marañón River. That same year, the explorer Alonso de Herrera trekked down the Casanare and Meta Rivers to reach the Orinoco, which he followed all the way to the mouth. Ordaz had sent 300 men on ahead to establish a colony but they soon found themselves lost in the tropical landscape. The natives made it understood that white men with beards, and greater in number than Orellana's company, were living inland. The captain offered some trinkets to the natives if they would lead him there, but they declined his offer and rowed back home.

A captured Indian woman was questioned about this tale of other white men in the region, and she informed Orellana that a short distance inland could be found a tribe where many Christians like them were held as slaves. The commander was able to ascertain through the use of sign language that these white, bearded Christian men were lost from another expedition. She said they now lived as members of the tribe, most having taken Indian wives and fathered children by them. The woman added that there were two white women who were married to other white men.

She offered to show them the way to the Christians and therefore was permitted to join the expedition. The Spaniards proceeded downriver with enough food to delay their need to go ashore for quite some time. The expedition continued to a large village, where the woman claimed they would find Christians. Unable to see any visible signs that corroborated her tale, Orellana was eager to press on toward the sea.

Father Carvajal, however, wished to continue searching for the whereabouts of the lost Christian men and women, but Orellana did not want to risk the lives of his men on such a dubious quest. After much discussion, Orellana decided that saving themselves was more important than rescuing lost Christians. He had good reason to be concerned that the natives might have set a trap, for his boats were coming under constant attack by a steady torrent of arrows and spears hurled from shore. While navigating down the middle of the river, the Spaniards saw glimmering white homes but were unable to investigate because of the powerful pull of the current.

The next day the Spaniards found themselves being pursued by a fleet of canoes determined to keep the strangers away from their villages. The warriors shouted loudly while waving their bows and arrows in a menacing manner. They also carried large poles and sharpened sticks. The adventurers heeded their warning and steered away from the villages.

Two days further downriver the Spaniards found a village where the natives offered no resistance. Here they discovered a large quantity of maize and oats, which the inhabitants used to make bread and chicha, the latter an intoxicating drink that resembled beer. They also sighted a quantity of hammocks that greatly exceeded the number of residents. The explorers witnessed a unique kind of arrow that whistled when fired. A number of natives were dressed in cotton clothing, which the Spaniards perceived as a sign of a more advanced society. They saw cotton robes of different colors and miters much like those worn by bishops, and a building storing various outfits believed for military and religious purposes. Seeing there were many roads leading inland, Orellana and his crew concluded that this village served as a trade depot for nearby villages.

The wandering Spaniards pressed on toward a wooded area that seemed a good place to spend the night. This plan was interrupted by the sudden appearance of numerous Indians advancing in canoes. Orellana and his men answered their war cries with shots fired by the arquebusiers, and the smoke and noise created by these weapons succeeded in scaring off the warriors. Not wishing to linger any longer at this hostile location, the soldiers resumed their voyage downriver. On the 22nd of June they saw off in the distance a well-populated region, but choppy waters and the tug of the current prevented them from reaching their intended destination.

The following day, Orellana and his comrades satisfied their need for food by capturing a village hidden up an inlet. They found the homes built in an orderly fashion along a single street. The Spaniards helped themselves to the tribe's plentiful supply of maize and some loaves of cassava bread, which was made from a mixture of yucca and maize. Near the large store of maize, the Spaniards discovered the drink that resembled beer. They also found a number of ducks and parrots. The village was situated at the end of a long savanna, and since it was not visible from the river the men christened this place Escondido Village, the Hidden Village.

The next day the Spaniards reached a small, vacated village along the river, which they suspected was a storage facility for Escondido's salt and maize, since these were the only items found at this location. That same day the soldiers aboard the smaller boat reached a fair-sized settlement, where they were surprised to find only maize. Orellana ordered the men to set off in search of a village with more varied food items, for meat, fish, or even turtle were desired by all to satiate their taste for flesh and complement a feast celebrating the birth of John the Baptist.

Carvajal noted in his journal, "We were proceeding on our way searching for a peaceful spot to celebrate and to gladden the feast of Saint John the Baptist, herald of Christ, when God willed that, on rounding a bend which the river made, we should see on the shore ahead many villages, and very large ones, which shone white. Here we suddenly came upon the excellent land and dominion of the Amazons."[8]

The Amazonian warriors were already aware of their approach. There soon appeared several canoes that had been concealed by trees along the banks. Noticing the natives were armed with bows and arrows, the Spaniards feared they had been lured into an ambush. Orellana and his comrades were startled by the strangely contorted gestures of the Indians, movements that appeared as if they were intoxicated. Their condition certainly seemed to boost their courage, for they showed no fear of Spanish weapons.

As they came within earshot, Orellana communicated through words and sign language that they had come in peace. The natives rebuffed his claim and continued to mass. The warriors responded with boisterous shouts and waving their bows and arrows in a threatening manner. Carvajal recalled, "As we began to come in close to land the Indians started to defend their village and to shoot arrows at us, and as the fighters were in great numbers it seemed as if it rained arrows; but our arquebusiers and crossbowmen were not idle, because they did nothing but shoot, and although they killed many, they [the Indians] did not become aware of this, for in spite of the damage that was being done to them they kept it up, some fighting and others dancing: and here we all came very close to perishing."[9]

However, the Spaniards dire need for food instilled in them a courage that would not be denied. Orellana had the boats advance toward the village, a path that steered them directly at the canoes. The armed Spaniards took steady aim at the enemy and unloaded a suppressing fire that provided enough cover for several soldiers to wade ashore. Once again, the muskets and crossbows provided the Spaniards with a deadly advantage.

Those who reached land found themselves pelted with arrows shot by both male and female warriors. The Tapuyan Indians had requested aid from their overlords, the Amazons, who responded by dispatching ten or twelve of their warriors to aid in their fight with the Spaniards. Padre Carvajal stated that when the Spaniards accepted their challenge they saw, "Indian women with bows and arrows who did as much fighting as the Indian men, or even more, and they led on and incited the Indian men to fight; and ... using the bows and arrows as sticks, would even club those who started to flee, and they served as captains, commanding the warriors to fight, and placed themselves in the front ranks and held others in position so that they would stand firm in battle, which, was entered into very resolutely."[10]

Recalling this hostile encounter that occurred on Saint John the Baptist day, 1542, Gaspar de Carvajal added, "They acted as leaders, took the foremost place in the battle. What is certain is that these women, who fought like Amazons, are the source of the stories widely disseminated among the Indians of a warlike race of women who have their kingdoms somewhere in this district without commerce with men...."[11]

Carvajal provided a detailed description of those he believed were the legendary Amazons: "These women are very white and tall, and have hair very long and braided and wound about the head and they are very robust and go about naked, [but] with their privy parts covered, with their bows and arrows in their hands, doing as much fighting as ten Indian men, and indeed there was one woman among those who shot an arrow a span deep into one of the brigantines and others less deep, so that our brigantines looked like porcupines."[12] The bow-staves of the natives measured 5 to 6 feet long, which propelled their arrows with tremendous force.

The battle on shore waged for more than an hour. The Spaniards fought with an unbridled fury, wounding and killing of a great many natives. Orellana and his troops felled seven or eight of the dozen female warriors who came to fight. Despite their losses the natives never lost heart. The barrage of arrows directed at the Spaniards was so heavy that even Carvajal was struck, "...and me too they hit in the side with an arrow, which went in as far as the hollow part, and had it not been for the folds in my clothes, through which the arrow first passed, they would have killed me."[13] Four other Spaniards were wounded during hand to hand combat in waist deep water. The men were relieved to learn that the arrows were not tipped with poison.

Orellana was forced to issue the call for retreat once he saw that warriors from surrounding villages were coming to the aid of their fiercely determined neighbors. Returning to their boats the Spaniards departed quickly once they saw an armada of canoes headed their way to aid the natives fighting on land. The soldiers summoned their remaining strength to push the boats away from shore and paddle as fast as they could to escape the grasp of the warriors. For their own safety, Orellana made sure the boats sailed down the middle of the river. Too exhausted to row, the Spaniards simply let the swift current carry them downriver.

An Enduring Legend

The encounter with warrior women who were well trained in warfare occurred near the mouth of the Trombetas, another of the many tributaries of the Amazon. These female warriors, who seemed to resemble the legendary Amazons of ancient Greek lore, were believed to reside in the Brazilian region now known as Belem. Carvajal estimated that they had traveled some 1,400 leagues from where they left Gonzalo Pizarro, to the point where they encountered the Amazons who fought alongside the Tapuyan Indians.

In their haste to elude the wrath of the natives, Orellana and his comrades departed without procuring additional food. They did, however, capture an Indian trumpeter whom Carvajal guessed was about 30 years of age. Orellana hoped to learn from his native prisoner the precise whereabouts of the rich kingdom of the Amazons. He used this opportunity to question the captured Indian about the region they had just passed through and the women they had been forced to fight. The native told him that inland there were a great many tribes and provinces, but the largest and mightiest region was ruled by a tribe inhabited by only females. The prisoner proceeded to tell a wondrous tale of fierce women warriors who occupied seventy inland villages, all of which were well barricaded. He claimed they resided in a province of more than three hundred leagues and their villages were linked by a series of roads. Coñori was the name of the empress who ruled over the region, inhabited by women who lived in stone houses. Besides those who were captured in war, the only men allowed into the heavily guarded city were those who came to carry on trade or pay tribute. He said the male overlords of the region had to pay tribute to the women who lorded over them, and in return Queen Coñori's warriors would come to their aid during times of trouble.

The native claimed "...that in the capital and principal city in which the ruling mistress resided there were five very large buildings which were places of worship and houses dedicated to the Sun, which they called *caranain*, and [that] inside, from half a man's height above the ground up, these buildings were lined with heavy wooden ceilings covered with paint of various colors, and that in these buildings they had many gold and silver idols in the form of women, and many vessels of gold and of silver for the service of the Sun...."[14]

The Waura tribe recounted in song and dance the legendary tale of Amazonian women who fled their jealous husbands by following an armadillo tunnel that led to a faraway land where they lived free of men. Orellana and his men were told that any male "who should take it into his head to go down to the country of these women was destined to go a boy and return an old man."[15]

The trumpeter claimed to have visited the homeland of the Amazons many times. He said they lived in stone cities, several of which he claimed to have seen with his own eyes while delivering his tribe's mandatory tribute. To the Spaniards the mention of inland stone cities conjured up images of those they had seen or heard about at Quito, Cuzco, and Cajamarca. The prisoner told Orellana that these tribes had an abundance of gold and silver, which was music to the ears of the Spaniards. He said they had grown so rich off the tribute paid to them that their homes were covered with sheets of silver—certainly plausible when taking into account that many Spaniards had seen, or at least heard about, the temples of the Incas sheathed in planks of gold or silver. The native claimed that gold and silver was used to make their plates, cups, and utensils, items which were reserved for the upper class. Women of lesser rank ate off plates and used eating utensils made of wood. The Amazonians were said to have made numerous idols to honor their gods, which were cast in precious metals. He said these gold and silver idols and effigies could be found housed inside five large temples located at the main city of the Amazons, much like the Coricancha at

Cuzco. He said all the women wore outfits made of wool sheared from the vast herd of llama they owned, an animal the Spaniards referred to as Peruvian sheep.

The male prisoner added that this mysterious tribe of women were a fierce warrior race who periodically waged war against tribes for the purpose of taking male prisoners who could satisfy their sexual needs for increasing their population. He also spoke of a white king who lorded over a region that the women frequently raided. The men were kept as their prisoners until the women were impregnated and then they were either sent back to their homeland or executed.

A great many conquistadors had previously heard tales of tribes in the New World who were similar to the Amazons of Greek lore. Carvajal, however, noted that these Amazons differed from the women warriors of ancient mythology: "These women that we are dealing with here, although they do use the bow, do not cut off their breasts nor do they burn them off."[16] Amazon in the Greek language means *having no breasts*. According to the accounts recorded by ancient historians women warriors supposedly cut off their right breast so that it would not hinder their pull of the bowstring. The dozen female warriors they fought against were the only such fighters they ever saw on their voyage. The great river first called the Marañón was later renamed the Amazon because of the oft reported tale of woman who fought like the legendary Amazons of Greek mythology. The Indian who traveled with Orellana and told this story of the Amazons would later die at the island of Cubagua.

According to Bartolomé de las Casas, a Spanish conquistador, historian, and Dominican missionary, Christopher Columbus returned to Spain with the claim that he had discovered an island in the Antilles that "was inhabited by women, who are visited by the men at a certain time of the year; and if they bear a female child they keep it with them, if a male they send it away to the island of the men."[17]

Many Spaniards viewed themselves as living the adventurous tales recorded in the fictional account of a chivalric knight named Amadis de Gaula, who traveled the world over performing many heroic deeds. Book V of the Amadis series told of this errant knight's encounter with the *Black Amazons of Californie*, which Orellana and his men believed they had discovered on their journey.

Hasty Departure

The expedition soon happened upon another village, which appeared to be empty. Since they were in dire need of food, the crew requested that

Orellana allow them to go ashore. The commander was hesitant, but he decided to indulge their request and steered the boat toward the village. Orellana sent a party ashore to gather food, a group which included Friar Carvajal. The Spaniards soon discovered they had walked into an ambush. Once on land, Carvajal and his companions were attacked by a great number of warriors who patiently laid in wait. The natives unleashed a barrage of arrows. Fortunately, the Spaniards were able to partially shield themselves from harm with their armor as well the shields made of manatee skins they had previously confiscated. Carvajal, however, was not quite as lucky as the others.

"They hit no one but me," states Carvajal, "for Our Lord permitted them, because of my faults, to plant an arrow shot over one of my eyes, the arrow passing through my head and sticking out two fingers' length on the other side behind my ear and slightly above it; from which wound, besides losing the eye I have endured much suffering and worry, and even now I am not free from pain...."[18]

Francisco de Orellana and the crew aboard the larger boat saw the desperate plight of their comrades and rushed to their aid. Those ashore took advantage of this timely assistance by returning to the boats. All sailed quickly out of harm's way. Orellana had given orders to depart once he saw the severity of Carvajal's wound. Though he lost an eye, the priest was fortunate to have escaped death. The expedition now had a one-eyed commander to lead the way and a one-eyed priest to offer spiritual guidance.

The Indians from the village continued to follow the Spaniards in their canoes but, having already felt the sting of Spanish weapons, they made sure to maintain a safe distance. Fearing to go ashore lest they should suffer another surprise attack, Orellana found a safe spot where the boats could be moored to some trees. Here the men slept aboard the boats while taking care to post sentries. This took place the night after Carvajal was wounded. The men sought to tend to the suffering and stem the flow of blood from the wound of the priest who had tended to their souls. The captain questioned his captive native about the tribes of this province. The prisoner told him that a vast stretch of the river was under the control of a mighty chief named Couynco, but even this powerful ruler answered to the Amazons, who lived further inland, an estimated seven-day hike from the river.

The following morning, which was the 25th of June, the boats resumed their voyage. The weary adventurers came upon a great number of islets in the middle of the river that appeared uninhabited. The Spaniards, whose transgressions had preceded them, were spotted by the local Indians. An armada of 200 large canoes, each carrying between twenty and forty armed warriors with elaborate feather decorations, suddenly came out to confront the Spaniards. All were suited in warlike attire and accompanied by musicians who played ominous tones on drums and various unique piped and stringed instruments. They followed the intruders for several hours before finally gaining on the Spanish boats. A deafening chorus of whoops and hollers were momentarily silenced by shots from the arquebuses and crossbows. The canoes continued to chase the boats down river.

Padre Carvajal wrote, "They surrounded our two brigantines and attacked us like men who expected to carry us off; but it resulted in just the reverse for them, for our arquebusiers and crossbowmen made it so uncomfortable for them that, many as they were, they were glad to stand off."[19] The warriors continued to give chase until the Spaniards had passed from their realm, a province that Carvajal estimated to be 150 leagues long.

Before leaving this hostile region, Orellana tried to make peace with the natives by offering a gourd containing some of their precious stones, small bells, and beads. The gourd was placed in the water and pushed in the direction of the warriors in the boats. One of the canoes came over and retrieved the gourd and showed its contents to the others. The Spaniards were disappointed to see that the Indians were mocking their offering. These were the same kind of trinkets that other natives of the New World had cherished, but clearly these items were of no value to these Indians.

After barely escaping the clutches of the persistent warriors, Orellana had the boats temporarily moored at an oak grove that overlooked a savanna. The Spaniards feared another confrontation when two canoes passed by and took note of them but this episode passed without incident.

The explorers managed to maneuver past the maze of islets as they continued their voyage downriver. It was the inhabited right side of river they had been navigating; the villages appearing to be less then half a league apart up to this point. After their latest altercation, Orellana had the boats stay closer to the opposite bank to avoid another canoe assault. Having reached this region on the day of Saint John, the Spaniards christened the province Punta de San Juan (Dawn of Saint John's Day).

13

Homeward Bound

The journey to the next region, which was heavily populated, offered the Spaniards little reprieve from those hostilities experienced in the previous province. The inhabitants of one village launched a fleet of canoes that attacked the two boats. These were tall and ominous looking warriors with closely cropped hair. They stained their skin black with injections of genipapo, which tempted Orellana to christen this region *Provincia de los Negroes*, the province of the black men. Carvajal remembered them as being physically large, comparing them to the strongly built Germans of Europe.

The warriors were effective at keeping the Spaniards from stopping at villages along the left bank of the river. Unable to replenish their dwindling store of food the adventurers were compelled to survive on a meager ration of bread. The natives ended their chase once the trespassers had crossed over to the next realm. The native who accompanied them said this new province, which he claimed extended for more than 100 leagues, was ruled by a mighty chief called Aripuna (a.k.a. Caripuna). Their homes were said to be made of stone and their city was fortified by a great wall. The guide told the captain that this realm was equal in wealth to the region lorded over by the Amazons. He spoke of five temples plated with gold, which sounded similar to the Coricancha temple of the Incas. After emphasizing that this chief had an abundance of gold and silver their prisoner warned that many of the tribes were cannibals.

A few days later a smaller village was spotted, and Orellana ordered his crew to make landfall so they could replenish their now depleted supply of food. The Indians resisted as best they could, but the desperate Spaniards soon prevailed. The defeated natives fled to another village that was a brief distance downriver. Because the village they had fought to possess was without food the Spaniards were forced to move on to the settlement where the natives had fled.

The combined inhabitants of the two villages fiercely resisted the

13. Homeward Bound

MATUÁ AND HIS BROTHER MANÚ, CARIPUNA BOY'S AND THEIR BARK CANOE

"Caripuna Boys and Their Bark Canoe" (from *Exploration of the Valley of the Amazons*, published 1854 under the direction of Navy Department for the U.S. House of Representatives).

Spaniards. Orellana and his men eventually triumphed but not without consequence. Before the Spaniards leapt out of their boats the warriors pelted them with arrows. The famished soldiers proceeded to raid and relieve the natives of their precious corn. One of the men was struck in the foot, and it quickly became evident that the arrow had been laced with poison. The area around Antonio de Carranza's wound rapidly turned black and the rot spread swiftly over his entire foot. The poison proceeded to rush up his leg and from there spread to his torso and arms. The concerned comrades cauterized the wound that afflicted Carranza, but there was little they could do to comfort his pain and suffering. Carranza died after three days of writhing in intense agony. Seeing first-hand the horrific effects of such projectiles, the adventurers lived in mortal fear of arrows tipped with poison.

At the village where Carranza died, the Spaniards took notice of the rise and ebb of the tide, an encouraging sign indicating they were nearing the ocean. Yet they still had another 300 miles to go before reaching the mouth of the Amazon. Further downriver Orellana and his crew halted briefly at a forest near the Tapajóz River, another tributary of the Amazon, where his men could rest before what, hopefully, was the final leg of their voyage. Since most of the men had long ago thrown overboard their cumbersome and rusted armor it was decided that they needed to barricade the *San Pedro* in a manner that would shield them from facing the same fate as Antonio de Carranza. Orellana knew there would undoubtedly be similar encounters during their trek through this province, so he decided to fortify the boats by having his men construct bulwarks to shield them from arrows, especially those dipped in poison.

Orellana and his comrades spent the next day and a half preparing their boats, and probably would have stayed longer had it not been for the sudden appearance of manned canoes and warriors on land shouting at them, which was interpreted as some manner of war cry. The soldiers chased them off with several shots delivered by their arquebuses and crossbows. Assuming that the natives were spying on them, Orellana had his men depart at once and cross to the other side of the river. They tied their boats to trees and attempted to get some sleep. They were periodically disturbed by the faint sounds of Indians whom they believed were searching for them.

The next morning Orellana had his men cast off as quickly and quietly as possible. They soon learned that the commotion they had heard during the night was a gathering of warriors in great numbers aboard an armada of canoes. The Indians surrounded the boats and unleashed a hailstorm of arrows at them. The improvised railings provided adequate protection. Once again, it was Spanish firepower that succeeded in driving off the enemy. One of the arquebus shots struck several warriors aboard an attacking canoe and the fearful excitement of the others caused their canoe to capsize and sink. More than a dozen natives were helplessly stranded in the water as their comrades rowed away in terror. The warriors treading water attempted to swim to shore but were chased down by the Spaniards, who killed all with shots from the crossbows or blows from their lances. Meanwhile, the canoes regrouped and launched another attack. A single arquebus shot by a soldier named Alferez felled two Indians, and a soldier by the name of Perucho successfully struck one of the chiefs, after which the canoes retreated.

The victorious Spaniards would mourn the loss of yet another comrade. During the heat of battle in the region ruled by a chief named Ichipayo (Nurandaluguaburabara, according to another account), one of the soldiers was mortally wounded in the thigh by a poisoned arrow. The bulwark had failed to protect Garcia de Soria from an arrow dipped in curare. The arrow, which had been shot from afar, had only grazed the flesh, but the wound was large enough and the poison was potent enough to carry out its deadly deed. Soria suffered terribly before dying within 24 hours after having been wounded.

Some native tribes of western and northern Amazonia used blowguns to propel darts dipped in curare, a powerfully concocted poison. Curare ingredients included stinging ants and ground snake fangs, but the main ingredient is the sap of the vine *strychos toxifera*. The silent but deadly blowgun was generally used to bring down monkeys, but it also proved to be an effective means of felling human intruders.

The natives continued to pursue the Spaniards downriver, but made sure to keep their distance so as to avoid the fate that had befallen their fellow warriors. The expedition passed by several large villages, where all came out to witness the fleeing strangers. To signal that Orellana and his comrades were not welcome, the inhabitants uttered ominous cries and performed bizarre gestures that involved the contorting of their bodies in a menacing fashion. As the adventurers passed by, they could see the people dancing and jumping for joy in celebration of having scared off the Spaniards. An even more ominous sight was the appearance of warriors, whom Carvajal estimated at more than five thousand in number, massing along a high bank. The fleet of canoes stopped pursuing once the Spaniards had passed their realm.

Orellana and his comrades were encouraged by the strengthening pull of the tide, a reassuring sign they were nearing the sea. Their journey downriver that day and the next brought them to a hilly region devoid of trees. They saw savannas on the left bank of the river with numerous dwellings. Their native guide told them that this region was comprised of many provinces, villages, and inhabitants who were subjects of a very powerful ruler. He also claimed the land was so rich with silver that all the people used the metal in the making of their utensils. A few days later the Spaniards went ashore to lay claim to a village, only to discover it had been abandoned; the inhabitants had been warned of their approach and left with all of their food.

Francisco de Orellana decided to settle for the night along a high bank near the river. He sent several companions ashore to inspect the region, instructing them to travel no further than a league inland and return with their report. The scouts did as they were ordered and returned to say the interior appeared promising. They also claimed to have seen many tracks, though not fresh, which were evidence that this region was often traversed by natives. Scouts told of seeing a village destroyed by fire, which their Indian companion said was surely done by natives further inland. The Spaniards stayed for two days at this location to renew their strength and morale.

The expeditionary force resumed their voyage downriver and soon encountered a great many islets, numerous enough to cause them much difficulty in navigating the river. They discovered that many of the islands were inhabited but feared to stop once they learned these villages belonged to the Caribs, a nation of natives the Spaniards were familiar with because of their penchant for feasting on human flesh. The explorers mustered enough courage to investigate an empty village where they were repulsed by the sight of roasted flesh cooked on gridirons as well as severed hands and feet that were unmistakably human. At one village they saw evidence that the Caribs had feasted on Christians, which was confirmed by finding a shoemaker's awl.

At another settlement the Spaniards were surprised to find "two crudely fashioned imitation brigantines, hung up, which the Indians had put together to look like copies, these having the proportions and shape which a real brigantine ought to have, [objects] which in my opinion must have been made [and placed there] in remembrance of some victory or for some other purpose connected with something they wished to remember, and [it was evident] that the Indians had seen brigantines, since they had learned how to shape and imitate them so well and so nearly like [real ones]."[1] The Spaniards also saw many finely crafted vessels for use in the home, some made of clay and others of wood. The natives had bowls, cups, and drinking containers that Carvajal compared to the classical workmanship of ancient Rome and which he stressed were equal or superior to any contemporary European artisan.

Into the Mouth

As the Spaniards continued downriver, the increasing surge of the tide further indicated they were getting closer to where the river joins the sea. The topography had begun to change; the dense jungle along the banks had begun to lessen. The mild weather of the highland regions gave way to a low land region that was extremely hot and humid. The river was dotted with many islands, few of which were inhabited but several of which provided them with food. Though free to scour for sustenance without fear of attack, the adventurers were still unfamiliar with which foods were safe to eat. Orellana decided to seek out a village that could provide them with food that was already collected and prepared.

A village was sighted along an estuary, and at the hour of high tide Orellana steered the boats toward the shore. Unfortunately, all failed to notice the numerous tree trunks lurking beneath the water. The smaller craft hit a large concealed log with such force that it tore a hole through one of the bottom planks, which caused the vessel to fill rapidly with water. Seeing that the Spaniards were in a dire situation, the natives used this opportunity to launch an attack. The soldiers still possessed the wherewithal to compel the warriors to retreat, after which they proceeded to collect food.

13. Homeward Bound

Meanwhile, the natives regrouped and attacked in even greater numbers. The Spaniards were forced to retreat to their boats only to discover that the tide had ebbed and the larger boat was now firmly lodged on shore and the damaged boat had sunk. Orellana and half the troops took up positions to combat the natives while the rest worked to extricate the smaller boat, the *San Pedro*, and repair the larger craft, the *Victoria*. The desperate soldiers held their ground for three hours, after which time the frustrated natives retired. This had given the others enough time to rescue their boats. They quickly patched the hull and set both vessels back on the river. Once the boats were loaded with a fair quantity of maize, salt, and other food items, the exhausted Spaniards slipped out to the middle of the river where they slept for the night.

The next day the Spaniards took refuge at an uninhabited islet. Here they made additional repairs to the small boat to ensure it would be seaworthy when the river emptied into the ocean. They would spend eighteen long days at this task, most of which was spent forging nails for the rebuilding of the small brigantine and repairing the larger boat. The men had to ration the maize, which was doled out by grains. Just as they were down to their last morsels of maize, they spotted a dead tapir floating their way. Orellana dispatched several men in a canoe to retrieve the animal. The tapir, which was nearly the size of a mule, was brought ashore. Carvajal noted, "The tapir had been dead for a short time, because it was warm and had no wound whatsoever on it."[2] There was enough meat on the animal to satisfy their bellies for nearly a week, which provided the sick and weak with enough energy to continue work.

As the adventurers sighted the mouth of the Amazon River they were surprised by a virtual sea of islets at this immense estuary. Finding the natives more receptive to their overtures, the Spaniards stopped at several villages to replenish their exhausted food supply. They were able to procure some fish but no maize.

As they neared the end of the river, Orellana decided they would need to thoroughly repair and adequately rig the boats for a lengthy sea voyage. To prepare the larger boat, the Spaniards ventured further downstream until they found a beach where they could freely work. Rigging was woven from vines, and sails were made from the Peruvian blankets they had carried since the beginning of the expedition. They improvised the making of anchors, which were buckets made of twigs filled with large stones. The soldiers managed to keep hunger at bay by eating roots the natives called *inanes*, which are yams. They also subsisted on a sparse diet of snails and shellfish. During this extended stay the soldiers caught a few crabs, but they were too small to satisfy their hunger. Their prolonged hunger pangs were the reason the Spaniards christened this desolate place as *Starvation Island*.

Both boats were deemed seaworthy after two weeks of intense labor, and on August 8, 1541, the Spaniards resumed their voyage downriver, their pace hastened by the newly made sails.

It has been estimated that at the time of their arrival there were some 200 to 250 independent villages along the Amazon Basin. The Spaniards met with a tribe willing to barter with them. These transactions yielded Orellana and his men pitchers of drinking water, roasted maize, edible roots, and other food items. Though these docile natives freely traded their items with the Spaniards they were not, however, willing to hand over all of their hard-earned food, which they hid from the prying eyes of the bearded strangers. The men of the village attempted to convey to Orellana that there had been other men like them who had come to this land, which they accomplished by pointing to their beards, pale skin, and clothes, while gesturing inland. The natives of this region informed the Spaniards that three days sailing along the coast would lead them to this Christian settlement. But Orellana was more interested in reaching a Spanish colony at the islands of either Cubagua or Margarita, two islands located near Trinidad, unaware that this was a voyage across 1,200 miles of open waters.

Orellana and his comrades had a difficult time overcoming the powerful tides that kept pushing them back upriver. In order to continue their voyage they had to time their sailing at ebb tide and then tack from one side of the river to the other. Torrential rains also hindered their progress. After the Spaniards camped at the mouth of the river for one day and night, they set out to find the Atlantic Ocean. It would take them 24 days to travel down the mouth of the river.

Ocean Voyage

Father Carvajal estimated that the mouth they entered was "four leagues wide." He also added, "and we saw other wider mouths than the one through which went out to sea; and to the minds of experienced men, and in view of the pattern of the many islands and gulfs and bays which the river formed fifty leagues back before we got out of it, it was quite evident that there remained other mouths to the right as we came down, on which side we encountered a heavier and rougher sea, although it was fresh water, than over the whole distance that we later traversed in salt water."[3]

After a grueling journey down the mightiest river on earth, Francisco de Orellana and his companions finally reached the Atlantic Ocean on August 26, 1542. The adventurers were unaware that they had traveled almost three-quarters of the nearly 4,000-mile river they had christened the Río Orellana, which was later renamed the Amazon. This marked the end of one ordeal and the beginning of another. Not knowing how long it would take to reach a Spanish outpost and unsure of which direction to follow, the intrepid explorers loaded the *San Pedro* and the *Victoria* with fresh water and roasted maize before undertaking their ocean voyage.

Carvajal wrote of their desperate effort to reach a Spanish settlement: "I am leaving out many other things we lacked, such as pilots and sailors and a compass, which are necessary things, for without any one of them there is no one, however devoid of commonsense, that would dare to set sail on the open sea, except ourselves—to whom this long and winding voyage came by accident and not by our will."[4]

Once at sea, Carvajal led the entire crew in a prayer of thanksgiving. They surely took a moment to reflect on the loss of fourteen comrades since having taken leave of Gonzalo Pizarro more than 240 days ago. Three men were killed by Indians and eleven perished from illness. Pedro de Empudia, Antonio de Carranza, and García de Soria were the three who died at the hands of native warriors.

The two vessels sailed together, and the men made every effort to remain within sight of the coast. The crew hoped to reach either the Christian settlement the Indians had mentioned or the Island of Cubagua, where they knew there were Europeans. Cubagua is situated approximately 150 miles west of Trinidad. In the beginning the seafarers were blessed with blue skies and favorable winds. The calm weather and water made for smooth sailing for these two boats. Orellana and his crew passed the island of Marajó and sailed northward along the coast. They managed to stay

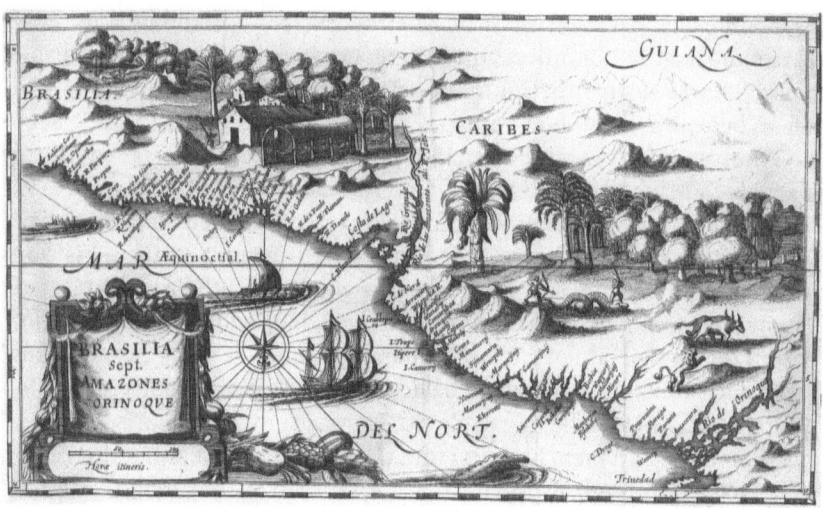

Map of Guiana (Library of Congress).

together for three days, but during the third night the vessels became separated by a sudden and terrible tempest. The crews of the *San Pedro* and *Victoria* quickly lost sight of one another. The next morning Orellana could not locate the other boat and assumed all aboard the *Victoria* had been washed out to sea or had plunged to a watery grave.

Friar Carvajal was aboard the missing *Victoria*, and after nine days of sailing was propelled to the Gulf of Paria, commonly referred to as the Dragon's Mouth. The men spent seven days and nights of constant rowing in a frantic battle with contrary winds and strong currents that kept them at bay before they were finally able to free themselves from the grasp of this vast gulf. Carvajal wrote, "Having escaped from this prison, we proceeded for two days along the coast [of Guiana] at the end of which, without knowing where we were, or where we were going, nor what was to become of us...."[5] Carvajal set a course for Cubagua, a pearl fishing settlement along the coast of Venezuela. All were convinced that the *San Pedro* and her crew had perished at sea.

Meanwhile, Orellana and his men continued on a northerly course until they safely reached the island of Cubagua, known to many as the Island of Pearls, which was under Spanish rule. They arrived at the town of Nueva Cadiz on Saturday the 9th of September 1542, and to their great delight, they were soon reunited with their comrades from the missing *Victoria*, which arrived two days later at the island. The 47 survivors aboard the two boats had managed to reach the island without the aid of a pilot, seasoned sailors, or a compass. It was a joyous end to their long ordeal.

After spending several weeks recuperating at Cubagua, Orellana and his men headed back to sea. They sailed to the larger island of Trinidad, a voyage of roughly 150 miles. Once there, Orellana chartered a small ship, one which was vastly superior to the vessel that had brought them to Cubagua, to take him to Santo Domingo. Cristóbal Enríquez, Cristóbal de Segovia, Alonso Gutiérrez, and Hernán Gutiérrez de Celis also sailed on this boat, which reached Santo Domingo on November 22, 1542.

During his stay at Santo Domingo, Francisco de Orellana met with the historian Gonzalo Fernández de Oviedo, who listened intently to his wondrous tale of adventure and survival in the wilds of South America. Oviedo later obtained a copy of Carvajal's journal, which provided additional information for his celebrated *Historia general y natural de las Indias*. Orellana decided to return to Spain where he hoped to parlay his exploits into a governorship of the lands he had explored. He was convinced that with proper ships, supplies, and men, he could find the hidden wealth of the vast region he had passed through, especially the lands lorded over by Aripuna and the vast realm of the women warriors he believed were the legendary Amazons.

While Orellana prepared for his return to Spain, Carvajal chose to remain behind at Isla de Margarita to seek medical attention for his lost eye. There he learned that Bishop Vicente Valverde, his mentor, had been killed by natives at the island of Puna. Valverde had been forced to flee Peru when Francisco Pizarro was assassinated by rebels seeking to avenge the execution of Diego de Almagro. Approximately forty of the expedition's survivors chose to return to Peru; counted among this group was Gaspar de Carvajal. They sailed first to Nombre de Dios, then Panama, and finally the city of Lima. Once there, the returning survivors of the Orellana expedition found themselves embroiled in the Spanish civil war for control of the former Inca empire. Carvajal was eventually appointed Vicar-General, which carried the title *Protector of the Indians*. He died at age 80 at the Lima monastery, where he had served as a strong voice for the rights of the natives.

14

The Final Voyage

Francisco de Orellana procured a ship that would transport him to Spain where he planned to seek a grant from the Crown to lead his own expedition to the great river he had navigated all the way to the sea. He was confident that he would be hailed as a hero for his many astounding feats, especially his exploration of the major river that cut across the vast continent of South America. Orellana hoped to obtain an appointment that would entitle him to lead a new expedition to discover the rich kingdoms he had heard about, and to be named governor of the region he had explored. He was unaware of the fact that Gonzalo Pizarro had survived his horrific ordeal and had dispatched a message to the royal court denouncing the actions of his former second-in-command.

Cristóbal Maldonado was the only member of the expedition to sail back to Spain with Francisco de Orellana. Their weather-beaten vessel was forced to call at the Lisbon port, where they were received at the court of the king of Portugal, who took a keen interest in the tale of his grand adventure and even offered to finance a second voyage. The monarch believed that the Amazon region fell well within the Portuguese boundary established by Pope Alexander VI. Orellana was compelled to remain in Lisbon for more than two weeks while members of the Portuguese court sought to learn more about his adventures in the New World. The king spent this time "acquainting himself in very great detail with the facts in connection with this voyage of discovery and making advantageous offers to him in an effort to get him to stay there, it being his intention, to make use of him in this matter."[1] The king offered him a prominent position, but Orellana politely declined the ruler's generous offer. Francisco felt confident that the Spanish king, who was also the Holy Roman Emperor, would be just as generous in his offer, if not more so.

Orellana and Maldonado reached the city of Valladolid, where the Spanish court was currently in session, around the middle of May 1543. Juan de Sámano, the secretary of the Council of the Indies, wrote to

Francisco de los Cobos, an advisor to Charles V: "There has arrived from Peru one who came out by going down a river which he navigated for a distance of 1,800 leagues and emerged at the Cape San Agustin; and because of the particulars which he has brought with him covering his voyage, Your Lordship will not hear him without fatigue. I shall not relate these particulars since he will shortly come himself."[2]

The one-eyed Francisco de Orellana expected to be lavished with honors and accolades, which he hoped to use as leverage for an appointment as governor of the New World region he had explored. Spanish officials, however, were not as elated as Orellana had expected. The cold reception of Emperor Charles V came as quite a shock, because his having met with the king of Portugal did not sit well at the Spanish court. Orellana was surprised to learn that he had to answer to charges of abandoning his commander and the expeditionary force in a remote forest of South America.

In his letter to Spanish officials Gonzalo Pizarro charged Francisco de Orellana with treason. He wrote, "And paying no heed whatever to what he owed to the service of Your Majesty, and to do what was his duty as he had been instructed by myself, instead of bringing back the food, he [Orellana] went on down the river without leaving any arrangements [to inform me].... And when my expeditionary force, having gone that far [saw] that there was no relief for them in the way of food ... they became greatly discouraged, because for many days they had eaten nothing but palm shoots and some fruit which had fallen from trees and which they found on the ground, together with all kinds of noxious wild beasts which they had been able to find since they had eaten in this wild country more than 1,000 dogs and more than 100 horses."[3]

Orellana was shocked to learn of Pizarro's letter accusing him of mutiny and treason, heinous acts that were blamed for the suffering and death of many Spanish soldiers. He had labeled his former lieutenant "the worst traitor that ever lived." Gonzalo sent his account of the expedition to the Council of the Indies on September 3, 1542, while Orellana and his men were still adrift at sea. Pizarro did not know that Orellana had survived, but he was positive that his second-in-command had betrayed him, his men, and Spain. According to Oviedo, Pizarro wrote "that Francisco de Orellana had shown the greatest cruelty that any faithless man could indulge in, in abandoning Gonzalo Pizarro [i.e. him] and the others in those wildernesses among so many rivers and without food."[4] It should be noted that Pizarro probably saw Orellana as an easy scapegoat for his disastrous expedition.

Gonzalo eventually learned of Orellana's survival, but by this time he was too embroiled in an effort to regain control of Peru to be bothered with returning to Spain to confront his former comrade. The Pizarros had many influential friends at court who made sure that the alleged misdeeds of

Orellana were not ignored. Francisco certainly could have used Father Carvajal's support before the inquisitive Spanish officials.

In his defense, Orellana reminded the Council of the Indies that it was Gonzalo Pizarro who selected which men were to travel downriver with him. Orellana stated, "why I should revolt, inasmuch as I was the principal man in the expeditionary force [next to Pizarro himself], and was not taking a chance on [securing] some personal gain by going, surrounded by so many dangers, down a river, starving, through a country which I knew nothing about...."[5] Francisco emphasized that he left behind his servants and personal belongings; pointed out that his voyage was out of necessity and not personal gain; and noted that the strong currents had made it impossible to return to camp. He ended by declaring that Pizarro was simply looking for excuses for his failed expedition.

The King and his council feared that the river Orellana and his companions had explored, as well as the surrounding lands, were on the wrong side of the demarcation established by the Treaty of Tordesillas. The mouth of the great river was clearly Portuguese territory and Orellana's river, which was the Marañón in the minds of many Iberians, was merely part and parcel of their papal grant. His discoveries therefore belonged to neighboring Portugal, as authorized under a papal decree signed by Pope Alexander VI. A dispute arose over where the course of the river trespassed onto Portugal's claims to the region. Orellana's oral account fueled concerns about which Iberian power had jurisdiction over the river and its surrounding regions. He was asked to provide the Council with a written report of his adventure. Unfortunately for Orellana, his report failed to allay the concerns of Spanish officials.

While at Spain, Orellana returned to his hometown of Trujillo, which was also home to the Pizarro clan. He continued to petition for remuneration of services rendered and an appointment that would permit him to explore and settle the region from which he had recently returned, a quest he emphasized would surely enrich the coffers of Spain. In true conquistador spirit, Francisco was convinced that he could locate the rich inland civilizations he had heard so much about from the natives. He reasoned that a large expedition would provide the military might needed to seek and conquer these realms, all of which were located in hostile regions. Many conquistadors viewed native aggression as evidence that they were protecting something of great value. The more belligerent the tribe, the greater the rewards—this was the lesson gleaned from the Spanish conquest of the Aztec empire.

The river that Orellana and his comrades had explored was generally referred to as the Great River and the surrounding province as the Amazon. This mighty South American river, which was christened the Orellana, in honor of the officer who had guided this epic voyage all the way to the end, was later renamed the Amazon, in remembrance of the female warriors who had captured the imagination of Europeans.

Preparation Problems

As was customary following the conclusion of a New World expedition, Francisco de Orellana was required to provide the Council of the Indies in Seville with a written account of his adventure. Orellana's report, which was read by many, was written with the aid of the journal maintained by Gaspar de Carvajal. The claim that the female combatants they encountered were Amazons was met with skepticism given that these warriors still had their right breasts, which was contrary to ancient Greek lore. Of much greater concern was whether or not the river Orellana and his men discovered and explored was within the realm granted to Spain by a papal decree.

Francisco helped his cause by writing to the king about the potential wealth of the vast region he had explored. He also stated that there were a great many tribes that could be brought into the Christian fold. Orellana requested that the king "see fit to give it to me as territory to be held by me as governor in order that I may be able to explore it and colonize it on behalf of Your Majesty."[6]

After much debate, the Council of the Indies ruled that many of his discoveries fell within the realm of Spanish claims under the Treaty of Tordesillas. Parts of the river, as Spanish authorities had feared, passed through the region granted to Portugal, but it was determined that the mouth of the great river was on the Spanish side of the demarcation line. Orellana was granted permission to return to the Amazon to further explore and colonize the region.

The members of the Council of Indies accepted Orellana's explanation that the river's swift current prevented their return to camp and therefore cleared him of charges that he had intentionally abandoned Gonzalo Pizarro and the rest of the soldiers. The Council knew that the king of Portugal had questioned Orellana and sought to retain his services with titles and money. It was feared that if they declined his request, he would simply offer his services to Portugal. Besides, who better to lead such an expedition than the man who had already navigated the river.

On February 13, 1544, following nine months of debate, appeals, and delays, Prince Philip agreed with the opinion of the Council of the Indies that Orellana should be granted authority to explore and establish a new province in South America, which was to be called New Andalusia. He was reminded to respect the line of demarcation and cautioned not to infringe upon regions that belonged to Portugal. Orellana was instructed to establish two colonies along the banks of the Amazon to serve as bases for exploring, settling, and exploiting the riches of the land for a distance up to two hundred leagues south of the great river. One colony was to be established at the mouth of the river to serve as a port of call for ships that would transport materials and wealth between the Old and New World.

Orellana was named Adelantado, a title often synonymous with governor, and elevated to the rank of captain-general. He was to be paid a salary of 5,000 ducats, which was to be drawn from the riches he expected to obtain on this expedition. He was also entitled to one-twelfth of the royal revenue obtained on this venture, but not to exceed a million maravedies annually. He was exempted from paying customs taxes for a decade. Prince Philip also stipulated that Orellana was to treat the natives kindly, which was in accordance with the *New Laws* inspired by the Bartolomé de las Casas account of Spanish cruelties committed against natives of the New World. Orellana agreed to all terms and conditions and attested to this obligation before a notary five days after presented with this royal decree—the date was February 18, 1544.

Orellana was required to procure ships and recruit 300 soldiers: 200 infantry and 100 cavalry. He was expected to purchase materials for the construction of two boats small enough to probe the tributaries of the Amazon. Eight friars were to accompany him to spread the tenets of Christianity. An inspector general was also appointed to ensure the king's interests were honored and to provide periodic reports. Eight black slaves would also accompany the expedition.

To avoid a potentially explosive diplomatic incident Francisco was warned: "If some governor or captain shall have explored or colonized some section of the river bank and shall be on it when you arrive, you should do nothing in detriment to his interests ... even though you may find this to be within your jurisdiction as governor, so that we can avoid this disturbances which have arisen out of such situations in Peru and elsewhere."[7]

The Spaniards were expected to barter for food and goods, or, if these efforts failed, they were to appeal to the generosity of the natives: "Under no circumstances were the soldiers to wage war against the Indians unless it was to defend themselves." The Crown also stipulated, "No occasion is to be allowed to arise to be an excuse wherewith the Spaniards may hold Indians or maltreat them or prevent them from becoming Christians."[8] They were expected to use every means available to convert the natives to Christianity.

Other key appointments for the expedition were Juan García de Samaniego, inspector; Juan de la Cuadra, keeper of accounts; Francisco de Ulloa, treasurer; Cristóbal Maldonado, chief constable; Vicencio de Monte, revenue collector; and the Dominican friar Pablo de Torres, inspector general. The latter appointee was to observe and report on how Orellana conducted himself. The friar also carried a message that contained the name of which person would succeed Orellana in the event of his death; there is no known record of this person's name. Torres was a spy for the crown, a fact that surely upset Orellana once he learned that he was being watched.

Orellana's task was made more difficult by the fact that the Spanish Crown refused to match Portugal's generous offer to fund his expedition. This meant that the newly appointed governor, a man with a small purse string, had to find the means to purchase ships, provisions, and other necessities for his grand venture. This was a standard practice for most Spanish expeditions to the New World. Even his request for guns from the Crown was denied. A great deal of time and effort was spent trying to find financial backing. Many of the captains and soldiers contributed financially to the fitting of the expedition.

A determined Orellana set out for Seville to prepare for his return to the Amazon. Though he had little difficulty enlisting soldiers, the recruiting of experienced seaman was an entirely different matter. Francisco sought permission to obtain the services of Portuguese sailors and pilots who were familiar with the Brazilian coastal waters, but the Crown would not sanction the use of a Portuguese pilot. This decision would prove to be a serious setback to the mission: Portuguese helmsmen were more knowledgeable of the eastern coast of South America, particularly Brazil. This inability to procure the services of an experienced pilot contributed greatly to the failure of the expedition. He was also not allowed to press sailors into service, for they had to volunteer.

Orellana worked quickly to prepare for his departure. However, during this period there were disturbing signs of the captain-general's mental instability. A mere three weeks after receiving his appointment as leader of the expedition Orellana publicly announced that he was nearly ready to sail, despite not yet having raised enough money or recruited the requisite number of men. He declared that he had readied at Guadalquivir two Spanish galleons and two smaller caravels, and added that the smaller boats needed for probing upriver were under construction, bold claims that clearly stretched the truth. On the very day that he was supposed to depart Francisco was forced to write to the king that he would have to postpone his launch. Spain's monarch had already learned from others that Orellana was far behind schedule.

The Adelantado wrote five letters to His Majesty to explain why he had not set sail when expected: The first letter was dated May 9, 1544; the second May 13; the third June 28; the fourth October 22; and the fifth letter was dated November 21, 1544. The last letter was of concern to royal officials because Orellana sounded paranoid, blaming delays on "powerful enemies" who were men of "evil purpose and intention"[9] committed to making sure his expedition never set sail.

Concerned by these continual delays, the king ordered Pablo de Torres, the Dominican friar, to provide a detailed account of what Orellana had on hand and an opinion as to whether or not he would be ready to depart anytime soon. Torres reported that the expedition was indeed far behind in preparations and that at the present pace they would not be ready to sail until the coming month of September. October rolled around and Orellana was still not ready to sail. Many who signed on for this venture jumped ship and joined expeditions that were ready to sail.

There were a number of unexpected difficulties that Orellana was compelled to endure, especially regarding the acquisition of supplies. Merchants who previously offered him credit suddenly demanded payment in cash after a number of financial backers suddenly withdrew their monetary pledge. Men who previously agreed to join his expedition suddenly had a change of heart. The Adelantado protested to the king that there was "a worm in our midst."[10] The commander requested that the king continue to "have confidence in him."

Many were convinced that Hernando Pizarro, Gonzalo's older half-brother who was in Spain at the time, was behind such political intrigue. Hernando was under house arrest but the vast wealth he accumulated during the conquest and continued to collect from his possessions in Peru permitted him to peddle his influence among Pizarro loyalists who sought revenge against the man they believed left Gonzalo Pizarro and his troops to die in the jungle.

Distressing news came from neighboring Portugal, where it was learned that the king, whose interest had been piqued by what he heard from Orellana, had authorized an expedition of four ships to sail to the Amazon region. It was also learned that the monarch was being supplied additional information from one of Orellana's former companions on the Amazon expedition, an individual who had fled to Lisbon after having killed a man in Seville. Many historians believe this person was Cristóbal Maldonado, who had a falling out with Orellana after returning to Spain. Maldonado found sanctuary at Portugal after being accused of murdering a man in Seville. The Crown feared that the Portuguese expedition would sail before theirs and therefore used its influence to induce merchants and others to help Orellana meet his quotas.

Portuguese agents may have been involved in a plot to prevent Orellana's return to the Amazon. Officials in Portugal feared that Spain might infringe upon their New World grants if they should succeed in establishing a colony in this region. An agent of Portugal had supposedly been attempting to persuade Spanish sailors to join a Portuguese expedition during this period; Don Juan de Sandi arrived in Seville claiming to be the captain of a Portuguese fleet that was preparing to sail to the Great River. Many believed that he had come to Seville to spy on their progress and to steal recruits. The Portuguese captain was briefly detained and freed once it was believed he could no longer interfere with their plans.

There were additional factors that conspired against Orellana's plans: foul weather conditions; failure of previously recruited men to show up at Seville; payment still owed for ships, he owed 2,000 ducats for one of the ships; and delays in obtaining and loading provisions were among the principle reasons for postponing their departure. It was also reported that Orellana had failed to recruit any seasoned sailors. Members of the Council of the Indies feared the expedition would never be ready to sail.

Orellana's fitness to command was called into question by the report of one inspector, "I am unable to give [any further clearer account] at this point, because in truth I do not understand either Orellana, or the affairs of this fleet, nor do I believe that he understands them himself."[11]

Pablo de Torres, the inspector-general, seemed to take pity on the plight of Orellana when he wrote that the captain-general was "so kindhearted that every time a person tells him something he believes it and acts on it, and so much gentleness at times is of little profit to one."[12]

Torres even tried to help Orellana's cause by writing, "I beseech Your Majesty, since up to now this enterprise has been so completely deprived of recognition and so utterly ignored, to take a more personal interest in it from now on, and that Your Majesty will bestow upon it some more special favor."[13] The priest's efforts were to no avail. Even the Council of the Indies sought to persuade Emperor Charles to provide financial assistance so Orellana's expedition could get underway, but the monarch still refused.

Orellana was saved from ruin by Cosmo de Chaves, his stepfather, who pledged 30,000 maravedies to help with the acquisition of ships and provisions. Having used up all his credit at Seville, the Adelantado found willing suppliers at his homeland province of Trujillo. Merchants obliged Orellana by extending him credit for provisions until his stepfather's money arrived, which finally occurred at the beginning of October.

Meanwhile, the eligible Orellana was receiving a number of marriage proposals, and many involved in the expedition hoped he would marry a woman who would bring a dowry large enough to benefit the needs of the expedition. Friar Torres had been desperately trying to find a wife for Orellana, especially someone who hailed from a family of financial means. In November of 1544, the *Adelantado* unexpectedly took Ana de Ayala, a mere teenage girl from a respectable but financially deprived family, as his wife. Ana agreed to sail with her husband to New Andalusia, a decision that did not sit well with the crew. Even Torres, his most ardent supporter, suspected Orellana lacked good judgment in this matter. The commander could have helped his cause by finding a wife who would provide a large dowry. Instead, he married a woman of low social status whom the Friar complained could not provide Orellana "a single ducat." All were greatly disappointed with their commander's poor choice.

The expedition's situation was further complicated by the inspector-general's discovery that one of the acquired boats was hardly seaworthy. Friar Torres chastised those who had not exercised good judgment in purchasing this ship. They had to replace it with a ship that was only half the size of the previously purchased boat.

Orellana refused to let Pablo de Torres examine the accounts, which prompted the frustrated inspector-general to write, "I do not wish to relate the infinite errors ... which have been perpetrated in connection with the enterprise. The man who has completely ruined things has been [Vincente] del Monte, who has made himself rich out of the money of the Genoese through deals and the *adelantado* [Orellana] has been putting up with all this. How could the fleet be fitted out if to his own wife, who is excessively poor, they have given jewels, silks and embroideries and the Genoese have handed over the 3,000 ducats in small change; and of the *Adelantado* and Del Monte had money in their pockets while the rest of the expedition is perishing from hunger and thirst."[14]

Torres also wrote to Philip II, regent of Spain, of Orellana's gross negligence, "I assure Your Highness that he is not carrying enough water to reach the Canaries nor jars in which to secure any if it takes them fifteen days to get there ... and also the deck of the ship on which the *adelantado* is sailing is full of women."[15]

After more than a year of preparations Orellana declared that he was finally ready to set sail. However, an inspection by royal officials did not reach the same conclusion: They found he was short of the required number of soldiers and friars, had only 24 of the 100 horses he was supposed to bring, the small boats for probing the river were not completed, and the expedition sorely lacked suitable pilots, shipmasters, and sailors.

Orellana countered that the remaining men were due to arrive shortly from Seville, Sanlúcar, and the surrounding villages. As for the horses, the rest were to be purchased during their stopovers at the Canary and Cape Verde Islands. He claimed that the parts for the small boats were already collected and would be assembled in the New World region. The inspectors decided to give Orellana one more chance to obtain all that he still lacked.

A second inspection conducted by Torres took place one month later on May 9, 1545. The inspectors took inventory and interviewed several members of the expedition. They wanted to make sure the pilots and shipmates were not foreigners; French, English, and Portuguese were unacceptable, for fear they would reveal to their respective homelands the expedition's findings. Orellana's appointment of a Genoese camp master was a point of contention. Adding to the commander's problems was the hiring of Francisco Sánchez as pilot, a navigator who was not familiar with the coast of Brazil. He had also hired a Portuguese sailor who did not know the region.

Friar Torres was annoyed to discover that Francisco de Orellana was not to be found on any of the boats. He searched for Orellana at Sanlúcar to tell him not to sail until they had gone over their findings and completed their report to the monarch. The pilots were ordered not to raise anchors or they would suffer harsh consequences for disobeying this directive.

Searching in Vain

Wishing to avoid any further disruptions to his plans, Orellana set sail on the morning of May 11, 1545, with four ships carrying a total of four hundred men. Defying the inspector-general's order, the boats departed the port of Sanlúcar de Barrameda at 10 o'clock and sailed two leagues away to a remote port, where they anchored until 6 o'clock that evening, at which time they cast out to sea. There was none of the usual fanfare for this expedition to the New World, for the captain-general and his crew had to leave without notice after having failed to pass the royal inspection. This rush to sail meant the expedition was not adequately prepared; it sorely lacked sufficient equipment and food, a shortage that would lead to needless suffering. Ana de Ayala sailed aboard her husband's ship.

The flotilla sailed to the Canary Islands in order to obtain additional provisions, enlist more colonists, and make sure the ships were seaworthy. The boats docked at the island of Tenerife for three months to store up on the many items they lacked. The expedition then sailed to the Cape Verde Islands where they docked for two months doing the same as they had done at their previous layover. Unfortunately, Orellana lost more than he ever gained during these extended stops. A great many aboard the ships took ill from an epidemic that had swept across the island—98 prospective colonists perished from this pernicious affliction. The loss was so great that there were no longer enough able bodies to man all four ships; one ship was abandoned and stripped of essential items to replace damaged parts on the other ships, which included anchors that had been lost. Once ready to set sail, fifty recruits, including the camp master and three captains, remained ashore. Some were either too weak or unwilling to continue the journey, the latter felt the evil tidings that seemed to plague this venture from the outset were simply too great. Many had concluded that their commander was either incompetent, insane, or possibly both.

The three ships finally sailed for the coast of Brazil around the middle of November. The crew was hampered by bad weather, during which time they ran out of drinking water and therefore had to rely on periodic rains, which were generally heavy, to quench their terrible thirst. Orellana's calamitous voyage culminated with the disappearance of one of the ships, which carried a crew of 77 recruits, eleven horses, and one of the brigantines that was to be used for probing the river. The lost ship and its crew were never seen or heard from again.

The remaining two ships eventually sighted the coast of Brazil and followed a southerly course along the distant outline for 100 leagues, where they happened upon a surge of freshwater that pushed them further out to sea. Knowing this was a clear sign that they were very near the mouth of the Amazon, Orellana ordered his crew to steer toward land.

The following day, December 20, 1545, the ships sailed into the vast mouth of the bay and dropped anchor between two inhabited islands where the famished Spaniards bartered their meager rations of trinkets for food, particularly maize, cassava, fish, and various fruits. Many of the men pleaded with Orellana to remain at the islands long enough to regain their strength as well as revive the vigor of their ailing horses. They also proposed that this would be an ideal spot to build the brigantine for probing the river, which had been brought over in sections. The captain-general, who was eager to locate the mouth of the river he had previously explored, told his crew there would be many other villages where they would find food, shelter, and opportunities to build a brigantine.

The expedition made periodic stops at the islands to gather additional wood for the building of a new riverboat. Bad luck, however, continued to haunt the crew. After having ventured some 100 leagues up a flood region devoid of villages, the company finally came upon some Indian huts. Unfortunately, these natives had little to offer in the way of sustenance. The powerful tide caused the ship to lose its hawser, which led to it being run aground on one of the islands inhabited by a friendly tribe. The crew went ashore to begin construction of a brigantine, a smaller boat more suitable for navigating the shallow waters. January, February and half of March 1546 were spent building this smaller boat. The stranded ship was stripped of nails and planking for the construction of a new vessel.

Overexertion coupled with a severe shortage of food exacted a terrible toll on the crew as they built their brigantine. The Spaniards sustained themselves by eating the horses and dogs that had accompanied them aboard ship, and they had little else to eat after these animals had been consumed. Exhaustion, hunger, and illness would claim the lives of 57 men during this ordeal. Their situation seemed hopeless after the boat ran aground, an accident which caused morale among the men to sink to new lows.

To save the rest from starving to death the commander sent a group of men aboard the newly built brigantine to find food. Orellana surely must have reminisced about how he had set out on such a task for Gonzalo Pizarro, however, since they were going upriver, he did not have to worry about the currents preventing their return. The search party encountered hostile natives; several men died from wounds and others perished from starvation. The survivors eventually returned without any food for their comrades.

Realizing he did not have enough men to establish a colony, a frustrated Orellana decided to resume his quest to locate the mouth of the river he had previously probed, where he knew there would be friendly villages that could provide food for his troops. The newly built brigantine would carry Francisco, Fray Pablo, and several members of his company on a search for the main river. The Adelantado planned to barter for gold or silver with the natives, which he would send back to Spain as a sign that his expedition had met with success and, hopefully, to entice others to join his venture.

Diego Muñoz and 28 crewmen remained with the grounded ship. This group of colonists busied themselves with the construction of a boat, which, once completed, they would use to search for Orellana's boat.

Meanwhile, the labyrinth of islands and tributaries would frustrate Francisco's efforts to locate the primary branch of the river, but Orellana refused to abandon hope. He was disappointed to learn that the river he chose to follow was not the river he sought, but instead an unfamiliar tributary of this vast estuary. The numerous channels explored all proved to be dead ends. After an absence of 27 days and the loss of 17 men to native assaults while searching for the elusive river, Orellana returned to the island where he had left his young wife and comrades only to discover that they were nowhere to be found. It is unknown if the captain-general grasped the irony of his predicament.

As mentioned, those who had remained behind did not idly await the return of Orellana and his companions. Having heard the stories of natives armed with poisoned arrows and the cannibalistic practice of some tribes, the Spaniards feared they were too few to fend off a native assault. Believing that their leader and his crew had perished while searching for the elusive tributary, the stranded crew spent their time repairing one of the longboats, making use of wood and material from the beached ship to reinforce their smaller vessel. They were aided by natives who provided them with food in exchange for their help in fighting an enemy tribe from the province of Caripuna.

The remaining crew departed the island once their boat was finished. They were accompanied by an armada of nearly 100 canoes to the islands of Marribuique and Caritán. The ruler of Marribuique guided them to where the river joined with another large river they estimated to be 12 leagues wide. The Spaniards feared that their lack of trinkets to trade, the worn condition of their leaky vessel, and so few men to man the boat, were sufficient reasons to head back downriver in the faint hope of catching sight of their commander. After wandering for 40 leagues they reached a fertile mainland that the natives called Comao.

The hospitable natives of Comao freely traded their food for Spanish trinkets, transactions which yielded an abundance of cassava, maize, sweet potatoes, fish, and fowl. When the Spaniards prepared to leave, six comrades who were weary of the journey and wary of the dangers ahead chose to remain behind with the tribe. The diminished crew sailed away, but four leagues into the voyage another Spaniard lost heart and returned to the village to live as a member of the tribe. He was soon followed by three more who rowed back in a small boat.

The Spaniards continued downstream, but their luck ran out when the water thrust their boat onto a mangrove swamp where they were tormented by a host of mosquitoes and a nagging sense of helplessness. Rafts were built and once they reached the coast, the grateful survivors hugged the shoreline for several hundred miles. Because their rafts leaked so badly the crew, who were already weakened by hunger and toil, had to constantly bale water to keep from sinking.

The remainder of Orellana's crew headed up the coast of South America, through the Gulf of Paria, before finally reaching the island of Margarita in early December 1546. The surviving Spaniards were elated to find twenty-five of their comrades and Orellana's wife at Margarita. The historian Francisco de Guzmán wrote that one of the men who was with Orellana informed the widow, "that her husband had not succeeded in getting to the main branch, which he was looking for, and consequently, on account of his being ill, he had made up his mind to come to a land of Christians; and during this time, when he was out looking for food for the journey, the Indians shot seventeen of his men with arrows. From grief over this and from his illness Orellana died."[16] It was reported that the despondent Orellana, after seeing that his wife and crew had abandoned him, sat down and stared at the water until his life slipped away.

Ana informed Spanish officials that her husband had failed to find the main river. She stated that Francisco de Orellana was ill and spoke of trying to locate a land of Christians. During this time, the natives attacked and killed many of his men while they were collecting food for an upcoming voyage. She added that the expedition was plagued by heavy rains and that,

14. The Final Voyage

"Everyone had endured great suffering because of our hunger and the illnesses ... we reached the point when we had eaten all the horses and dogs, and for a period of eleven months we wandered about like lost men in the region of the said river, during which time the greater part of the expedition had died ... among them my husband."[17]

An official inquiry into the affairs of this disastrous expedition states that Orellana took 450 men on his voyage to the New World. There were only 44 survivors, which included Ana de Ayala, Orellana's widow. The title of Adelantado had been granted in perpetuity but Francisco de Orellana died without a legitimate heir. Despite the failed expeditions of Gonzalo Pizarro and Francisco de Orellana, the search for the rich kingdom of Eldorado and the legendary realm of the Amazons remained an eternal quest for an untold number of future adventurers seeking fortune and glory.

Chapter Notes

Epigraphs

1. Robert Silverberg, *The Golden Dream: Seekers of El Dorado* (Athens: Ohio University Press, 1996), 144.
2. William Lewis Herndon, Lieutenant United States Navy. *Exploration of the Valley of the Amazon* (Washington, D.C.: Robert Armstrong, Public Printer, 1854), 17–18.
3. Edgar Allan Poe, *The Unabridged Edgar Allan Poe* (Philadelphia: Running Press, 1983), 1163.

Introduction

1. Sources differ in rendering the name as either El Dorado or Eldorado. This book will refer to the legendary ruler as El Dorado and his land as Eldorado.
2. Pedro Cieza de Leon, *The Incas of Pedro de Cieza de Leon* (Norman: University of Oklahoma Press, 1959), xxxviii.
3. Nicholas Hordern, *God, Gold and Glory* (London: Aldus Books, 1971), p.180.

Chapter 1

1. John A. Crow, *The Epic of Latin America* (Garden City: Country Life Press, 1946), 119.
2. Victor Wolfgang von Hagen, *The Golden Man: The Quest for El Dorado* (Westmead: Saxon House, 1974), 32.
3. *Ibid.*, 39.
4. John Hemming, *The Search for El Dorado* (London: Phoenix Press, 2001), 21.
5. Victor Wolfgang von Hagen, *The Golden Man: The Quest for El Dorado* (Westmead: Saxon House, 1974), 43.
6. John Hemming, *The Search for El Dorado* (London: Phoenix Press, 2001), 23.
7. Victor Wolfgang von Hagen, *The Golden Man: The Quest for El Dorado* (Westmead: Saxon House, 1974), 44.
8. *Ibid.*, 45.
9. *Ibid.*, 47.
10. *Ibid.*, 50.
11. *Ibid.*, 50.
12. *Ibid.*, 54.
13. Germán Arciniegas, *The Knight of El Dorado: The Tale of Don Gonzalo Jiménez de Quesada and his Conquest of New Granada, Now called Colombia* (New York: Viking Press, 1942), 159.
14. John Hemming, *The Search for El Dorado* (London: Phoenix Press, 2001), 31.
15. Victor Wolfgang von Hagen, *The Golden Man: The Quest for El Dorado* (Westmead: Saxon House, 1974), 61.
16. John Hemming, *The Search for El Dorado* (London: Phoenix Press, 2001), 33.
17. *Ibid.*, 35.
18. *Ibid.*, 35.
19. *Ibid.*, 35.
20. *Ibid.*, 37–38.
21. Hugh Thomas, *The Golden Empire: Spain, Charles V, and the Creation of America* (New York: Random House, 2010), 378–379.
22. Robert Silverberg, *The Golden Dream: Seekers of El Dorado* (Athens: Ohio University Press, 1996), 408.
23. Hugh Thomas, *The Golden Empire: Spain, Charles V, and the Creation of America* (New York: Random House, 2010), 408–409.
24. John Hemming, *The Search for El Dorado* (London: Phoenix Press, 2001), 56.
25. Germán Arciniegas, *The Knight of El Dorado: The Tale of Don Gonzalo Jiménez de Quesada and his Conquest of New Granada,*

Now called Colombia (New York: Viking Press, 1942), 162.
26. Victor Wolfgang von Hagen, *The Golden Man: The Quest for El Dorado* (Westmead: Saxon House, 1974), 96.
27. *Ibid.*, 99
28. *Ibid.*, 100.
29. Germán Arciniegas, *The Knight of El Dorado: The Tale of Don Gonzalo Jiménez de Quesada and his Conquest of New Granada, Now called Colombia* (New York: Viking Press, 1942), 163.
30. Hugh Thomas, *The Golden Empire: Spain, Charles V, and the Creation of America* (New York: Random House, 2010), 166.
31. John Hemming, *The Search for El Dorado* (London: Phoenix Press, 2001), 70.

Chapter 2

1. Robert Silverberg, *The Golden Dream: Seekers of El Dorado* (Athens: Ohio University Press, 1996), 141.
2. John Hemming, *The Search for El Dorado* (London: Phoenix Press, 2001), 103.
3. *Ibid.*, 104.

Chapter 3

1. Germán Arciniegas, *The Knight of El Dorado: The Tale of Don Gonzalo Jiménez de Quesada and his Conquest of New Granada, Now called Colombia* (New York: Viking Press, 1942), 37.
2. *Ibid.*, 38.
3. *Ibid.*, 40.
4. R.B. Cunninghame Graham, *The Conquest of New Granada: Being the Life of Gonzalo Jimenez de Quesada* (London. William Heinemann, 1922), 6.
5. Robert Silverberg, *The Golden Dream: Seekers of El Dorado* (Athens: Ohio University Press, 1996), 119.
6. Bernardo de Vargas Machucha, *The Indian Militia and Description of the Indies* (Durham: Duke University, 2008), 131.
7. John Hemming, *The Search for El Dorado* (London: Phoenix Press, 2001), 43.
8. John A. Crow, *The Epic of Latin America* (Garden City: Country Life Press, 1946), 118.
9. Victor Wolfgang von Hagen, *The Golden Man: The Quest for El Dorado* (Westmead: Saxon House, 1974), pp. 123–124.

10. J. H. Parry, *The Discovery of South America* (New York: Taplinger Publishing, 1979), 227.
11. R.B. Cunninghame Graham, *The Conquest of New Granada: Being the Life of Gonzalo Jimenez de Quesada* (London. William Heinemann, 1922), 46.
12. John A. Crow, *The Epic of Latin America* (Garden City: Country Life Press, 1946), 122.
13. Germán Arciniegas, *The Knight of El Dorado: The Tale of Don Gonzalo Jiménez de Quesada and his Conquest of New Granada, Now called Colombia* (New York: Viking Press, 1942), 93.
14. Robert Silverberg, *The Golden Dream: Seekers of El Dorado* (Athens: Ohio University Press, 1996), 86.
15. John Hemming, *The Search for El Dorado* (London: Phoenix Press, 2001), 88.

Chapter 4

1. Germán Arciniegas, *The Knight of El Dorado: The Tale of Don Gonzalo Jiménez de Quesada and his Conquest of New Granada, Now called Colombia* (New York: Viking Press, 1942), 104.
2. R.B. Cunninghame Graham, *The Conquest of New Granada: Being the Life of Gonzalo Jimenez de Quesada* (London. William Heinemann, 1922), 79–80.
3. Germán Arciniegas, *The Knight of El Dorado: The Tale of Don Gonzalo Jiménez de Quesada and his Conquest of New Granada, Now called Colombia* (New York: Viking Press, 1942), 119.
4. Victor Wolfgang von Hagen, *The Golden Man: The Quest for El Dorado* (Westmead: Saxon House, 1974), 146.
5. Hugh Thomas, *The Golden Empire: Spain, Charles V, and the Creation of America* (New York: Random House, 2010), 383.
6. R.B. Cunninghame Graham, *The Conquest of New Granada: Being the Life of Gonzalo Jimenez de Quesada* (London. William Heinemann, 1922), 135.
7. John Hemming, *The Search for El Dorado* (London: Phoenix Press, 2001), 96.
8. *Ibid.*, 97.
9. Germán Arciniegas, *The Knight of El Dorado: The Tale of Don Gonzalo Jiménez de Quesada and his Conquest of New Granada, Now called Colombia* (New York: Viking Press, 1942), 145.
10. *Ibid.*, 146.

11. *Ibid.*, 147.
12. *Ibid.*, 149.
13. John Hemming, *The Search for El Dorado* (London: Phoenix Press, 2001), 101.

Chapter 5

1. Victor Wolfgang von Hagen, *The Golden Man: The Quest for El Dorado* (Westmead: Saxon House, 1974), 184.
2. Germán Arciniegas, *The Knight of El Dorado: The Tale of Don Gonzalo Jiménez de Quesada and his Conquest of New Granada, Now called Colombia* (New York: Viking Press, 1942), 205–206.
3. *Ibid.*, 217.
4. Hugh Thomas, *The Golden Empire: Spain, Charles V, and the Creation of America* (New York: Random House, 2010), 412.
5. *Ibid.*, 412.
6. *Ibid.*, 413.
7. *Ibid.*, 410.

Chapter 6

1. Michael Wood, *Conquistadors* (Los Angeles: University of California Press, Berkeley, 2000), 189–190.
2. J. H. Parry, *The Discovery of South America* (New York: Taplinger Publishing, 1979), 212.
3. Peter O. Koch, *The Spanish Conquest of the Inca Empire* (Jefferson, NC: McFarland Company, Inc., 2008), p.172.
4. John Hemming, *Red Gold: The Conquest of the Brazilian Indians, 1500–1760* (Cambridge: Harvard University Press, 1978), 185.
5. Gaspar de Carvajal, *The Discovery of the Amazon* (New York: AMS Press, Inc., 1970), 36.
6. Brendan Bernhard, *Pizarro, Orellana, and the Exploration of the Amazon* (New York: Chelsea House Publishers, 1991), 40.
7. Gaspar de Carvajal, *The Discovery of the Amazon* (New York: AMS Press, Inc., 1970), 43.
8. *Ibid.*, p.245.
9. Michael Wood, *Conquistadors* (Los Angeles: University of California Press, Berkeley, 2000), 192.
10. *Ibid.*, 192.

Chapter 7

1. Hugh Thomas, *The Golden Empire: Spain, Charles V, and the Creation of America* (New York: Random House, 2010), 291.
2. Robert Silverberg, *The Golden Dream: Seekers of El Dorado* (Athens: Ohio University Press, 1996), 146.
3. Gaspar de Carvajal, *The Discovery of the Amazon* (New York: AMS Press, Inc., 1970), 51.
4. *Ibid.*, 246.
5. *Ibid.*, 52–53.
6. Pedro de Cieza de Leon, *The Travels of Pedro de Cieza de Leon: The First Part of His Chronicle of Peru* (Boston: Adamant Media Corporation, 2005), 38.
7. Robert Silverberg, *The Golden Dream: Seekers of El Dorado* (Athens: Ohio University Press, 1996), 150.
8. *Ibid.*, 149–150.

Chapter 8

1. Michael Wood, *Conquistadors* (Los Angeles: University of California Press, Berkeley, 2000), 204.
2. *Ibid.*, 204.
3. Gaspar de Carvajal, *The Discovery of the Amazon* (New York: AMS Press, Inc., 1970), 56.
4. Brendan Bernhard, *Pizarro, Orellana, and the Exploration of the Amazon* (New York: Chelsea House Publishers, 1991), 17.
5. *Ibid.*, 17.
6. J. H. Parry, *The Discovery of South America* (New York: Taplinger Publishing, 1979), 263.
7. Brendan Bernhard, *Pizarro, Orellana, and the Exploration of the Amazon* (New York: Chelsea House Publishers, 1991), 44.
8. J. H. Parry, *The Discovery of South America* (New York: Taplinger Publishing, 1979), 263.
9. Michael Wood, *Conquistadors* (Los Angeles: University of California Press, Berkeley, 2000), 206.
10. Robert Silverberg, *The Golden Dream: Seekers of El Dorado* (Athens: Ohio University Press, 1996), 157.
11. Brendan Bernhard, *Pizarro, Orellana, and the Exploration of the Amazon* (New York: Chelsea House Publishers, 1991), 19.

12. Robert Silverberg, *The Golden Dream: Seekers of El Dorado* (Athens: Ohio University Press, 1996), 157.
13. Brendan Bernhard, *Pizarro, Orellana, and the Exploration of the Amazon* (New York: Chelsea House Publishers, 1991), 45–46.

Chapter 9

1. Brendan Bernhard, *Pizarro, Orellana, and the Exploration of the Amazon* (New York: Chelsea House Publishers, 1991), 19.
2. Gaspar de Carvajal, *The Discovery of the Amazon* (New York: AMS Press, Inc., 1970), 416.
3. *Ibid.*, 183.
4. Hugh Thomas, *The Golden Empire: Spain, Charles V, and the Creation of America* (New York: Random House, 2010), 297.
5. Gaspar de Carvajal, *The Discovery of the Amazon* (New York: AMS Press, Inc., 1970), 185.
6. Robert Silverberg, *The Golden Dream: Seekers of El Dorado* (Athens: Ohio University Press, 1996), 159.

Chapter 10

1. Michael Wood, *Conquistadors* (Los Angeles: University of California Press, Berkeley, 2000), 214.
2. Robert Silverberg, *The Golden Dream: Seekers of El Dorado* (Athens: Ohio University Press, 1996), 153.
3. Michael Wood, *Conquistadors* (Los Angeles: University of California Press, Berkeley, 2000), 206.
4. Stuart Stirling, *Pizarro: Conqueror of the Inca.* (Gloucestershire: Sutton Publishing, 2005) p. 131.
5. Michael Wood, *Conquistadors* (Los Angeles: University of California Press, Berkeley, 2000), 215.
6. Garcilaso de la Vega, *Royal Commentaries of the Incas and the General History of Peru, Part II* (Austin: University of Texas,1966), 916.
7. Robert Silverberg, *The Golden Dream: Seekers of El Dorado* (Athens: Ohio University Press, 1996), 179.
8. Hugh Thomas, *The Golden Empire: Spain, Charles V, and the Creation of America* (New York: Random House, 2010), 301–302.
9. Brendan Bernhard, *Pizarro, Orellana, and the Exploration of the Amazon* (New York: Chelsea House Publishers, 1991), 90–91.

Chapter 11

1. John Hemming, *Red Gold: The Conquest of the Brazilian Indians, 1500–1760* (Cambridge: Harvard University Press, 1978), 188.
2. Brendan Bernhard, *Pizarro, Orellana, and the Exploration of the Amazon* (New York: Chelsea House Publishers, 1991), 59–60.
3. Robert Silverberg, *The Golden Dream: Seekers of El Dorado* (Athens: Ohio University Press, 1996), 159-160.
4. Brendan Bernhard, *Pizarro, Orellana, and the Exploration of the Amazon* (New York: Chelsea House Publishers, 1991), 61.

Chapter 12

1. Gaspar de Carvajal, *The Discovery of the Amazon* (New York: AMS Press, Inc., 1970), 425.
2. Robert Silverberg, *The Golden Dream: Seekers of El Dorado* (Athens: Ohio University Press, 1996), 160.
3. Brendan Bernhard, *Pizarro, Orellana, and the Exploration of the Amazon* (New York: Chelsea House Publishers, 1991), 69.
4. Hugh Thomas, *The Golden Empire: Spain, Charles V, and the Creation of America* (New York: Random House, 2010), 298.
5. Brendan Bernhard, *Pizarro, Orellana, and the Exploration of the Amazon* (New York: Chelsea House Publishers, 1991), 72.
6. Gaspar de Carvajal, *The Discovery of the Amazon* (New York: AMS Press, Inc., 1970), 205.
7. David M. Jones and Brian L. Molyneaux. *The Mythology of the Americas* (New York: Lorenz Books, 2001), 389.
8. Robert Silverberg, *The Golden Dream: Seekers of El Dorado* (Athens: Ohio University Press, 1996), 164.
9. *Ibid.*, 164–165.
10. Brendan Bernhard, *Pizarro,*

Orellana, and the Exploration of the Amazon (New York: Chelsea House Publishers, 1991), 81.
  11. David M. Jones and Brian L. Molyneaux. The Mythology of the Americas. (New York: Lorenz Books, 2001), 389.
  12. Anthony Smith, Explorers of the Amazon (New York: Viking Penguin Inc., 1990), 73.
  13. Gaspar de Carvajal, The Discovery of the Amazon (New York: AMS Press, Inc., 1970), 434.
  14. Ibid., 221.
  15. Brendan Bernhard, Pizarro, Orellana, and the Exploration of the Amazon (New York: Chelsea House Publishers, 1991), 84.
  16. Robert Silverberg, The Golden Dream: Seekers of El Dorado (Athens: Ohio University Press, 1996), 169.
  17. David M. Jones and Brian L. Molyneaux. (The Mythology of the Americas. New York: Lorenz Books, 2001), 389.
  18. Gaspar de Carvajal, The Discovery of the Amazon (New York: AMS Press, Inc., 1970), 103.
  19. Robert Silverberg, The Golden Dream: Seekers of El Dorado (Athens: Ohio University Press, 1996), 167.

Chapter 13

  1. Gaspar de Carvajal, The Discovery of the Amazon (New York: AMS Press, Inc., 1970), 442.
  2. Robert Silverberg, The Golden Dream: Seekers of El Dorado (Athens: Ohio University Press, 1996), 171.
  3. Ibid., 172.
  4. Michael Wood, Conquistadors (Los Angeles: University of California Press, Berkeley, 2000), 225.
  5. Hugh Thomas, The Golden Empire: Spain, Charles V, and the Creation of America (New York: Random House, 2010), 303.

Chapter 14

  1. Gaspar de Carvajal, The Discovery of the Amazon (New York: AMS Press, Inc., 1970), 125.
  2. Hugh Thomas, The Golden Empire: Spain, Charles V, and the Creation of America (New York: Random House, 2010), 304.
  3. Ibid., 301.
  4. Gaspar de Carvajal, The Discovery of the Amazon (New York: AMS Press, Inc., 1970), 79.
  5. Ibid., 92.
  6. Hugh Thomas, The Golden Empire: Spain, Charles V, and the Creation of America (New York: Random House, 2010), 304.
  7. Ibid., 306.
  8. Ibid., 306.
  9. Gaspar de Carvajal, The Discovery of the Amazon (New York: AMS Press, Inc., 1970), 335–340.
  10. Brendan Bernhard, Pizarro, Orellana, and the Exploration of the Amazon (New York: Chelsea House Publishers, 1991), 99.
  11. Anthony Smith, Explorers of the Amazon. (New York: Viking Penguin Inc., 1990), 85.
  12. Brendan Bernhard, Pizarro, Orellana, and the Exploration of the Amazon (New York: Chelsea House Publishers, 1991), 101.
  13. Ibid., 101–102.
  14. Hugh Thomas, The Golden Empire: Spain, Charles V, and the Creation of America (New York: Random House, 2010), 308.
  15. Ibid., 308.
  16. Gaspar de Carvajal, The Discovery of the Amazon (New York: AMS Press, Inc., 1970), 151.
  17. Michael Wood, Conquistadors (Los Angeles: University of California Press, Berkeley, 2000), 229.

Bibliography

Arciniegas, Germán. *The Knight of El Dorado: The Tale of Don Gonzalo Jiménez de Quesada and his Conquest of New Granada, Now called Colombia.* New York: Viking Press, 1942.
Bernhard, Brendan. *Pizarro, Orellana, and the Exploration of the Amazon.* New York: Chelsea House Publishers, 1991.
Burland, Cottie. *The People of the Ancient Americas.* London: Hamlyn Publishing Group, 1970.
Burland, Cottie, Irene Nicholson, and Harold Osborne. *Mythology of the Americas.* London: Hamlyn, 1970.
Carvajal, Gaspar de. *The Discovery of the Amazon.* New York: AMS Press, Inc., 1970.
Chagnon, Napoleon A. *Yanomamö: The Last Days of Eden.* New York: Holt, Rinehart and Winston, 1983.
Coe, Michael, Dean Snow, and Elizabeth Benson. *Atlas of Ancient America.* New York: Facts on File, Inc., 1986.
Crow, John A. *The Epic of Latin America.* John A. Crow. Garden City: Country Life Press, 1946.
Descola, Jean. *The Conquistador.* New York: Viking Press, 1957.
Graham, Cunninghame R.B. *The Conquest of New Granada: Being the Life of Gonzalo Jimenez de Quesada.* London. William Heinemann, 1922.
Hagen, Victor Wolfgang von. *The Ancient Sun Kingdoms of the Americas.* Cleveland: The World Publishing Company, 1961.
_____. *The Golden Man: The Quest for El Dorado.* Westmead: Saxon House, 1974.
_____. *South America: The Green World of the Naturalists.* London: Eyre & Spottiswoode, 1951.
Hardoy, Jorge E. *Pre-Columbian Cities.* New York: Walker and Company, 1973.
Hemming, John. *Red Gold: The Conquest of the Brazilian Indians, 1500-1760.* Cambridge: Harvard University Press, 1978.
_____. *The Search for El Dorado.* London: Phoenix Press, 2001.
Herndon, WM Lewis. *Exploration of the Valley of the Amazon.* Washington, D.C.: Robert Armstrong, Public Printer, 1854.
Hordern, Nicholas. *God, Gold and Glory.* London: Aldus Books Limited, 1971.
Howard, Cecil. *Pizarro and the Conquest of Peru.* New York: American Heritage Publishing Co. Inc., 1968.
Innes, Hammond. *The Conquistadors.* New York: Alfred A. Knopf, 1969.
Jones, David M., and Brian L. Molyneaux. *The Mythology of the Americas.* New York: Lorenz Books, 2001.
Jones, Dr. David M. *The Lost History of the Incas.* London: Hermes House, 2007.
Kamen, Henry. *Empire: How Spain Became a World Power 1492-1763.* New York: HarperCollins Publishers, 2003.
Koch, Peter O. *The Spanish Conquest of the Inca Empire.* Jefferson, NC: McFarland, 2008.
Leon, Pedro de Cieza. *The Incas of Pedro Cieza de Leon.* Norman: University of Oklahoma Press, 1959.

_____. *The Travels of Pedro de Cieza de Leon: The First Part of His Chronicle of Peru.* Boston: Adamant Media Corporation, 2005.
Machuca, Bernardo de Vargas. *The Indian Militia and Description of the Indies.* Durham: Duke University Press, 2008.
Mann, Charles. *1491: New Revelations of the Americas Before Columbus.* New York: Alfred A. Knopf, 2006.
Markham, Clements R. *Expeditions into the Valley of the Amazons 1539, 1540, 1639.* Boston: Adamant Media Corporation, 2005.
McIntyre, Loren, *The Incredible Incas and Their Timeless Land.* Washington, D.C.: National Geographic Society, 1975.
National Geographic, editors of. *Lost Empires, Living Tribes.* Washington, D.C.: National Geographic Society, 1982.
The New Encyclopedia Britannica. 29 vol. Chicago: Encyclopedia Britannica, 1990.
Novaresio, Paolo. *The Explorers: From the Ancient World to the Present.* New York: Stewart, Tabori & Chang, 1996.
Parry, J.H. *The Discovery of South America.* New York: Taplinger Publishing, 1979.
Pennington, Piers. *The Great Explorers.* London: Bloomsbury Books, 1979.
Poe, Edgar Allan. *The Unabridged Edgar Allan Poe.* Philadelphia: Running Press, 1983.
Prescott, William H. *The Conquest of Peru.* New York: Random House, 1953.
Reader's Digest, editors of. *The World's Last Mysteries.* Pleasantiville: Reader's Digest Association, Inc., 1981.
Salmoral, Manuel Lucena. *America 1492: Portrait of a Continent 500 years Ago.* New York: Facts on File, Inc., 1990.
Silverberg, Robert. *The Golden Dream: Seekers of El Dorado.* Athens: Ohio University Press, 1996.
Smith, Anthony. *Explorers of the Amazon.* New York: Viking Penguin Inc., 1990.
Stirling, Stuart. *Pizarro: Conqueror of the Inca.* Gloucestershire: Sutton Publishing, 2005.
Thomas, Hugh. *The Golden Empire: Spain, Charles V, and the Creation of America.* New York: Random House, 2010.
Time-Life Books, editors of. *Age of Exploration.* New York: Time-Life Books, 1974.
_____. *The Search for El Dorado.* Alexandria: Time-Life Books, 1994.
Vega, Garcilaso de la. *Royal Commentaries of the Incas and the General History of Peru, Part II.* Austin: University of Texas,1966.
Wasbard, Simone. *The World's Last Mysteries.* New York: Reader's Digest, 1976.
Wood, Michael. *Conquistadors.* Los Angeles: University of California Press, Berkeley, 2000.
Yenne, Bill. *Cities of Gold: Legendary Kingdoms, Quixotic Quests, and the Search for Fantastic New World Wealth.* Yardley: Westholme Publishing, 2011.

Index

Acarigua (river and village) 33
Acosta, Juan de 175
Aguado, Pedro de 43, 118
Aguarico, village 149
Aguarico River 171, 173
Aguilar, Cristobal de 184
Alcantara, Juan de 143, 154
Aldana, Lorenzo de 52
Alderete, Juan Fernández de 41, 43
Almagro, Diego de 46, 47, 49, 51, 52, 123, 178, 179, 180, 217
Alvarado, Pedro de 48, 49, 126
Amazon River 5, 33, 36, 137, 149, 157, 158, 160, 166, 172, 175, 193, 194, 203, 205, 209, 213, 214, 216, 220, 221, 222
Amazon warriors 4, 5, 37, 101, 151, 196, 198, 201, 202, 203, 205, 206, 208, 221, 231
Ampudia, Juan de 50
Ampudia, Pedro de 185
Añasco, Pedro de 50
Andes Mountains 1, 35, 44, 48, 65, 90, 114, 125, 127, 129, 132, 148, 157
Aparia the Greater 156, 161, 162, 163, 165, 168, 187
Aparia the Lesser 149, 150, 151, 162
Apure River 34, 38, 43
Arauca River 34
Araucana tribe 24
Ariari River 38
Ariguani River 67,
Aripuna 208, 216
Aristotle 36
Atacari tribe 17
Atahualpa, Inca ruler 2, 31, 47, 48, 55, 95, 123, 124
Atunquijo 131
Avila, Pedro Arias de (Pedrarias) 46, 47
Ayala, Ana de (Orellana's bride) 225, 227, 230, 231
Ayoman tribe 13, 14
Aztecs 1, 2, 48, 55, 69, 85, 95, 108, 127, 137, 193

Balboa, Vasco Núñez 10, 21, 46, 47
Barquisimeto 16, 115
Bastidas, Rodrigo 32, 57, 59
Belem 152, 203
Benalcázar, Sebastián de 1, 2, 3, 53, 54, 113, 124, 125, 126; Eldorado 50, 51, 52, 122; encounter Quesada, and Federmann 54, 103, 104; at Quito 46, 47, 48, 49, 52; return to South America 113; Spain 105, 106, 107, 108, 109, 112, 116
Bezos, Antonio 59
Bobure tribe 10
Bogotá 3, 45, 54, 85, 87, 88, 89, 97, 98, 99, 100, 101, 103, 104, 105, 109, 110, 116, 118, 119, 120, 121
Bondas, tribe 59, 60
Brazil 152, 157, 192, 203, 223, 228
Busongota 88
Bustamante, Diego de 176, 177

Cabot, Sebastian 18, 64
Cajamarca 47, 123, 204
Cajicá 89
Cali 52, 176
Cañari tribe 48
Canary Islands 57, 58, 62, 227
cannibalism 26, 27, 29, 30, 51, 59, 72, 76, 90, 133, 198, 208, 212, 229
Cape Verde Islands 227
Caprigueri Indians 30
Capua, native settlement 137
Caqueta River 37
Caquetio, native tribe 13, 16, 19, 31, 32, 33
Carahana 14
Cardozo, Antonio Diaz 65
Caribbean Sea 16, 55, 72
Caribs 42, 43, 72, 115, 212
Caripuna 229
Caritan 230
Carora hills 40
Carranza, Antonio de 209, 210, 215

Index

Carrare River 74
Cartagena 58, 62, 72, 73, 106, 107, 108, 113, 117, 118
Carvajal, Gaspar de 4, 125, 147, 148, 149, 150, 151, 152, 154, 162, 163, 166, 167, 168, 169, 182, 186, 187, 191, 193, 194, 196, 197, 200, 201, 202, 203, 205, 206, 207, 212, 214, 215, 216, 217, 220, 221
Carvajal, Juan de 114, 115, 116
Carvajal, Sancho de 134, 175
Casa de la Contratación 8
Casanare River 199
Casas, Bartolomé de las 9, 110, 205, 222
Casas, Domingo de las 65, 94
Castellanos, Juan de 65, 70
Castillo, Bernal Díaz de 46
Castro, Cristóbal Vaca de 180
Catatambo River 10
Cauicuri tribe 36
Celis, Hernán Gutierrez de 187, 216
Cerro Negro 91
César River 66, 71
Cespedes, Juan de 65, 77, 78, 80, 90
Charles V, Holy Roman Emperor 2, 3, 7, 8, 14, 31, 39, 56, 57, 58, 63, 64, 101, 108, 109, 110, 111, 116, 126, 150, 219, 225
Chaves, Cosmo de 225
Chaves, Francisco de 124
Chía 90, 98
Chibcha 1, 2, 3, 26, 34, 35, 36, 45, 50, 51, 53, 60, 65, 78, 80, 84, 85, 86, 87, 88, 89, 90, 91, 93, 95, 96, 97, 98, 99, 101, 103, 104, 105, 106, 112, 118, 120
Chimili 66
Chipatá, village 79
Chiri Indians 22
Chiriguana tribe 67, 70
Choque village 37, 38, 39
Cindahuas 24
Cinnamon 50, 51, 112, 122, 123, 125, 133, 135, 136, 171, 178
Ciparícato, tribe 19, 20
Coaheri River 17
Coari 15
Coca River 137, 139, 142, 144, 148, 170, 171, 172
Cocunubá 90
Cofanes, 144, 176
Cojedes River 15
Colombia 1, 2, 3, 8, 22, 50, 55, 57, 60, 64, 84, 90, 101, 112, 122
Columbus, Christopher 8, 205
Comao 230
Comiti, native settlement 25
Coniupuyara, Amazon ruler 152, 196, 197, 204
Coricancha 128

Coro, Spanish settlement 2. 9, 10, 11, 12, 13, 14, 15, 17, 19, 20, 21, 23, 24, 25, 29, 30, 31, 32, 34, 37, 38, 39, 40, 43, 44, 53, 104, 114, 115, 147
Cortejo, Juan 41
Cortés, Hernán 2, 8, 32, 41, 55, 63, 69, 83, 84, 95, 108, 109, 116, 126, 137
Council of the Indies 8, 59, 105, 106, 108, 112, 114, 218, 219, 220, 221, 225
Couynco, native ruler 206
Coyon tribe 34
crocodiles and alligators 22, 33, 53, 66, 67, 69, 70, 74, 75, 140, 160, 161
Cuadra, Juan de la 222
Cuba 108, 129
Cubagua 42, 114, 205, 214, 215, 216
Cuiba tribe 16, 17
Cumujajua, native ruler 23
Cundinamarca 50, 84, 97, 103, 104, 105
Curaray River 156
Cuzco 47, 48, 123, 124, 126, 191, 204, 205

Dalfinger, Ambrosius. 9, 10, 11, 12, 13, 20, 21, 22, 23, 25, 26, 27, 28, 31, 32, 40, 64, 66, 69, 70
Dávila, Gil González 41, 42
Delicola, native ruler 137, 138, 139, 144
dogs 20, 33, 51, 66, 69, 79, 82, 100, 129, 136, 140, 170, 171, 172, 175, 176, 219, 228, 231
Dortal, Jerónimo 41, 42, 43
Duitma tribe 100

Ecuador 48, 49, 51, 57, 126, 149
Eldorado (El Dorado) 1, 2, 3, 5, 9, 11, 26, 35, 42, 44, 50, 54, 85, 86, 89, 103, 106, 109, 112, 114, 116, 118, 119, 120, 122, 124, 125, 126, 127, 128, 129, 135, 136, 137, 139, 145, 146, 174, 178, 192, 231
Elmene, native settlement 25, 26
emeralds 22, 50, 51, 58, 80, 83, 85, 86, 88, 89, 90, 91, 93, 94, 96, 97, 101, 107, 108, 110, 112, 143
Empudia, Pedro de 191, 215
Enriquez, Cristóbal 186, 216
Escondio Village (Hidden Village) 201
Espinosa, Gaspar de 52, 63

Federmann, Nicolaus 2, 51, 61, 112, 114; banished from Venezuela 20, 21; feud with Welsers 108, 109, 113; in search of Xerira 40, 41, 43, 45; meets Quesada and Benalcázar 104, 105, 106, 107; return to Coro 21, 32, 33, 38, 39; search for the South Sea 11, 12, 13, 14, 15, 16, 17, 18, 19, 20
Fonte, Lázaro 64, 79, 80, 82, 94, 95, 104, 106, 111, 112
Fugger, banking firm 7

Index

Funes, Cristóbal de 131
Funis, Villegas 175

Gallego, Diego Hernandez 94, 107
Gallegos, Juan 71, 73, 75, 76, 80, 81
Gasca, Pedro de la 81
Gayon, native tribe 15, 17
Ghent 108
gold 2, 3, 8, 10, 11, 13, 16, 17, 21, 22, 23, 24, 25, 29, 30, 31, 34, 35, 36, 37, 42, 48, 50, 51, 55, 56, 57, 58, 59, 60, 61, 62, 67, 77, 78, 79, 80, 81, 83, 85, 86, 87, 88, 89, 90, 91, 92, 93, 94, 95, 96, 97, 99, 100, 101, 102, 105, 107, 108, 110, 112, 118, 122, 124, 127, 128, 136, 137, 143, 150, 187, 191, 204, 208, 229
Gomara, Lopez de 58, 59
Gordo, Juan 93, 111
Guacheta, native town 89
Guadalquivir River 223
Guahibo tribe 35, 36
Guaicari tribe 17
Guajira 43
Gualies 121
Guarjibo 33
Guatavita, Lake 2, 86, 90, 105, 112
Guatemala 48
Guaviare 44
Guayaquil 124, 126, 129, 134
Guayupés Indians 44, 114
Güejar River 118
Guiana 41
Gundelfinger, Andreas 32, 34
Gutierrez, Alonso 216
Guzman, Francisco de 230
Guzman, Gonzalo de 108
Guzman, Nuño de 63

Heredia, Pedro de 58
Herodotus 196
Herrera, Alonso 41, 42, 199
Hispaniola 8, 62
Hohermuth, Georg 31, 32, 33, 34, 35, 36, 37, 38, 39, 44, 92, 114,
Huanaco, 124
Huascar 47, 48
Huitotos tribe 37
Hunsa 92
Hutten, Philipp von 32, 33, 34, 36, 37, 38, 39, 114, 115, 116

Ica, native ruler 187
Ichipayo, chief 210
Icononzo 45
Imara 150, 151, 152, 155, 161, 162, 163, 193
Incas 1, 2, 3, 36, 47, 48, 50, 55, 81, 82, 85, 93, 94, 95, 108, 123, 124, 127, 128, 131, 132, 133, 141, 166, 176, 191, 193, 196, 208

Inza, Jerónimo de 75
Iraca 96, 97
Irimarais 156
Isásaga, Francisco de 153
Itabana, native village 17, 18, 19

Jaguars 20, 67, 70, 74, 75, 158, 195
Jamaica 129
Jirajara tribe 10, 13
Junco, Juan de 64
Jurua River 192

La Canela, cinnamon groves 4, 5, 122, 123, 124, 125, 126, 127, 129
Lebrija, Antonio de 64, 88
Lebrón, Jerónimo 81
Lenguazaque 89
Lengupá River 91
León, Pedro de Cieza de 57, 122, 125, 127, 128, 135, 141
Lerma, Garcia de 55, 56, 57, 59
Lescano, Anton 65
Lima 125, 217
Limpias, Pedro 11, 21, 40, 41, 44, 45, 104, 114, 115
Lisbon 109, 112, 218, 224
llamas 4, 36, 37, 128, 132, 179, 193, 205
Lugo, Alonso Luis de 57, 58, 61, 62, 69, 109, 110, 117
Lugo, Don Javier Alonso de 57, 58, 111
Lugo, Pedro Fernandez de 40, 57, 59, 60, 62, 63, 65, 71, 73, 76, 77, 83, 107, 110, 111

Macatoa, village 114
Machángara River 131
Machiparo 154, 162, 182, 185, 187, 188, 189
Madeira River 198
Madrid 108, 109
Madrid, Juan 64
Magdalena, Río Grande 3, 23, 24, 25, 53, 55, 62, 64, 65, 69, 70, 71, 72, 74, 75, 76, 77, 85, 97, 102, 103, 106, 107, 121
Magellan, Ferdinand 10
Malambo 73
Maldonado, Cristóbal 168, 184, 185, 191, 218, 222
Manco, Inca ruler 123, 126
Manjarres, Luis de 65, 73
Manoa 42, 116
Maracaibo, Lake 5, 9, 10, 11, 12, 21, 28, 30, 32, 40
Marajo Island 215
Marañón River 157, 180, 199, 205, 220
Marcobaré, rescued donkey 61, 65
Margarita, Isla de 214, 217, 230
Mariquita 121
Marribuique 230

Index

Martín, Esteban 10, 11, 21, 23, 24, 25, 26, 28, 29, 30, 32, 33, 34, 35, 37
Martin, Francisco 25, 29, 30
Martínez, Diego 43
Masparro (river and tribe) 34
Matahambre 119
Matienzo, Otiz, de 42, 43
Medina, Blas de 184
Medrano, Antonio de 118
Mercadillo, Alonso de 171
Meta province 41, 102
Meta River 40, 42, 43, 44, 199
Mexía, Diego 166, 167, 169
Mexico 8, 31, 41, 57, 63, 84, 107, 109, 127, 193
Moniquirá 83
Monte, Vicencio de 222, 226
Montes, Diego de 114
Montezuma 95
Muequetá, native town 89, 90
Muisca *see* Chibcha
Muñoz, Diego 229

Napo River 133, 137, 142, 144, 147, 148, 149, 156, 170, 171, 172, 175
Naveros, Antonio de, p. 17, 23
Neiva, village 2, 53, 96, 103, 104
Nemoncón village 87
Nicaho, native chief 23
Nicaragua 47, 126

Olaya, Anton de 65, 79, 93
Omagua 114, 138, 154, 162, 189
Oniguayal 189
Opia River 114
Opón, native chief 79, 80
Opón River 71, 74, 79
Ordaz, Diego de 41, 42, 43, 199
Orellana, Francisco de 4, 5, 138, 169, 176, 177, 180, 188, 189; Amazon voyage 156, 157, 158, 160, 161, 162, 163, 165, 166, 167, 168, 170, 171, 172, 173, 174, 175, 182, 183, 184, 185, 186, 187, 191, 192, 193, 194, 197, 198, 199, 200, 201, 206, 207, 208, 209, 210, 211, 212, 213, 214; Amazon warriors 152, 190, 191, 196, 201, 202, 203, 204, 205; disastrous search 227, 228, 229 230, 231; leaves Pizarro 148, 149, 150, 151, 152, 153, 154, 155; Pizarro expedition 126, 127, 129, 130, 133, 134, 136, 142, 145, 146, 147; preparations for return to the Amazon 221, 222, 223, 224, 225, 226, 227; return to Spain 218, 219, 220; voyage to Cubagua 214, 215, 216, 217
Orinoco River 36, 41, 42, 43, 118, 199
Oviedo, Gonzalo Fernandez 66, 120, 122, 128, 216, 219

Pacabuey Indians 23, 40, 69
Paguana 162, 193
Panama 21, 46, 47, 52, 63, 125, 126, 217
Panches 90, 98
Pandi 45
Papamena 37
Paria 41, 42, 43,
Paria, Gulf of 216, 230
Pasacote River 44
Pasca, native village 3, 97, 104
Pasto 142
Pauto River 44
Pauxoto village 23, 24
Pemeno, tribe 10, 22, 28, 30
Pericón 78, 79, 89
Perijá 24
Peru 2, 53, 55, 57, 73, 84, 107, 109, 112, 127, 131, 157, 178, 180, 191, 193, 213, 217, 219, 222
Perucho (soldier) 210
Philip II 116, 117, 221, 222, 226
pigs 4, 53, 103, 104, 105, 118, 120, 125, 128, 132, 140, 179
Pijao tribe 53
Pineda, Gonzalo Díaz de 51, 52, 123, 124, 171, 172, 176, 177
Piura 124
Pizarro, Francisco 3, 4, 21, 31, 47, 49, 51, 52, 55, 56, 73, 81, 99, 105, 108, 109, 112, 116, 122, 123, 123, 124, 126, 131, 137, 150, 178, 180
Pizarro, Gonzalo 3, 4, 5, 107, 138, 139, 140, 141, 142, 177, 203, 215, 229; complaints against Orellana 173, 180, 218, 219, 220, 221, 224; parting ways with Orellana 146, 147, 152, 153; return to Quito 170, 171, 172, 173, 174, 175, 176, 178, 179, 180; in search of La Canela and Eldorado 124, 125, 126, 127, 128, 129, 130, 131, 132, 133, 134, 135, 136, 137, 143, 144, 145
Pizarro, Hernando 55, 56, 57, 109, 123, 126, 180, 224
Pizarro, Juan 123
poison 10, 13, 17, 19, 24, 27, 28, 36, 60, 66, 148, 160, 161, 172, 203, 209, 210, 211, 229
Popayán 51, 52, 53, 104, 112, 113, 142, 176
Portugal 192, 218, 221, 222, 223, 224
Potosi 124
Province de Picotas (Province of the Gibbets) 198
Pueblo de la Loza, (Porcelainville) 191
Pueblo de los Bobos (Village of the Idiots) 193
Pueblo Vicioso (Viciousville) 194
Puelles, Pedro de 52, 53, 107, 122, 124, 125, 129
Puerto Ayacucho 42

Index

Puerto Viejo 124, 127, 129, 134
Puna, island 217
Punta de San Juan 207

Quema, native settlement 134, 140
Quemados Village (Village of the Burned People) 199
Quesada, Alonso 117
Quesada, Francisco 64, 117
Quesada, Gonzalo Jiménez de 3, 114; back to Spain 106, 107, 108, 109, 110, 111, 112; meets Federmann and Benalcázar 45, 103, 104, 105, 106; returns to South America 116, 117, 118, 119, 120, 121; search for Eldorado 40, 51, 53, 58, 62, 63, 64, 65, 66, 67, 69, 70, 71, 72, 73, 74, 75, 76, 77, 78, 79, 80, 81, 82, 83, 84, 85, 86, 87, 88, 89, 90, 91, 92, 93, 94, 95, 96, 97, 98, 99, 100, 101
Quesada, Hernando 64, 65, 74, 96, 98, 101, 103, 106, 111, 112
Quijos 131
Quillasinga 52
Quinto Real (royal fifth) 17, 105
Quito 1, 2, 4, 47, 48, 49, 50, 51, 52, 103, 122, 123, 124, 125, 126, 127, 128, 129, 130, 131, 132, 133, 172, 174, 175, 176, 177, 178, 179, 180, 204

Rellejo, Juan 106
Rendon, Gonzalo Suárez 64, 65
Rentz, Sebastián 12, 21
requirement, Spanish proclamation 14, 17, 22, 92
Ribera, Antonio de 128, 131, 134, 142, 175, 176
Río Ariari 36, 44
Río César 22
Río Guaviare 36, 114
Río Guayboro 36
Río Itacha 40
Río Negro 114, 157, 194
Río Opon 77, 78
Río Tocuyo 115
Río Zulia 28
Robledo, Jorge de 113
Robles, Alonso de 168, 183, 191
Rodríguez, Sebastián 154
Rumiñavi 48, 50

Sagipa, native ruler 98, 99, 100, 110, 112
Saint Eulalia Confluence 157
salt 3, 13, 22, 25, 35, 38, 51, 76, 77, 78, 80, 81, 82, 85, 86, 88, 90, 129, 201
Samaniego, Juan García de 222
Sampollón 71, 76, 77
San Martín, Juan de 64, 71, 76, 77, 78, 80, 81, 82, 90, 91, 92, 100

San Miguel 42, 47, 48, 49
San Pedro, boat 143, 147, 148, 155, 167, 210, 213, 215, 216
Sánchez, Francisco 227
Sandi, Juan de 225
Sanlúcar 31, 41, 226, 227
Santa Cruz, Francisco de 29
Santa Fe 113
Santa Marta 8, 21, 32, 40, 45, 51, 53, 55, 56, 57, 58, 59, 60, 61, 62, 64, 65, 67, 69, 71, 73, 75, 76, 77, 80, 81, 94, 101, 103, 107, 109, 110, 111
Santo Domingo 8, 9, 11, 12, 20, 31, 32, 39, 40, 43, 73, 114, 115, 216
Saravita River 83
Sarobai village 34
Sedaño, Antonio 42
Segovia, Cristóbal de 216
Seissenhofer, Johannes 11, 12
Seville 9, 12, 21, 31, 57, 109, 112, 114, 221, 223, 225, 226
Socuy River 22
Sogomosa River 85
Sogomosa, trade center 35, 91
Soleto, Diego 118
Somondoco 85, 90, 91
Soría, Garcia de 215
Sorocatá 87
Soto, Hernando de 46
South Sea 3, 7–8, 10, 11, 12, 13, 16, 17, 18, 21, 30, 107
Spain 52, 58, 61, 62, 63, 99, 101, 105, 106, 107, 108, 112, 117, 165, 192, 205, 216, 220, 221, 224
Starvation Island 213
Suesca 90, 120
Suma Paz 44, 45

Tairona Indians 57, 60, 61
Tamalameque, native trade center 23, 24, 25, 64, 69, 70, 71, 77, 78
Tapajóz River 209
Tapir 35, 158, 182, 213
Tapuyan Indians 202
Temple of the Sun 96, 97
Tenerife 58, 59, 227
Tocaima 106, 121
Tocuyo 14, 33, 41, 43
Tomara, native settlement 23, 24
Torres, Pablo de 222, 223, 224, 225, 226, 229
Trinidad 42, 214, 216
Trinity River 189
trinkets 10, 14, 15, 16, 17, 25, 34, 42, 79, 163, 165, 207, 230
Trombetas River 203
Trujillo 4, 125, 126, 220, 225

Tundama, native chief 96
Tunja 85, 91, 92, 93, 94, 96, 97, 98, 101, 106
Tupinambarana, island 198
Turmeque 85
turtles 158, 160, 161, 162, 163, 165, 183, 184, 185, 187

Uaupés, native tribe 114
Ulloa, Juan de 222
Ulm, German city 9, 11
Ulma, Spanish settlement 10, 21
Upar Valley 22, 39
Upia River 35
Urbina, Diego de 72, 73
Uyapari 42

Valenzuela, Pedro 64, 90, 91
Valladolid 109, 218
Valley of the Ladies 16
Valverde, Vincent 125, 217
Vanegas, Hernando 92
Vargas, Hernán Sánchez de 154, 172, 173
Vascuña, Iñigo de 24, 25, 29, 30
Vega, Garcilaso de la 143, 154, 172, 173
Velasco, Ortun Velasquez de 64
Velez, native town 106
Venezuela 2, 5, 8, 9, 10, 11, 12, 21, 31, 39, 41, 57, 58, 105, 109, 114, 122
Vera, Gonzalo de 147

Victoria 167, 213, 215, 216
Villegas, Jerónimo de 178
Villegas, Juan de 36

Waipis Indians 44
Wangari River 38
Wauri, tribe 204
Welser, Anton 7, 8, 9, 10
Welser, Bartolomé (the Younger) 114, 115
Welser, investment firm 2, 7, 8, 11, 12, 21, 31, 32, 40, 41, 57, 58, 61, 62, 108, 109, 115, 116

Xagua, native tribe 15
Xerira, golden kingdom 5, 21, 22, 32, 35, 40
Xiriguana, native tribe 25

Yalcones 50
Yaracuy River 19, 20
Yuldama, native ruler 121
Yuma River 22

Zapatosa (lagoon) 22, 66
Zárate, Agustín de 179
Zipaquirá 78, 85, 88
Zipia, grand ruler of Chibcha 2
Zorro, Gonzalo Garcia 65
Zumaque (Sumaco) 132, 133, 134, 135, 138

www.ingramcontent.com/pod-product-compliance
Lightning Source LLC
Chambersburg PA
CBHW032036300426
44117CB00009B/1084